The case of Walter Pater

'He was always a seeker after something in the world that is there in no satisfying measure, or not at all.'

—*A Prince of Court Painters*

The case
of Walter Pater

MICHAEL LEVEY

THAMES AND HUDSON

© 1978 Michael Levey

Library of Congress Catalog card number 78-53030

Printed in Great Britain by
Latimer Trend & Company Ltd Plymouth

Contents

List of Illustrations

Acknowledgments

In writing such a book as this one is bound to incur numerous debts, and I acknowledge gratefully much help from family, friends and colleagues. My prime debt must be to Maureen Duffy who not only drove me to various places connected with Pater (usually, it seemed, graveyards) but who undertook a great deal of genealogical research, with valuable results. Thanks to her serendipity and persistence, members of the Grange, May and Glode families assumed new significance in the story of Pater. I am also grateful to Mr Peter Nutt for his research on my behalf.

I should like to record the helpful attitude of the staff at St Catherine's House, at Somerset House, at the Public Record Office and – more personally and particularly – at the London Library. A general acknowledgment must cover my indebtedness to archivists and local history officers who responded to my queries, even when the results were negative. But I want to single out at Enfield Mr D. O. Pam and Mr G. C. Dalling who took so much trouble over my many questions. At the King's School, Canterbury, Mr Paul Pollak kindly communicated some unpublished letters of Pater's and guided me about aspects of his school career. At Oxford Dr Bernard Richards of Brasenose College gave me useful information; Dr William Parry, Librarian of Oriel College, helped me over portraits of Charles Shadwell, and I am grateful to the Governing Body of the College for permission to reproduce the painting by Fiddes Watt. I am especially grateful to the Principal of Somerville College, Mrs Barbara Craig, and to the Governing Body, for permission to reproduce the drawing of Clara Pater, and to Lady de Villiers for generously allowing me to see and make use of her biographical note on Clara Pater. At Sidmouth Dr G. H. Gibbens, Hon. Curator of the Museum, took great pains to inform me of visits there by Pater, his godmother and his sisters.

I am very much indebted to the Librarian, Dr W. H. Bond, of the Houghton Library at Harvard University, for providing me with copies of Pater MSS there; Mr Rodney G. Dennis, Curator of Manuscripts, has kindly given me the Library's permission to make

7

quotation from these and to reproduce a page. I am also indebted to Miss Saundra Taylor, Curator of Manuscripts at the Lilly Library, Indiana University, Bloomington, for copies of J. R. McQueen's correspondence, and allied material, and for the Library's permission to utilize this. My quotations from these manuscript sources are, in fact, slight, but I apologize to any copyright holder whom I have been unable to trace. Quotations from Walter Pater's letters are from the volume *Letters of Walter Pater* edited by Lawrence Evans, © Oxford University Press 1970; by permission of Oxford University Press.

For other positive help, gratefully recalled, I should like to express my thanks to: Allan Braham, Giles Gordon, John Hale, Paddy Kitchen, Sheila Reid, David Rodgers, Seymour Slive, Luisa Vertova Nicolson and Christopher White (who regularly read work in progress and retained an encouraging interest). I must record, yet once again, my sustained debt to Mrs Grace Ginnis whose typing brings calm and order to fevered manuscripts of mine; and I value also her response to my work.

Finally, in as terse a manner as he would wish, I express my gratitude to my editor, Stanley Baron.

MICHAEL LEVEY

September 1977

London 1890 - '91

1 PATER IN LONDON, 1890–91:
a sketch by Charles Holmes, an undergraduate at Brasenose who
later became Director of the National Gallery, London. In his
autobiography Holmes contrasts Pater's lack-lustre air in Oxford
with his spruce, semi-military appearance during the period he
lived in London.

2 PATER AT OXFORD, 1872:
drawn by Simeon Solomon and noted by him as done
at Brasenose. Pater early admired his art, and became a
friend of Solomon's.

3 CLARA PATER, 1870:
drawn by Theodore Blake Wirgman, probably in
Oxford. Clara Pater was then aged about twenty-
nine, and the drawing well conveys her distinguished
appearance, often commented on by
contemporaries.

4 SIMEON SOLOMON, 1859:
a self-portrait at the age of eighteen. Solomon was taken up by
Swinburne, among others, but his arrest in 1873 for importuning
in a public urinal caused scandal leading to his eventual wreck
as artist and as man.

5 CHARLES SHADWELL:
painted by George Fiddes Watt late in the sitter's life. Shadwell
presented the portrait to Oriel College when he retired as
Provost in 1914, aged seventy-four. In the mid-1860s he had
probably been Pater's closest friend.

6 HARBLEDOWN PLACE, HARBLEDOWN (*left*):
an old photograph of the house near Canterbury where Pater
lived while at the King's School, 1853–58.

7 2, BRADMORE ROAD, OXFORD (*right*):
an old photograph of the house, today lacking its gate and
railings, in which Pater lived from 1869 to 1885.

8 12, EARL'S TERRACE, KENSINGTON:
Pater's London home from 1885 to 1893.

9 MANUSCRIPT OF 'TIBALT THE ALBIGENSE':
the first page of Pater's draft of an unfinished, unpublished
imaginary portrait, one of several begun in his late years and
never completed. Acquaintances recalled Pater speaking of
intending to write a portrait set at the period of
the Albigensian heresy.

Introduction

W̲ALTER P̲ATER is a case – in many senses, including the one
admitted as colloquial by the *American College Dictionary:* 'a
peculiar or unusual person'.

He is a case also of someone generally neglected, and where not
neglected often misunderstood. His writings have not seemed vital
enough to keep alive some interest in the man; and his life was not in
itself sufficiently stirring to make him one of those popular figures
for biography today, whose personality is frankly preferred to their
work. This book is very much about the man – and also about his
work.

Never tremendously famous, enormously influential or prolific –
not even long-lived – Pater can easily appear a case of the second-rate
nineteenth-century figure, of some brief interest possibly at or for the
period but now of little concern except to a few devoted students.
Dim, prim, faded and faintly absurd is the personality suggested
by such associations as his name now raises: a mid-Victorian bachelor
don at Oxford, hyper-aesthetic and unadventurous, who wrote
something about burning with a hard, gem-like flame and a purple
passage on the *Mona Lisa* at once familiar, stale and vulnerable to
parody.

In their drab blue-green binding, first selected by him, the
volumes of his writings tend to look not so much daunting as plain
dull. And their diversity seems bewildering rather than stimulating:
essays on Plato, though Pater was not a great classical scholar;
personal, semi-evocative 'notes' on a few painters, though Pater was
no art historian; some strange 'imaginary portraits' and *contes* in a
tradition more French than English. It is hard to place Pater as a
writer, for he assumes a startling freedom to move between fiction
and fact. As a result, he lacks a convenient niche. And although his
writings were posthumously assembled into a 'Library Edition', it is
part of the irony of his case that there is still no complete collected
edition even of everything published in his lifetime. Of his quite
extensive surviving work in manuscript there has been no systematic
publication at all.

But at least the major portion of his writings is accessible. His life is very much more buried and difficult to disinter – and cemetery metaphors are particularly appropriate. He never reached that high plateau of Victorian acceptance and approval which would have entitled him at death to a two-volume authorized biography. On the other hand, his life has for posterity lacked the glamour of secret passions, madness, grave scandal or dramatic religious doubts which flash excitingly around figures like Ruskin, Darwin, Newman and Browning. At first sight, Pater looks to have passed through life much as he passed acquaintances in the street, not pausing but with a distant, distancing wave of a well-gloved hand politely fending off their intrusion.

No proper biography of Pater has been attempted since the unauthorized, naive, disconnected, unreliable though partly invaluable efforts of Thomas Wright, whose well-illustrated two-volume *The Life of Walter Pater* appeared in 1907. Some of Wright's errors of fact have crept into even the longest and most detailed studies of Pater, so that there is good reason for an up-to-date examination of his life. Besides, nobody's existence could have been as negative as Pater's has gradually come to appear. The impression was in part disseminated by Pater himself after his early tendency to daring explicitness had exposed him to hostile criticism at Oxford. One aspect of the complex case he presents is therefore the deliberate public toning-down by him, in a concern for social survival, of his private nature. After his death, his two sisters devotedly did their quite successful best to discourage scrutiny of him. They refused to help Wright, though they had given support of a kind to A. C. Benson's *Walter Pater*, which appeared the year before in Macmillan's English Men of Letters series. In that slim volume, far more sensitive and perceptive than Wright's, though much less seriously researched, Benson quotes Pater as once saying of the past (apropos the French Revolution): 'I am all for details. I want to know how people lived, what they wore, what they looked like.' Fiercely and not especially intelligently, Pater's elder sister Hester (who died only in 1922) saw to it that the minimum details became known about her brother. She may have meant well, but she served him ill.

Pater was not the dim, prim, funereally staid person which Miss Pater may conceivably have supposed, or wished, him to be and which – ironically – might be extrapolated from a hasty glance at the well-wrought mask of his prose. When the dust is disturbed on the somewhat musty, meagrely documented case he presents, there emerges a personality of extreme emotional ardour, keen sensibility and high, often satiric, humour. It was not by chance that he was to

18

be a good mimic and at school a good actor – or that he should there have played Hotspur. His closest friend from his schoolboy and early Oxford days testified to his being 'as amusing a companion as there could be . . . It was almost like having a Charles Dickens book, *viva voce*, as one's companion.' And after Pater's death Lionel Johnson described the character he had known as 'instinct with veritable *fun*' (his italics). An acquaintance who later became a friend soon found him 'both humorous and witty'.

Time has increased the difficulty of recovering this true personality, never revealed probably except to intimates and increasingly concealed in the constricting milieu of conventional, academic, Victorian Oxford. Yet it is essential to understanding Pater. Well before Wilde he forged the paradox and the amusingly outrageous remark as weapons – tipped with steel, for all their lightheartedness – with which to challenge established opinions, now of Swiss scenery and now of Christianity. It would be hard to say which will have been found the more offensive, but remarks about Christianity were certainly the more damaging to the speaker's reputation. Combined with an openly stated love of beauty, however strange, and an almost eighteenth-century belief in the importance of pursuing pleasure, the result had a power to cause scandal – that is, collective fright – which might have been tolerated in London but was bound to be explosive in the narrow environment of a mid-nineteenth-century English university.

To these views and a careless, possibly sometimes wounding, wit Pater could not help adding the most dangerous element of all in his situation: a frank response to youthful male beauty which his Oxford contemporaries speedily noticed. They might have said, in Lord Queensberry's famous words to Wilde, 'I don't say you are it but you look it.' Even Benson's tactful little monograph did not fail to hint, even while protesting in lip-smacking phrase that there was in Pater 'no luxurious yielding to lower satisfactions,' that the secret of his temperamental isolation, struggles and mystery was told in his writings for those who could read it. More clearly did Ingram Bywater, a close friend of Pater's as an undergraduate, privately tell an enquirer about his early Winckelmann essay: 'You will notice, I think, a certain sympathy with a certain aspect of Greek life.'

This stigma, for it was no less, probably underlay a good deal of the moral opprobrium Pater brought to a head when as a young don in 1873 he published *Studies in the History of the Renaissance*. His Oxford career never recovered from it. Although he grew increasingly discreet in his life, expressed opinions and friendships, it is perfectly true – as Benson suggested – that his writings contain the 'secret'; indeed, he needed this outlet for such sensations. Just how turbulent they remained, repressed behind the grave, literally buttoned-up, formal exterior of Pater in middle age, is shown by the bloody and erotic *Apollo in Picardy*, a variation of the story of the god and the boy Hyacinth, published in 1893, the year before Pater's death.

But perhaps the most significant damage to his reputation, and the undisclosed reason for the extreme reaction of the Misses Pater to any probing of his life, arose through the trials and conviction of Oscar Wilde. Never Pater's pupil, Wilde had greatly admired him, borrowed from him more than is usually realized and had even, apparently, added something at Pater's instigation to prevent some unpleasant misconstruction in *The Picture of Dorian Gray* (which received a review from Pater (omitted from the Library Edition of his works)). Twice during Wilde's cross-examination by Carson in the libel suit he brought against Queensberry in April 1895 was Pater's name thus introduced into the proceedings. After the withdrawal of the prosecution Wilde was arrested. At his first trial the opening speech for the defence referred again to the suggestion made by Pater, 'one of the most accomplished critics of our age'. On 25 May 1895, after the re-trial, Wilde was sentenced to two years' hard labour.

The sensation was immense. Not only did the newspapers rejoice at Wilde's own downfall, but they saw in his condemnation the sternest rebuke – in the words of the *Daily Telegraph* – to 'some of the artistic tendencies of the time', and a warning to, among others, young men at the universities. The *Evening News* described Wilde as being, *before* he broke the law and outraged human decency, 'a social pest . . . one of the high priests of a school . . . which sets up false gods of decadent culture.'

Pater had died in July of the previous year. After some initial enthusiasm, his attitude to Wilde seems to have become increasingly wary, even censorious. In reviewing *Dorian Gray* he had singled out the character of Lord Henry Wotton for surprisingly strong moral disapproval (possibly displeased, or alarmed, by Wotton's echoes of his own earlier hedonism) and he may even have surmised that there was gathering around Wilde far greater opprobrium than he himself had endured. Wilde had introduced Alfred Douglas to Pater in the autumn of 1891. 'He becomes the spoiler of the fair young man': Pater's comment on Wotton might almost have been his private prophecy about a relationship which soon set society gossiping and culminated in the most resounding of scandals even in a century of great scandals.

Though safely dead, leaving behind him an air of disapproval of Wilde's excesses, Pater and his reputation could not escape the association. Many of the 'artistic tendencies of the time' could be traced back to him. Even in his obituary *The Times* had prudishly remarked of his influence, 'that that was always wholesome, we do not pretend to say.' The cult of beauty in everything, the pursuit of pleasure, a taste for the bizarre – these were the very things for which Pater had pre-eminently stood. Unlike most Victorian figures, he had not lectured or hectored his audience, preferring rather the method of hypnotic suggestion; but Wilde had boldly and publicly trumpeted what Pater whispered, and his own life was like an attempt to cram together all the experiences which Pater had described as passing into the image of the *Mona Lisa*. Sought in reality, the pagan world, the animalism of Greece, the lust of Rome and the sins of the Borgias dwindled to shoddy, blackmailing street-boys, society's vituperation and the crushing misery of Reading Gaol. That was exactly where many people would have expected the aesthetic movement to lead. Nor could they know it, but one of the first books Wilde received in prison was Pater's *Renaissance*.

When Benson discussed Pater and the aesthetic movement, he obviously felt he had to step with rather heavy-footed earnestness, denying any moral laxity in Pater's own case, though admitting that others may have taken his irony and paradoxes to sensual extremes. Wilde he could not bring himself openly to name. 'It is', he wrote, 'a difficult subject to treat discreetly, because the *epigoni* of the school, in certain notorious instances, ended in complete moral and social shipwreck.'

Since Wright was able the following year to give a full and comparatively sensible chapter to Wilde in his biography of Pater, it seems as if Benson's nervous allusiveness, along with his somewhat contorted protests, stemmed from the Misses Pater – drawing no doubt the firmest of lines between their dead brother's persona and the most execrated literary figure of the period. Perhaps they unconsciously understood that Wilde acted out fantasies of which Pater had only dreamt. Pater had taught himself to be content with re-telling the story of Apollo and Hyacinth, while in about the same year Wilde was writing ecstatically to Douglas, 'My own Boy . . . I know Hyacinthus, whom Apollo loved so madly, was you in Greek days.'

No letter of Pater's, his sisters could congratulate themselves, was likely to be the cause of blackmail or be read out at the Old Bailey in a criminal libel trial. In fact, the banality of such letters as Pater did write, and which survive, is positively disturbing and almost inhuman – conveying such a painful suppression of personality as to suggest the writer was haunted by the dangers for him of betraying direct emotion of any kind.

The discretion he had forcibly imposed on his naturally passionate temperament – the caging of intense, even wild instincts – left him lonely and somewhat weary, despite all his courtesy, as if expiating a secret sin. Some sympathetic observers quickly penetrated the carapace of politeness and detected fundamental fears underneath. Perhaps they did not always realize how completely Pater shared their analysis and that his writings – so distinct from the outpourings of most Victorians – are one sustained, conscious, subtle exploration of his own nature and his dilemma. 'There are few more autobiographical writers,' shrewdly noted William Sharp in probably the clearest, least evasive sketch of Pater produced by anyone who knew him. In many ways Pater was closer, as an artist, to Henry James than to Ruskin; and it was a very Jamesian note he made to himself about his transparently personal, almost psychoanalytic 'portrait', *The Child in the House*: 'voilà, the germinating, original, source, specimen, of all my *imaginative* work' (his italics). Instinctively, he understood that he had to go back to his boyhood to uncover what he was and how he became it. And instinctively, he made a dream the occasion of that exploration: '. . . it happened that this accident of his dream was just the thing needed for the beginning of a certain design he then had in view, the noting, namely, of some things in the story of his spirit . . .'

The case of Pater would scarcely be of any general interest if it was merely that of any timid, repressed Victorian don at Oxford, teaching classics and dabbling in art appreciation. Even the breath of early scandal quietening down into conformity and regular attendance at chapel lends it little novelty. Such a limp figure was commended and consecrated by his friend the Reverend F. W. Bussell, preaching on Pater in Brasenose Chapel a few months after his death. 'The entire interest of his later years was religious,' declared Bussell, with unpardonable exaggeration. His statement might have had to be taken at its face value had not Pater left the evidence of his own late writings and projects to show the complex nature of his interests. If Bussell had not been utterly indifferent to art, and apparently proud of being so (reporting that he and Pater never discussed the subject: 'I should have been but an inept scholar and listener'), he might have been aware that Pater's very last projects included preparation not only of a lecture on Pascal, which Bussell thought significant for the religious trend of his thought, but also one on Rubens.

Perhaps anyone would deserve to be rescued from the pious, genteel trivializing inflicted, doubtless from the highest motives, by Bussell on the personality of Pater. The quietly humorous, conscientious, domestic don, a pattern for the student life, assiduous at chapel attendance and remarkable for ascetic habits (he never smoked, we learn from the sermon, and 'rarely took tonic or medicine of any kind'), is not merely a stock figure but one put forward by Bussell to counter any impression gained from actually reading Pater. Rather cleverly inverting the facts, he spoke of Pater's writings as 'a sort of disguise' to those who knew him well, whereas the 'disguise' lay rather in Pater's adoption, by middle age, of conventional attributes – not out of hypocrisy but out of defeat and disillusion. At the end of his life he returned – outwardly – to being the amiable Christian child of his earliest years.

In Pater's writings lie the real reasons for re-examining and rescuing him from misconceptions of all kinds. Because he had always to begin with himself, define his own attitude and express the effect on him of a work of art (in whatever medium), he was born to cut away the nineteenth-century, notably Ruskinian, moral ground for enjoying art as good, true and improving. Instead, Pater encouraged the concept of personally scrutinizing a work of art to see what savour it possesses for the individual, and whether it is pleasurable rather than morally 'good'. For that release we are indebted particularly to him.

Ruskin had assumed a Jehovah-like authority, and laid out a strict, ethical garden of art with defined flowerbeds and a large amount of forbidden, poisonous fruit. Pater turned it into a jungle rich and rank, where anyone was free to wander as he liked and where the very fruits condemned by Ruskin might prove not only the most alluring to eat but entirely harmless. Constantly exercising his own imagination, Pater extended – and mutely defended – the power of the imagination. He opened up the worlds of art and nature to limitless exploration by the senses. Acutely aware of ambiguities in his own personality, with its hidden fears and desperate longings, he daringly chose to express them: at first by re-creating the effect on him of works of art, most famously in writing of the *Mona Lisa*, and then by creating his own works of art. What he was telling was the story of himself, testifying to how seriously he took art because art had always given him a pleasure he could find nowhere else. In that alone lay its justification.

Pater had been practising what he not so much preached as propounded since he was a child. It had all begun for him as a developing, predominantly visual consciousness awakening to unforgettably detailed images like that of white pear-tree blossom seen against the sky through a window, or of glass beads, empty scent-bottles and discarded tufts of coloured silks found in the attic. More disturbing yet pleasurable sensations came from being assailed by the sudden appeal of the animate: faces of fascinating, almost flower-like beauty, with curving lips, perhaps the more vivid for being sometimes glimpsed and then lost.

Such responses early came heightened by another overwhelming, obsessive and more sinister sensation, of ubiquitous mortality. Amid even the finest manifestation of physical beauty death lurked; and Pater was seized with a terror he never shook off. There was no escaping sorrow, he understood instinctively; and boyhood experiences confirmed it. He grew up with adults who had suffered, and learnt that even children die. His pet bird or fine white cat might undergo its own mortal agonies, exacerbating to the sensibility of those who loved them.

The unexpected sting of a wasp concealed in the perfect-seeming, tranquil still-life of a basket of yellow apples in a cool room on an autumn afternoon was for him a foretaste of much deeper pain. But the incident already suggested how intermingled would be the two streams which fed his work. There was to be no trite reconciling of of them, any more than there would be any appeasement of his restless desire for what is beautiful. In the end, and often horribly, death mars all – as the flying metal discus saws through the face of Hyacinth 'crushing in the tender skull upon the brain'. No previous English prose writer had so intimately and passionately proclaimed a belief in sheer beauty: a belief given poignant intensity by his no less passionate awareness of everything that threatens it.

The more seriously the case of Pater is examined, its clouds of indifference, prejudice or misleading association dispelled and something of a once living, actual man substituted for a grey wraith, the more it becomes the case *for* Pater. To state the nature of that case requires a book, and this is it.

One   Surgeons in Stepney

O N SUNDAY 4 August 1839 the third child of Richard and Maria Pater was born at No. 1, Honduras Terrace, Commercial Road, Stepney. It was a boy. He was given the names of Walter Horatio and was baptized on 2 October at the old parish church of St Dunstan's, where five years previously his parents had been married.

The first week-end of August 1839 proved typically stuffy in London, though Sunday was slightly cooler. 'Today we can breathe again,' the young Queen Victoria reported to Lord Melbourne, having complained of the oven-like heat of the Saturday, both in the Park during the day and at the opera in the evening when she had found it intensely hot.

The weather can hardly have been less oppressive for her subjects in Stepney. They lacked not merely the amenities of parks or theatres but, in most cases, adequate living-space and even basic drainage. Poverty, dirt and disease had begun to grip the area during the eighteenth century. The early nineteenth century carelessly encouraged these conditions, while improving and expanding industrialization.

The 'pleasant prospect' of Stepney which Sir Thomas More had praised three hundred years before, with its pure air and its riverside fields, had grown to be the 'East End', with its shameful, hopeless squalor, its over-crowded inhabitants and the inescapable presence of the Docks, at once cause of the conditions and source of employment. Splendid new buildings and basins had been designed for the West India and East India Docks, swallowing land and dwelling-houses in the process, and at the same time, attracting a vast increase in the working population who had to live as they might. Sailors, dockers and seamstresses – not to speak of children – struggled for existence in virtually a prison-camp environment, shocking to the conscience not of society but of a few philanthropic individuals who came, saw and attempted to alleviate its insanitary urban misery. For what the nineteenth century was so rapidly creating a new word was needed and now came significantly into common use: slums. In London by the 1830s Stepney had become a slum.

Between the river and Commercial Road lay some of the most squalid lanes and stifling tenements in the district, lodgings often for seamen and casual labourers, where human bodies huddled at night in too-small rooms, foetid yet far preferable to the alternative of homelessness. Commercial Road itself – as its name suggests – was part of the recent development of the area, a broad route cut in the first decade of the nineteenth century to run conveniently from the Docks to the City. Regular terraces of simple, quite small, though elegant houses of the period lined – and in patches still line – Commercial Road. Honduras Terrace, on the south side, was one of the shortest, consisting of just five houses. Its name recalled the import of timber – mahogany. Immediately round the corner from it lay what was vulgarly known as Vinegar Lane (Hardinge Street), notable even in that area for its poverty and lack of drainage. But the south side of Commercial Road at this point and date represented a rim – a thin rim – of respectability. It was the best part of the neighbourhood. Here, amid houses serving as lodgings and many then as now turned on the ground floor into shops, were similar houses occupied by professional men and their families: a prosperous ironfounder, for example, owning a good deal of local property, a lawyer or two, and several surgeons.

Richard Pater was one of these. Above apothecary but below the select, highly restricted rank of physician (alone then entitled to be called Dr), a surgeon was the equivalent of today's general practitioner. It is easy to see how much need of surgeons the district had. Indeed, it needed everything; and a remarkable amount of practical work was being done by the Reverend William Quekett, a clergyman later to be featured by Dickens in *Household Words*. In Quekett's own rambling and otherwise tedious memoirs, written when he was old, a sober, terrifying and partly statistical account is provided of conditions around and behind Commercial Road. Only a misunderstanding had originally brought Quekett as a curate to St George-in-the-East (he supposed he was to serve at the fashionable West End church of St George's, Hanover Square). Profoundly shaken by what he discovered, he remained to start a school under a railway bridge, devise a penny bank (at a time when the remuneration for sewing a shirt by hand was $2\frac{1}{2}$d) and – well before Mayhew – to chronicle in detail some facts about poverty in nineteenth-century London (fifty-one children wandering the streets homeless on a single November night in 1843).

To counter disease Quekett planted his own brother Edwin as a doctor in the parish. But Edwin Quekett died young of diphtheria, perhaps not surprisingly. The practice he had taken over had itself become vacant ominously, only through the sudden death of the previous occupant. Individual action was powerless against grim facts. Statistics for life expectation in Stepney by 1842 showed that the average age of labourers, servants and their families dying there was twenty-two; for tradesmen and their families, twenty-seven; for professional men and gentlemen, forty-five. To this last figure, the senior male members of the Pater family in Stepney were closely to conform.

Richard Glode Pater shared his practice with his younger brother, William Grange, who was then living a few doors down the same side of Commercial Road, at 6, Hardwick Place. They must have come to the area as boys when their father (John) Thompson Pater, moved from Highgate early in the century. He too had been a surgeon, advertising himself also as a 'man midwife' in the days when his Highgate address was no more precise than 'near the ponds'.

The status of the family at this period is hard to establish. Thompson Pater had married a Miss Hester Grange, one of several children of George and Elizabeth Grange who lived in the City parish of St Swithin's London Stone. Thompson and Hester Pater presumably called their elder son after Sir Richard Glode, a brick-layer who rose to be a sheriff of London, whose residence was Mayfield Place, near Orpington. Not far from Orpington is the small and still charming village of Hadlow near which Hester Pater's elder sister Sophia lived with her husband John Porter, of Fish Hall, a fine eighteenth-century house; their daughter and heir, Mary Susanna, married a local landowner and was to be Walter Pater's godmother, as well as a hospitable friend generally to his family.

Exactly when, or indeed why, Thompson Pater settled in Stepney is not clear. Certainly he was living there by 11 November 1808 when 'T. Pater . . . Surgeon', of Shadwell, is listed among some creditors in a notice in *The Times*. He apparently chose Commercial Road (dwelling conceivably at No. 1, Honduras Terrace) and must therefore have been among the first occupants of property in the newly-built thoroughfare. Earlier still, as a fairly young married man, he had gone out to America, where at least one of his children was born. In 1808 he was aged probably no more than forty-two. Perhaps it seemed to him that the rapid development around the Docks offered a larger, if not more lucrative, practice. Perhaps he also felt the effect of a less healthy environment. 1812 is always given as his date of death (though there seems no documentary evidence as yet for this). He left a widow, who long outlived him, and three children. Of the boys, Richard may have been already apprenticed to his father before his death; he would be about sixteen, slightly older than Keats was when he was first apprenticed to a surgeon. William would be about twelve. The eldest child was Elizabeth (in full Hester Elizabeth Mary), aged then about nineteen; she never married but became not only a favourite aunt of Pater himself and his sisters but virtually their mother by adoption.

When Richard and William Pater grew up, and were qualified, they presumably preferred to remain working in the area they knew well – and where they had good reason to know that medical care was desperately needed. Nothing concrete exists to establish their attitude, but Pater was to touch frequently in his writings on sympathy with suffering, and on poverty, along with a constant almost desperate emphasis on cleanliness. In the partly autobiographical *Marius the Epicurean*, he speaks of the priesthood or 'family' of Aesculapius, whose temples were also 'a kind of hospitals for the sick, administered in a full conviction of the religiousness, the refined and sacred happiness, of a life spent in the relieving of pain.' It was certainly a family tradition in which Pater believed; his own elder brother was to represent a third generation of doctors, and Pater dedicated a book to his memory with terse yet explicit reference to his 'useful and happy life'.

Duty and compassion were keynotes in the character of Walter Pater also, early present in him and likely, if not positively inherited, to have been fostered in his home environment. As a child he built up an image of his dead father as still an active presence in the world, somehow still on duty and protectively watching over him. And had he cared to trace it, perhaps he would have felt proudly that something hereditary informed his own sympathy for sick animals and that 'devoted nursing' which an acquaintance recalled him and his sisters as adults giving to a paralyzed cat.

By 1826 Richard Pater appears in London directories as practising at Honduras Terrace. Most probably his widowed mother and his sister lived with him. Although his brother William is not apparently listed as in the practice until later, he was undoubtedly in the district on 10 June 1834. On that day he and Elizabeth Pater witnessed Richard's marriage at St Dunstan's, Stepney, to Maria Hill.

In the register the bride gave her previous residence as Alverstoke in Hampshire, but she had been born in London (in Aldermanbury, in the City) probably about 1801. Of her family nothing seems known, nor of how she had met her husband. Since the name Hill is so common, it may be a mere coincidence that in 1801 a firm of muslin manufacturers called George Hill had premises at 70, Aldermanbury. By the time of her marriage Maria Hill possibly had no immediate living relatives. Her husband's family and friends seem to have absorbed her. Judging by Pater's very slight allusions in his semi-autobiographical writings, she was a rather faint figure to her own children – perhaps less active, less loving, or less healthy, than their aunt Bessie. Not everything Pater put into the boyhood of Marius can be exactly from his own boyhood, but the remark about the widowed mother's life as 'languid and shadowy enough' chimes with the general impression one has of some elusiveness about Maria Pater, herself early widowed and her existence conceivably 'like one long service to the departed soul.' At least, she preserved and in her will dutifully handed on to her two sons their father's gold watch, his chain and seals.

Her eldest child and first son was born in 1835 and baptized on 7 May with the names William, for his uncle, and Thompson for his grandfather and great-grandfather. Over the next six years, at regular two-year intervals, three children were born to her. The house in Honduras Terrace was gradually filling up. Meanwhile William Pater had married Matilda Margaret Knight Macdonald, herself a doctor's daughter, and had moved along Commercial Road, to Hardwick Place; their first child was a girl, Matilda, born and dying a few months old in 1838. The year before, Richard and Maria Pater's first daughter, Hester Maria, had been born and baptized at St Dunstan's on 21 March. Walter Horatio followed in 1839 and presumably in 1841, the second daughter, Clara Ann. For some reason there is no trace of a birth certificate for her (or of her being baptized) and it must be concluded that her father failed to register her birth. Extraordinary though this seems, it is possible that he delayed – he had taken a month to register Walter's birth – and was then overtaken by illness.

On 28 January 1842, at Honduras Terrace, Richard Pater died. The cause was stated to be 'affection of the brain'. The diagnosis was no doubt that of his brother, who had been present at the death. His age was forty-five.

Although Pater was probably too young to be directly aware of what had happened, the event profoundly marked him. He lost his father before he had ever really known him and would probably continue to wonder about him all his life. As late as 1889, in a relaxed moment, he certainly talked much about his father to Lionel Johnson, who bothered to note the fact without disclosing what he said. Even if Pater's extreme youthfulness allowed him to escape being present at the deathbed, his elder brother and sister are unlikely to have been so fortunate. What Pater certainly could not escape realizing as he grew up was the effect of his father's death on the surviving household of three women. 'Impressible, susceptible persons indeed, who had had their sorrows, lived about him', he was to write of the child, Florian, in *The Child in the House*, the first and most openly autobiographical of his fictional essays. And this passage leads straight on to what he calls the most poignant of that child's recollections – 'in unfading minutest circumstance' – of the 'cry on the stair . . . struck into his soul for ever', uttered by his father's aged sister in announcing the father's death: a death located as happening 'in distant India'.

Things the boy Pater was told or assumed about his father's death have here perhaps been crystallized into one coherent, dramatic account, where the patently fictional elements may well be truthful to his earliest impression. Thomas Wright, relying on Edmund Gosse, for some reason took the 'cry on the stair' to have been sounded at the death of Pater's grandmother six years later; her death certainly seems to have deeply affected Pater himself, to judge from the passage describing Gaston's reaction to a grandmother's death in *Gaston de Latour*, his last, unfinished, semi-autobiographical narrative.

Yet it is hard to think that the death of Mrs Hester Pater at the age of eighty-four can have precipitated quite the wild grief Pater conveys as felt by her daughter ('sounding bitterly through the house'), by then in her mid-fifties. More truly heart-rending had been the death of Richard Pater, yet Pater can scarcely have recalled that moment itself. Between the two deaths, however, another was to intervene. On 19 September 1845, William Pater died at his home in Stepney, also aged forty-five. His death was accidental, brought on by a shock to the system, according to the death certificate, from a fall downstairs. The news of this second, unexpected loss of a brother might indeed have drawn a cry of almost despairing sorrow from Elizabeth Pater, all the keener no doubt for thinking of her mother's sorrow.

The premature deaths of the two brothers, at the same age, in the same profession, may even have become slightly blended in Pater's own mind. At the time William died, Richard's widow and her family had moved away from Stepney to Enfield. Distance of place, as well as of time, would increase any blur in Pater's recollection as he grew up. Enfield was always to stand for him as quiet, sheltered, glowingly beautiful and basically secure: an enclosed, almost ideal childhood place.

Any associations he learnt to have with Stepney must have been sordid, morbid and threatening. Fatally easily, death had bridged the gap which seemed to exist between the bastion of a respectable doctor's residence in Commercial Road and the stinking squalor of Vinegar Lane. Even the garden calm of Enfield was not proof against death. The 'cry on the stair' signalled the rending of the childhood cocoon in which Pater had been happily wrapped. That moment of grief was, as he clearly implies, experienced by him only faintly and vicariously – like the pain of the adults around him. At first he could bear to hear of his father's death. He says as much in *The Child in the House*. It was something long past; and in the biblical reference to the resurrection of the just he detected a comforting sense of his father spiritually still alive and a guardian-presence.

So it seemed, until reality forced itself on him abruptly in the shape of an open grave. He writes of the boy who is patently himself wandering on a brilliant summer day with his mother through a churchyard and how he discovered the dark patch of a grave newly dug and prepared for a child. Then the full physical horror of death came on him. The image of his father shrank to being 'only a few poor, piteous bones'. He realized that no benign, protective figure existed of the kind he had liked to imagine; instead, though perhaps only briefly, it was replaced by a fearful, ghostly, half-hostile *revenant*.

When as an adult Pater probed – with extreme perceptiveness – the roots of the person he had become, he was led back to the fact of pain and death in ways bound up most closely with his own early experience. That happened to be sadder than the average child's. It began with a death he did not directly suffer, but certainly suffered from: that of his father. The wound which that inflicted on the whole Pater household must have been partly re-opened with the death some three years later of his uncle. In Pater's own case, other family deaths were only to reinforce what he already felt and was to describe again and again with a sort of fascinated and frozen horror.

For him there is always a grave gaping half-hidden among even the lushest grass on the brightest day. Indeed, it was exactly at the point when emotions of beauty or love are most actively stirred that Pater seems to have been seized by a panic fear of death. The 'Conclusion' to *The Renaissance*, especially in its first unrevised form, is itself a desperate 'cry on the stair', in which the beauty of life and art is seen inextricably bound up with human evanescence: 'We have an interval, and then we cease to be.'

No less fascinating to him, probably pondered on already as a fatherless child, is how and in what manner we cease to be. His protagonists, whether the imaginary Marius, that reflection of himself, or even Leonardo da Vinci, are made to prompt speculation – a curious questioning – as to their last, dying impressions. Of Florian, the child of *The Child in the House*, Pater was to state that it was not, as often with children, religious books which suggested his sombre speculations but an innate tendency, 'further strengthened by actual circumstances.'

Facts of Richard Pater's existence and death were transmuted to make him more positively heroic, doubtless because this is how he came to appear to his son. Fiction was bound to be involved, since Pater had to create a character he never knew. Young Marius can recall little about his dead father. But the father, with pride and a pious concern for his home, had the authority given by belonging to 'a local priestly college'. Marius thinks of him almost exclusively with awe. Remembering only 'a tall, grave figure above him in early childhood, Marius habitually thought [of him] as a *genius* a little cold and severe.' To this deliberately faint impression – which is not claimed as correct – is added the widow's sustained mourning and regret, 'together with the recognition, as Marius fancied, of some costly self-sacrifice to be credited to the dead.' Nothing more explicit is said, but the implication of the giving up of a career, a fortune – or perhaps life itself – is clear; behind it may lie Maria Pater's unconscious reproach to the husband whose self-sacrifice had led to his leaving her a widow.

In *The Child in the House* the father is made to seem a soldier (soldiers and a surgeon were to be brought together in the story of *Emerald Uthwart*), though Pater lets his exact career be ambiguous. We hear first that he is 'Latin-reading'; he taught his children, 'while he was with them', to call wallflower *flos parietis* – a literal translation which perhaps hints at some sub-donnish joke, since that is not its Latin name. Nothing more is learnt about him except his death in India. The second mention of this seems strangely to overlook the implied drama of the overheard cry on the stairs. 'The child had heard indeed of the death of his father, and how in the Indian station, a fever had taken him, so that though not in action he had yet died as a soldier . . . he could think of him . . . [as] a grand, though perhaps rather terrible figure, in beautiful soldier's things, like the figure in the picture of Joshua's vision in the Bible.'

The idea of a warrior-father, which this passage suggests, may have become particularly fixed in Pater's mind later when he was a schoolboy at Canterbury where the father of his best friend was a dashing, splendidly-dressed colonel in command in Canterbury during the Crimean War. Both Florian and Marius possess fathers whose profession or status suggests authority, and therefore some responsibility for other people; even the two lines from a Virgil eclogue which Pater quotes in the context of Marius's father refer to Daphnis: prematurely dead and now glorified, on earth a shepherd with a flock. And it is easy to see that Richard Pater could be figured as having enlisted in the fight against disease, and as giving his life in that cause, 'though not in action'. According to Edmund Gosse, he refused to move out of the East End. His family may well have suspected that some infection caught during his work, if not the work itself, had brought on a fatal affection of the brain – not totally different from the 'fever' by which Florian's father dies. As for the unexpected reference to his death occurring in India, that might be not so much a dab of totally fictional colour as the real echo of something heard by Pater in early childhood about the possibly fatal proximity to Richard Pater's practice of those Docks of East and West India.

To heal the experiences of Stepney must have been the reason for the retreat of the bereaved family from London. Abruptly widowed, with four children under the age of ten, Maria Pater became the head of a household which included her spinster sister-in-law and a mother-in-law approaching eighty. She did not entirely sever links with the Commercial Road area, even after William Pater's death, but she gave up the house in Honduras Terrace – conceivably in 1842 – and carried her family to the then country village of Enfield, eleven miles north of London. There they were to remain until 1852.

Richard Pater had left no will, and in April 1842 Letters of Administration were granted to the widow. His estate was valued at £5,000. That was not in itself a meagre amount – twice what Pater would leave half a century later – but it was probably the only money to support the four children and the three women for the rest of their lives. Away from London, they might hope to be healthier, if not happier, and to manage more cheaply.

To Pater the home at Enfield ('the *old house*, as when Florian talked of it afterwards he always called it') was the birthplace of his consciousness. There it unfolded, rapidly revealing its disturbingly sensuous character. The shape of the rooms and the scents of the garden were absorbed into the structure of his individual 'house of thought' which, once built, would never change. Before he reached adolescence, he reached a sort of maturity – isolating in its intensity and in its burden of a ceaseless response to physical beauty shot through with pain.

High walls and blossoming trees could not quite shut out some floating taint to be traced back to Stepney: an underlying fear about the powerlessness of love in the face of death (testified to by the trio of sad, semi-conventual women around him). In Stepney his father had served his fellow men, and had tragically died. Something too of what had impelled him might seem already at work in his son, a child whose quivering joy at the spectacle of the world was accompanied by what he himself, in the person of Florian, would describe as 'an almost diseased sensibility to the spectacle of suffering.'

Two   The house, the family and the child

THE HOUSE settled in by Mrs Pater at Enfield survives only in Pater's vivid yet allusive pages. It had gone by 1894, and the sparse references to where exactly the family lived are vague.

The rural nature of Enfield at the period, part of its attraction, is also part of the reason. Around its central grouping of church, grammar school and market-place were then loosely scattered over half-wooded hills and riverside meadows several imposing mansions in extensive grounds, while nearer the centre smaller houses, with often their own charming gardens, dotted its lane-like roads, identified not by number but by merely the occupant's name.

More than one house may later have been claimed as that lived in by the Paters, or they may have changed houses. Thomas Wright stated categorically that they lived in Chase Side, a long street then containing only a few houses, and he called theirs 'a small decorous white tenement'. The sole firm piece of evidence is the 1851 census return, where certainly Maria Pater is shown as living in Chase Side, though this is less revealing than it might seem, since at the period that term designated apparently an area and not just the still existing street. Pater's grandmother died at Enfield, but her address was not at that time given as Chase Side. The point is of more than minute concern since it is usually assumed that Pater in his semi-autobiographical references endowed his home with a more glamorous standing than it had in actuality possessed. Country houses he was to visit elsewhere might have coloured his recollection, but Enfield offered sufficient examples; and there are scattered hints that it was there, and around at least one house he had known there, that his imagination crystallized.

Much of the area had been the royal preserve of Enfield Chase, commemorated in an almost confusing number of local place-names. Many of the larger lodges and manors were architecturally fine and had historical associations. Though the grammar school building dates back to the sixteenth century, and early nineteenth-century activity had enlarged or altered some of the older houses, the general feel of the place must have been still rustic eighteenth century.

34

Despite its proximity to London, it probably retained very much the character suggested by Charles Lamb (who had lived there) in humorously complaining of the excessive number and height of its stiles. He developed indeed a dislike of it as a 'dreary village' of intolerable dullness, where nothing happened and where even the doctors (so he wrote to Mary Shelley) seemed to have no patients. Until 1848 there was no railway; public transport between Enfield and London was provided by Glover's bus, at the cost of two shillings and sixpence a journey.

It was on 'a brooding early summer's day' in the fields at Enfield that Pater heard the cuckoo for the first time – as he briefly mentions in a uniquely direct reference to his own childhood, suitably in his essay on Lamb. Looking back as an adult on that suburban-pastoral world, he too found its surface humdrum, its streets dingy and its green places, 'where the child goes a-maying', tame enough. Yet he recalled how significantly in such an environment bright weather altered appearances; shifts between sunlight and rain were keenly sensed; and there was pleasure in looking at the rolling clouds towards London, 'touched with storm or sunshine'. This last reference comes from *The Child in the House*, written earlier in the same year as the essay on Lamb (1878), at a date when Pater was in recollective mood, perhaps already girding himself for the major task of beginning *Marius* (thought of at first, it may be, as an extended self-portrait, 'the noting, namely, of some things in the story of his spirit').

Enfield itself clearly meant most to him as the location of that house within which had developed the consciousness of his own essence and individuality. It was a sort of house of the spirit, home-like in the sense of giving him a profound feeling of security and perhaps a wish never to have to grow up and leave its protective walls. It was at once womb and tomb. The end of *The Child in the House* is actually departure from this home, a departure looked forward to and yet shown – in an incident symbolically if not literally true – to be against all the child's instinct. The family have started out for the new place (as the Paters were indeed to do, moving to near Canterbury, in 1852) when it is discovered that they have left a pet bird behind in the empty house. The boy Florian returns, passes through the denuded rooms searching for it and is overwhelmed by nostalgia: 'the aspect of the place touched him like the face of one dead; and a clinging back towards it came over him so intense that he knew it would last long, and spoiling all his pleasure . . . himself in an agony of home-sickness.'

For most of Pater's imaginary people the home in which they

grow up takes on an importance emotional and moral. And, in many ways, it is really the same home each time, never very large or grand, countrified, even untidy, yet austere, cared-for, clean and white (a favourite adjective in this context), furnished with a few used and cherished objects, and fragrant from the proximity of flowers, garden trees or hayfields. In his essay on Rossetti Pater was to expand excitedly implications of the title of the sonnet-sequence, *The House of Life*, in directions entirely, typically personal and of little relevance to the physical passion which is Rossetti's theme. He conjures up the dwelling-place in which every object has its association, somewhat faded, sad and of Baudelairean mystery: dim mirrors, hair-tresses of the dead and visionary magic crystals in secret drawers. It is 'the house one must quit, yet taking perhaps, how much of its quietly active light and colour along with us! – grown now to be a kind of raiment to one's body . . .'

If Pater could hardly help physical detail accumulating around the reverie stimulated by Rossetti's title, he was bound to enjoy lingering in greater detail over the boyhood environment of his own creations, blending with dreams no doubt his real memories, but repeating certain motifs. Plaster and carved wainscot, warm bricks, mouldering tiles, lumber-rooms and cool attics where a boy might wander (like Florian and like young Duke Carl of Rosenmold) – these are the materials and rooms of the house he fondly built again and again to fit – like a garment – the imaginary inhabitant who is a shadow of himself. The house too must be at least a shadow of the house at Enfield.

Little is conveyed about the exterior, but the suggestions are of the picturesque rather than of the architecturally distinguished. Yet always the house is old. Where Marius lives is *Ad Vigilias Albas* (White-nights) in 'the fragment of a once large and sumptuous villa . . . mellowed by age.' Gaston de Latour is brought up in very much the French country equivalent, made up of two houses, the Château of Deux-manoirs: 'the old walls, the old apartments still existed . . . the race of Latour, still full of loyalty to the old home.' In *Emerald Uthwart* the house is positively called Chase Lodge, though shifted to Sussex, and built of 'oldish brick and raftered plaster', the old rooms filled with 'old black mahogany furniture' – and the churchyard full of old Uthwart tombs.

The emphasis on their age is part of the sense of security these homes exude. It was not fanciful snobbery which led Pater to stress the family tradition of inhabiting such places but something of the same longing for continuity, to find a fixed pattern amid human flux. In *The Child in the House* he says explicitly of Florian's home that it

36

'really was an old house.' There was, too, 'an element of French descent in its inmates – descent from Watteau, the old court-painter, one of whose gallant pieces still hung in one of the rooms.'

The latter reference is easily decoded. The unusual surname of Pater gave the family an apparent link with Jean-Baptiste Pater, Watteau's only pupil. Members of the family may well have encouraged a vague assumption (almost certainly wrong) that they were descended from him. The adult Pater appears to have been sensibly sceptical about, though not indifferent to, this link; it obviously gave him the idea in the imaginary portrait, *A Prince of Court Painters*, of seeing Watteau through the eyes of Jean-Baptiste Pater's sister (and perhaps it was some sense of unusual affinity which prompted him untypically to write this portrait entirely in the first person, as 'extracts from an old French journal' – one which might almost be presumed to have descended in the family). That a painting by Pater – still less one by Watteau – actually hung in the house at Enfield seems unlikely; when Mrs Pater made her will she would surely have mentioned it, if only as an heirloom. But the idea of a house with a room painted by Watteau, and lived in once by the Pater family, finds full imaginative expression in *A Prince of Court Painters* where their old, sombre salon at Valenciennes is gracefully transfigured by Watteau's redesigning and decoration. 'I am struck', the girl notes in her journal, 'by the purity of the room he has re-fashioned for us.' The result (with its 'dainty panelling . . . quite aerial scroll-work . . . delicate harmony of white and pale red and little golden touches') sounds close enough to the 'noticeable trimness and comely whiteness' of the house in which Florian lives.

That house has a garden with a large poplar growing in it, a tree, Pater suggests, most often despised by the English but loved by the French. In fact, poplars seem to have been something of an Enfield speciality. The garden of Lamb's house there had poplars in it at the end of the nineteenth century, and twenty years earlier a row of fine Lombardy poplars is specifically mentioned as having stood in front of Enfield Court, one of the fine properties in the neighbourhood. And perhaps Pater named the house of Marius 'White-Nights' in recollection of the name of another large house there, White-Webbs.

The first positive indication of the Paters being at Enfield comes with the death of Hester Pater on 21 February 1848. The death certificate gives her address as simply Chase Hill, which is also given as the address of the woman who registered her death, having been present at it, a certain Fanny Wood. That this is neither a slip, nor synonymous with Chase Side the street, would seem indicated by the entry for Hester Pater's burial in the Parish register; there she is recorded as of Windmill Hill. Vague though designations may be at the period, Windmill Hill and Chase Side are two different places. Then as now they ran at right angles to each other. The area of Chase Hill, today heavily built over and further altered by extensions to the railway, lies between them. Judging from maps, it seems to have been the site in the mid-nineteenth century of only very few, quite large houses, somewhat isolated and surrounded by their own grounds.

One of these was probably Chase Hill House, then owned by Daniel Harrison, a local landed proprietor and J.P. who is otherwise recorded confusingly with addresses simply of Chase Hill and Chase Green. In the census of 1851, his dwelling of Chase Hill House is separated from Maria Pater's only by an empty house; and though it is not possible to estimate the distance, the fact is suggestive. Conceivably, Chase Hill House was where Pater's grandmother died. She might have leased it from Harrison. It is even possible that the Pater family occupied, during her lifetime, two houses, she being looked after by Fanny Wood. In this connection it is worth noting that the general servant living in Maria Pater's household at the time of the 1851 census was Eliza Wood (born in Essex), likely enough to be a relation of Fanny Wood.

The theory of there being for a period two adjoining households cannot be proved, but it would be tempting to see some echo of such a situation in *Gaston de Latour* where it is at the significantly-named Deux-manoirs that Gaston grows up: 'two houses, oddly associated at a right angle . . . that the two families, in what should be as nearly as possible one abode, might take their fortunes together.' Perhaps it is just a coincidence that the same book should contain a distinct echo of one real event at Enfield, in the death of Gaston's grandmother 'to whom he had always turned for an affection, that had been as no other in its absolute incapacity of offence.'

The house Pater grew up in at Enfield may have been both old and comparatively spacious (at least not the 'tenement' described, though probably never seen, by Wright). Very easily could he have assumed that it had for long been in his family; and about that family as such he – even more than most children – is likely to have wanted to know more.

Although the family appear to have believed that their surname was rare, it occurs a little more widely than they may have realized and sometimes with people of a lower class than their own. Grocers in Hammersmith and labourers in Limehouse are among Paters recorded in the late 1830s and 1840s. John Pater was the name of the then manciple of Trinity College, Oxford. Clara Pater, daughter of a

38

carrier, married at Godalming in 1838. Oddly enough, a Maria Pater, *née* Hill, and her husband were living in Stepney in 1841, not far behind Commercial Road; he was employed as a boot-closer (that is, in sewing the uppers of boots and shoes).

Equally distinct from Richard Glode Pater and his anyway immediate family seem to have been Admiral Charles Pater and Lieutenant-General John Pater, the latter a cavalry officer serving for long at Madras, dying there in 1817 and commemorated there by 'Pater's Road' and 'Pater's Gardens'. This is, admittedly, a death in India which Pater *might* somehow have heard of and decided to appropriate for Florian's father in *The Child in the House*, but it was already well in the past at the time he himself was born.

The branch of the Pater family from which Richard Glode descended lived first at Newport Pagnell and then at Weston Underwood, near Olney, in Buckinghamshire, and seems first certainly recorded by Thompson Pater, Richard's grandfather, who married Mary Church at Newport Pagnell on 3 October 1763. The Paters are said by Wright to have been involved for generations in the lace trade and to have been settled first at Beccles. Mary Church's mother was a Miss Gage, of the Roman Catholic family of Norfolk. At Weston the couple were in the district of the lace trade, but their choice of where to settle may also have been governed by other considerations. Not far away, at Thornton, a Robert Pater and his family are recorded by at least 1618, and some connection seems likely.

Thompson Pater's children were baptized as Roman Catholics (very probably only because of the fact that Mary Church was a Roman Catholic) but though the majority may have retained this faith, there was a break made by Pater's own father – or possibly first by his grandfather – who adopted no religion. Of the nine children of Thompson and Mary Pater's marriage, some of the girls remained living as spinsters at Weston, and Pater was to note in a letter of 1859 the death there 'of my Aunt Anne'. She was probably the last of Thompson Pater's children to die, and her death severed such slight connections as may have existed between the place and Pater. In his work he never refers to either Weston or Olney, or to Cowper who had lived for long in both villages.

Pater's grandfather, John Thompson, the eldest son, seems certainly to have broken with family tradition by becoming a surgeon, and establishing this as a tradition for his own descendants. But trading, mercantile and financial interests characterized the large family and descendants of his younger brother John Church Pater. Some of them held clerkships in the Bank of England. Others settled in Liverpool and became prosperous merchants. Contacts between these cousins and the family at Enfield are unlikely to have been great, but some contacts there probably were – especially when it came to finding a job for Pater's brother, William. He indeed seems to have had closer relations altogether with the Liverpool branch of the family. His attachment to some of them was mentioned by Pater, writing after his death in 1887, in reply to a letter of condolence from Frederic Loudon Pater, himself a merchant and the second son of Joseph Pater, also a merchant of Liverpool. Perhaps significantly, that death is the only known occasion of letters exchanged between the two sets of cousins.

It is, strangely, in another direction not strictly concerned with the Paters as such, where the family ties might have been weaker, that there seems to have been a much stronger and more enduring bond, emotionally more valuable to Pater's mother if not to her children. And in Pater it was all symbolized. His godmother was Mary Susanna May, only child of the widowed Sophia Porter (*née* Grange) of Fish Hall near the small village of Hadlow, in Kent, and thus Hester Pater's niece. She had married an eccentric local landowner, Walter Barton May, of Hadlow Castle. Their eldest child was born in 1822 and christened Walter Horatio. It was after him that Pater was named.

By the time Pater was born, Mrs May had become estranged from her husband. She had left him and returned the short distance from Hadlow to Fish Hall, where she lived with her children and her mother. Walter May, increasingly eccentric, had been inspired by the example of Beckford's Fonthill to design and have built at Hadlow a Gothic folly, the most prominent feature of which is the still surviving, though dilapidated tall tower, soaring but somehow prosaic, and only too aptly described as 'May's folly'. Perhaps May saw himself as another Beckford, a hermit withdrawn in disillusionment from society, almost the sort of figure – given youth and philosophical if cold detachment – to be described by Pater in the personality of Sebastian van Storck, who abruptly leaves his home and his fiancée and is finally found dead in a desolate house, one of the old lodgings of his family, 'in an upper room of the old tower.' May's own death, in 1855, was commemorated by a grandiose funeral, followed by burial in an equally grandiose family mausoleum in the south-western corner of the simple local churchyard, close to his mock-Gothic castle.

Fish Hall (now Great Fish Hall) is in every way the architectural opposite of that: unpretentious, compact though quite extensive, a well-proportioned red brick house of the eighteenth century entirely hidden from the road, and expressive not of folly but of good sense. Mary Susanna May possibly enshrined as much herself. At least, she seems to have proved a good friend to her godson's mother and entertained her family at Fish Hall. Maria Pater's will was witnessed by Mary Susanna May and her daughter (also Mary Susanna), and her death was to take place at Fish Hall. Its layout and grounds are almost certainly far grander than the house and garden of Pater's childhood at Enfield, but its emotional atmosphere was probably little different and certainly no less emphatically female. Indeed, the two households might have been drawn to one another as much for these reasons as for family ones.

At Fish Hall the trio of women consisted at first of widowed grandmother, mother and daughter (Walter Horatio May married early and set up his own household). Although not positively widowed until 1855, Mrs May lived without a husband and in more than one way could perhaps have claimed to be among the susceptible persons 'who had had their sorrows', within Florian's youthful environment and also Gaston de Latour's. When Gaston thinks intently about the 'little tombs which had recorded almost the minutes of children's lives' (Elizabeth de Latour, Cornélius de Latour, aged so many years, days and hours), it recalls Hadlow churchyard where lie buried the very young sons of Mary Susanna May, aged five and thirteen months respectively, and also – possibly more poignant a loss to the family – her infant grandson, Walter Reginald May, who died in 1846, at the age of six months.

And it might be of Hadlow again that Pater is thinking in *Emerald Uthwart* (where Sussex is made to sound remarkably like Kent, with its 'little velvety fields'): 'Here all was little; the very church where they went to pray, to sit, the ancient Uthwarts sleeping all round outside under the windows, deposited there as quietly as fallen trees on their native soil, and almost unrecorded, as there had been almost nothing to record.'

Granges, Paters, Mays – they too over the centuries had been born and had died, leaving little memorial of themselves except their tombstones. Yet these shadowy people probably stirred, and even reassured, the young Pater by the very fact that they had once lived, undergone suffering and joy, and had now ceased to be. Proof of their having existed lay in the people who had known them, had been begotten by them and had in turn begotten other people, one day to slip silently back to rejoin them. Nothing had disturbed their restful obscurity, seeming to be continued in the stillness of the grave. They formed a sort of leaf-mould to his imagination, itself more easily taking root in the past than the present, often more stimulated by some name carved in a simple stone epitaph than by an actual, living person. 'Dead, yet sentient and caressing hands seemed to reach out of the ground and to be clinging about him,' Marius muses, on returning to his old home not long before his own death; and a sense of finding peace by descending into literally familiar earth seems to have come early to Pater – and never as something to be dreaded.

Within the narrow family circle, it was probably old people – or those who appeared old– who gave him the strongest feeling of comparable shelter and peace. Their slight withdrawnness from the world would appeal to him, as would any gravity, or even sadness, inculcated in them by life. To them, with time and affection to spare, he in turn probably appealed as a boy unusually thoughtful, affectionate and retiring: happier to listen or talk to them than to mix with other children and to play conventional children's games. To other boys he might seem odd – indeed, he did. To those regarding him lovingly, he probably appeared not only serious but marked out for some special, possibly religious, future.

No doubt his grandmother and his aunt Bessie were foremost among the admiring circle, but another elderly female figure must at least be recorded. This is Miss Susanna Grange, younger sister of Hester Pater and Sophia Porter though like them surviving to the age of eighty-four. Her existence remains inevitably tenuous and has previously not been remarked. But in the 1851 census she is listed as present in Maria Pater's household at Enfield, conceivably only as a visitor – in which case she is likely to have lived at Fish Hall. It was there that she died in April 1855, a few weeks before the death of Walter Barton May, and her death was registered by Bessie Pater who must herself have been staying then at Fish Hall. Nothing in Pater's writings explicitly refers to this spinster great-aunt; to him too she perhaps remained shadowy, but the very unobtrusiveness of her presence may have added to the sensibility he gives Florian of growing up among 'those who pass their days, as a matter of course, in a sort of "going quietly".'

The extraordinarily intense absorption of Pater in the spectacle of himself coming to increasing awareness in the enclosed environment of Enfield, watched over by a group of women gentle, cloistered, subdued and more than slightly sad, makes it easy to forget that he was not an isolated only child but one of a family of four. At best, a few hints of this situation percolate through his writings, but rarely with much emotional weight. Indeed, without knowing that he had a brother and two sisters, a casual reader would find even the hints hard to detect, so oblique are they. Pater's imaginary heroes inhabit houses of the spirit which barely have room for anyone else – least of all for siblings. Something of his own detachment seems in reality to have characterized the attitude of his siblings to him and among each

42

other. An exception to this was probably the relationship between him and Clara, the youngest child, who grew up gravely beautiful and intellectually gifted.

The rapport between them finds its place, significantly, in *The Child in the House*, where Florian openly weeps with relief when his little sister returns at last from a day's outing to a wood, bringing him a treasure of fallen acorns and black crow's feathers, 'and his peace at finding her again near him mingled all night with some intimate sense of the distant forest . . .' Otherwise, although there is a reference in the same piece to the 'children's room', and a brief abrupt mention of 'Lewis' (presumably Florian's brother) falling ill, everything combines to suggest the solitariness of Florian as a child. Of all the later studies, it is only Emerald Uthwart, 'the youngest son, but not the youngest child', who has brothers and sisters (and he also, like Pater, has his birthday in August), though little is said of them except that they all liked gardening.

In temperament the boy Pater seems already to have felt utterly detached from at least his elder brother and sister. The gap in their ages was not great, and it must have been that his intense, imaginative interior life created a distance which no amount of physical proximity could bridge. Hester Pater's image as an adult is faint enough, coloured by domesticity and some suggestions of residual sourness; of her as a child there are no indications whatsoever. She was to share with Clara the dedication of *Marius the Epicurean*, but, since by then the two sisters lived with and looked after Pater, she could scarcely have been omitted. On the evidence, slight though it inevitably is, of *The Child in the House*, she appears to have had no distinct place in his emotional life. There is not even a passing reference to an elder sister, and it may be that she early faded, or was absorbed, into the circle of women around him who stood for quiet domestic activity. Fated to live long, outliving her siblings, and never to marry, intellectually in no way equal to her younger brother and sister, Hester was possibly assigned prematurely a Martha-like Victorian household role which never allowed other aspects of her personality to find expression. Even her name within the family is not quite clear. In letters to friends Pater calls her 'Tottie' – perhaps a childhood nickname. Mrs Pater entered her name in the 1851 census form merely as Maria which suggests that this is what she was called during anyway her mother's lifetime, though she herself as an adult uses Hester in such letters of hers as exist.

Hester was ever-present but perhaps rather shadowy to Pater while growing up. Clara, two years his junior, may not yet have been a companion, but like Florian's 'little sister' she must have stirred his tender, almost frighteningly strong susceptibility to the suffering and pain of other people. In art and in life, imaginatively and actually, tragically and trivially, it is all fused in *The Child in the House* by Florian's sight of a reproduction of David's sketch of Marie-Antoinette going to the guillotine (her face now mute and resistless, yet calling on men 'to have pity and forbear'), and by the appeal in his small sister's frightened face, out in the garden under the lilacs, when a spider falls on to her sleeve. To her look at that moment is traced back 'a certain mercy he conceived always for people in fear, even of little things,' and a concurrent impulse towards self-sacrifice. Clara is thus given her place in Pater's emotional development, though less as a person than as a stimulus to discovery of his own nature.

A good deal more is known about her character – as about her appearance – than about Hester's, but her shyness, reserve and perhaps pride prevented any profound impression of her personality surviving. Her temperamental affinities with Pater were strong – possibly stronger even than either of them ever quite recognized, at least when they were children. And though it is true that his imaginary portraits are always of men without sisters, there may be something a little more than accidental in his adopting the *persona* of a sister of Jean-Baptiste Pater's for the 'portrait' of Watteau conveyed through her journal. That lonely, sensitive, half-sad girl is represented as far from illiterate or naive, provincial though she is, and perhaps some faint family resemblance to Pater's own sister and her situation shines through. Clara might have noted, as the girl does, 'a certain immobility of disposition in me'. And Clara never received the education her intellect deserved. Her Latin and Greek were to be self-taught in adult life. When Mrs Humphry Ward first met her as a young woman, she was 'without much positive acquirement', despite her intelligence. What she would or could have become with proper schooling and fairer opportunities can only be guessed. Little though Pater can have wished to dominate, it was he alone who received a serious education among the children and he who, in life and after death, became the focal point of his sisters' lives.

More complex seems to have been Pater's relationship to his elder brother, William, someone whose character also remains rather obscure. Thomas Wright stressed his strikingly good looks, both as a boy and as a man, in contrast to Pater's own appearance, but Wright for some reason was obsessively concerned with conveying an idea of Pater as almost grotesquely ugly – a fact contradicted by portraits of him as a young man and by some contemporary comments. No portrait or photograph of William seems to exist, but if

44

Wright is correct about him Pater may well have felt what flaws there were in his own appearance the more strongly, and envied William's physical beauty.

The only story Wright relates of the two boys suggests no particular sympathy between them. Pater early developed a horror of snakes – mentioned as a trait of the young Marius and in Pater's life documented by several factual instances. Wright (giving no source for his information) says that William, well aware of his brother's antipathy, once put a viper round a door-handle and that Pater 'nearly died of fright' when he realized what he had grasped. Perhaps the incident was merely an isolated practical joke at a period when such repugnance – especially in a boy – would have seemed just funny or cowardly, but perhaps it also indicates the elder brother's impatience altogether with Pater's character and interests. To him Pater may have seemed bookish, if not priggish, over-sensitive, if not solemn, and generally in need of being brought to face practical life.

By 1851 William had left school and was a clerk in a merchant's office, possibly at Enfield or more probably in London. He was then fifteen. The choice of occupation is likely to have been governed in one way or another by the fact that prosperous members of the Pater family were merchants. Nevertheless, William must have decided against such a career. In 1857 he was admitted to the Royal College of Surgeons at Canterbury. He joined the army, but soon left it. There was talk later of his going out to Brazil with one of his Liverpool cousins though he may never have gone. Eventually, he became assistant medical officer at the Fareham Lunatic Asylum, moving from there to a more senior post in the asylum at Stafford.

'William', Pater writes almost petulantly in a letter of 1859, when he was an undergraduate at Oxford and William in the army, 'never informs us of any of his movements.' This may have become less true once William found a post that suited him, but his detachment from the trio of Pater and his sisters seems always to have been marked. No friend of theirs ever records meeting him, either in Oxford or London, or being even aware that Pater had a brother. Only at the very end of his life, when he was suffering from heart disease and dropsy, did William leave Stafford for London, to be looked after by Hester and Clara in the temporary Paddington lodgings (not their own Kensington home) where he died. Like his siblings, William never married. He bequeathed everything he possessed to Hester and Clara, and in his will made no mention of Pater.

It would be easy to declare that Pater's writings make virtually no mention of him. But his good looks may well have been borrowed as the suitable outward expression for several of Pater's fictional people whose characteristics otherwise are so close to Pater's own. In *Emerald Uthwart*, written after William's death, there is perhaps a recollection of further real facts when the young Emerald is told he would ' "do for the army" '. Emerald is – even among Pater's handsome heroes – outstandingly handsome, graceful, healthy and eager to be a soldier ('and what he reads most readily is of the military life . . .').

The strange end of this strange story, with its extract from the 'Diary of a Surgeon', can scarcely have been written without reflecting on that line of surgeons in the family, of which William was the last. William perhaps had been uncertain about what career to adopt, or had at first been given small choice. He obviously took some years to settle down, yet seems to have felt no less strong an urge than Pater to serve his fellow human beings. In the unfinished, unpublished, imaginary portrait, *Tibalt the Albigense*, the boy brought up a heretic early decides 'to be a healer of the body'. Had he been a Catholic, Pater states, he would have been a priest. The grim people who surrounded Tibalt did not discourage him but found a way to the realization of his desire/purpose (both words are in the manuscript) to become a physician. With that sentence the fragment tantalizingly ends.

Already at Enfield, even while employed in a merchant's office, William may have dreamt of following the profession of his grandfather, father and uncle, perhaps within an army context. Of Pater's dreams we can be more sure: the idea of becoming a priest was then firmly in his mind, expressed by dressing-up, giving sermons and acting as a priest. With perhaps conscious emphasis on his surname, as well as in allusion to his quiet manner and his strange ways, his schoolfellows at Enfield Grammar School called him 'Parson Pater'.

Marius experiences and never loses 'That first, early, boyish ideal of priesthood, the sense of dedication . . .' Gaston de Latour has an 'early-pronounced preference for the ecclesiastical calling', and is shown in the opening chapter as a boy receiving the tonsure, his first step towards the priesthood. Another unfinished, unpublished imaginary portrait, inspired by Romanino's painting of S. Gaudioso, Bishop of Brescia, deals with Domenico Averoldi (a 'second Gaudioso') who never denies the story of how his naive delight in holiness when a child led him solemnly to bless his comrades.

If other boys agreed to join in Pater's liturgical games, as Wright states, it was probably for the mere fun. To him they meant something much deeper, as they appear to have done to the women in the household, especially his aunt. Like Florian, he felt a kind of 'mystical appetite' for sacred things and enjoyed yielding to 'religious impressions'.

46

One aspect of this was patently a precocious aestheticism, more concerned with altar-lights and vestments, and the apparatus of religion, than with its substance; there may even have been an appeal to his sense of theatre, with the priest, rapt and apart, moving amid ritual and attendants. The vicar of St Andrews', Enfield, was soon to be causing scandal and dissension by his High Church proclivities (a churchwarden, an M.P., was struck in the church by Daniel Harrison of Chase Hill a year or two after the Pater family left Enfield), but to Pater he must have given intense, sensuous delight.

Yet vague though Pater's 'impressions' of religion may have been, they cannot have been entirely aesthetic. The vessels and vestments and so on represented things he desired: order, purity, cleanliness. The priest or clergyman represented a dedicated way of life, a sublimation of self and the disturbing currents of earthly love in love of God and service of others – always providing God exists. 'The doubts never die,' Pater was to write in the last months of his life, referring to Pascal, though with a distinct autobiographical echo. But as a boy first awakening to the literal charm of religion, and deliberately needing a bulwark against tremors of mortal fear, he probably experienced no doubts. 'For a time', the pre-adolescent Florian finds, 'he walked through the world in a sustained, not unpleasureable awe,' generated by what sounds an almost Blake-like sense of mystic correspondences.

'For a time . . .' It could not last, partly because Pater was to discover the probing, disturbing power of his own intelligence. And, besides, those fierce waves of visual beauty which swept over him created their own disturbance, stirring as he grew up turbulent emotions of longing and no doubt lust. The real world, of people as much as things, was too physical, too palpable, too alluring, to be treated as just a shadow of some divine world presumed existing behind it.

Nuances in his attitude can have become clear to him only gradually as he ceased to be a child. To the fond women around him they possibly never became clear. He seemed, without hypocrisy, to be a saintly boy. That he was destined for the Church would naturally occur to them. His aunt especially, herself pious as well as affectionate, must have felt he was marked out in every way for such a life, thinking of him perhaps less in terms of a Victorian prelate than as a holy man, or even hermit, of medieval tales. His intellectual precocity, too, was rapidly apparent ('his mother taught him to read, wondering at the ease with which he learned', he says of Florian) and would soon deserve more encouragement than Enfield Grammar School provided at the period. He probably looked older, graver, than his contemporaries: set apart already in temperament from the majority of them, and not yet conscious of the full burden of that separation.

Enfield and Hadlow, countrified, tranquil environments, easily blended into each other to leave the impress of a single one: an old house sheltering a child who was in his imagination perhaps fixed forever as its sole occupant, emotionally alone though not lacking in exchange of affection, his personality taking shape under pressure of a myriad trivial-seeming yet intense sensations, to be absorbed and never forgotten. Everything helped to feed the flame of his imagination; it was for that cult that he had a real vocation, became and remained its true priest, tending it until the end of his life.

But though time might appear for a while to stand still for Pater – most completely perhaps in moments of overwhelming perception – neither he, nor the people around him, any more than their pets or indeed the fabric of their house, was impervious to change. Constantly, it seems, his enjoyment of sheer beauty was shot through with painful awareness of its frailty, and even by pain itself. The flowers of red hawthorn which Florian picks to fill the children's room lose their fiery brightness and fade to being a few dry petals perishing 'in the drawers of an old cabinet.' Even art, Pater half-understood, is not without pain. When he describes how Florian was taught by an older boy to make flowers out of sealing-wax, it is apt – and doubtless a true recollection – that he should mention how he burnt his hand badly in a lighted taper. Shock seems still pulsing years later behind the sentence in *The Child in the House* which tells of his white angora cat – first of the cats Pater owned – with its flower-like face and dark tail, which fell into a lingering sickness, could no longer stand the light and finally flickered into death, 'after one wild morning of pain.'

Ironically, it was most probably Pater's own ability which led to the move away from the 'old house' and broke the seclusion of Enfield. Possibly on the advice of the headmaster of the local grammar school, it was decided that he should go to the King's School at Canterbury. The Enfield home was given up and by the beginning of 1853 Maria Pater and her family were living close to Canterbury in the village of Harbledown.

To a certain extent Pater's childhood was over and an enchantment was broken. Nevertheless, what followed was very far from disillusion. At the King's School he was to encounter boys quite as idiosyncratic as himself, make his first – perhaps only – serious friends and, most important of all, begin to write. New qualities in his character, including wit and mimicry, developed and found a perhaps more appreciative audience at school than at home. His

48

academic gifts also developed and he was encouraged to work successfully for a scholarship at Oxford. He felt the stirrings of ambition. He was to leave the school with the rather guarded yet public commendation of the clerical headmaster (who did not basically care for him), hinting at the prospect of his having a distinguished career.

But the achievements of those years at Canterbury were not to escape being darkened by disappointments and by sudden death. Already, by 1851, before leaving Enfield, Maria Pater had made her will, prompted possibly by ill-health. She chose three trustees for her children: her sister-in-law, Bessie, Charles Sturges, a surgeon living in Stepney, and John Pendergast, a lawyer whose home and offices were in Commercial Road, comparatively close to Pater's birthplace. Three winters after having had the will witnessed by Pater's god-mother and her daughter, she was on another visit to Fish Hall, this this time from Harbledown, and at Fish Hall she apparently unexpectedly died, on 25 February 1854. She was buried in Hadlow churchyard, near to the May and Porter monuments but in a grave by herself. Stark truth gives poignant force in this case to the familiar words carved on her simple tombstone: '. . . leaving a family to sorrow for her loss.'

Three   The triumvirate

PATER was not yet fifteen when his mother died. He had been exactly one year at the King's School, a year which had probably been lonely for him if not miserable. He returned to it in the winter of 1854 not merely dejected and in mourning but with self-reproach – if the incident connected with the death of Marius's mother is, as seems likely, autobiographical. 'She died away from home,' Pater relates, but before dying managed painfully to send for Marius, so that he should not always feel guilty over what occurred before she left. 'For it happened that, through some sudden, incomprehensible petulance there had been an angry childish gesture, and a slighting word, at the very moment of her departure, actually for the last time.' And Pater records the peculiar bitterness of that 'marred parting' for one who set so much store on the principle and habit of home. As for the event itself, it 'for a time seemed to have taken the light out of the sunshine.'

Most of Pater's other heroes scarcely have mothers. Even the mother of Emerald Uthwart, who helps the surgeon extract the bullet from her son's corpse, is in no sense *there*; all that is previously implied of her is indeed a lack of emotional engagement about this boy, the youngest son but not the youngest child: 'you conceive', Pater directly addresses the reader, 'the sort of negligence that creeps over even the kindest maternities in such case.' Perhaps in those words lies some echo of his own experience, feeling possibly that what attention his mother could muster was directed towards her youngest child, Clara. One of the few mothers in his work, that of the young poet in *An English Poet*, an unfinished, posthumously published study, is early widowed and 'really stricken at heart underneath', dies while her son is still a boy.

The actual circumstances of the death of Maria Pater may have given her for Pater a place, and a positive quality, which she had somehow lacked in life. Besides, however faint and languid her existence might seem, its abrupt end must have made her children aware of how alone they now were. Only their aunt Bessie, some years older than their mother, was left to look after them. No more is heard of Mrs May, Pater's godmother, bothering with the family.

Maria Pater had scrupulously divided her possessions equally between the four children, except for the furniture and household effects whose sale she stipulated might be postponed during their minority or for so long as Bessie lived with them. Apart from the money in trust, and as well as a portion of silver, each child received a legacy of appropriate trinkets: Hester a diamond brooch, for example, and two seals, one 'my seal marked *Maria*'; Clara a small gold watch, an amethyst seal and also a seal engraved with Shakespeare's head. William was bequeathed his father's gold watch and seal, and his mother's wedding ring. To Pater had come a large gold watch, 'his late father's chain and seal' and his mother's guard-ring.

As the owner of those rather sad mementoes, he must have once again walked down to Canterbury a few weeks after the beginning of the Lent term, taking his usual way, the footpath from the village of Harbledown, where in a small, late Regency-style terrace house the bereaved family continued to live. Expense perhaps had prevented Mrs Pater from taking a house in Canterbury itself. But from the edge of the hill at Harbledown, the city was easily seen, with the towers of the cathedral rising in its midst, lying at the end as it were of the still surviving bridle-path which must be that taken so regularly by Pater.

The associations of the King's School with Henry VIII, its famous pupils like Marlowe, even his own daily lessons – such things probably meant less to him than the cathedral and constant attendance at its services. There was, too, the spectacle of a not too cloistered – often indeed positively worldly – existence led by the canons, among whom was the future Dean Stanley. At Canterbury there was grandeur as well as antiquity, and a far more complex history of mingled secular and religious strains for Pater to brood on than anything offered by Enfield. When in *Gaston de Latour*, Gaston travels through a bitter frost on Candlemas morning (that is, on 2 February) to Chartres, 'to the great western portal', Pater is surely recollecting his own first journey at the same time of year down to Canterbury. Though in *Marius* the city is Pisa where Marius goes to school, and the landmark of a building is necessarily 'the great temple of the place', Pater's walk home up to Harbledown comes to mind when Marius recalls 'turning back once for a last look [at it] from an angle of his homeward road.'

Not until *Emerald Uthwart*, written under the emotional impetus of a visit again to the King's School in the summer of 1891, did Pater deal with a cathedral and a closely-linked school in an English setting, barely disguising the Canterbury location. By then the school had mellowed, as it was bound to in almost any middle-aged man's eyes, into being a perfect setting for the jewel-like, popular Emerald.

Yet even while glamorizing his corporate environment, Pater cannot help wryly remarking, 'A school is not made for one.' And he is too honest or too disillusioned to believe that either sympathetic companionships or passionate friendship formed at school can survive beyond it. Not only does Emerald experience the profound charm of the place and feel diminished, not disagreeably, in the cathedral amid the 'grand waves, wave upon wave, of patiently-wrought stone', but he makes one firm friend, James Stokes. The two boys, thinking of military glory, even in ecclesiastical surroundings, half dream of being brought back after dying splendid soldiers' deaths, for ever to lie together in the cathedral aisle under a tattered flag and a single epitaph: 'in hac ecclesia pueri instituti . . .' This mood of high romanticism is quite consciously contrived to contrast the more ironically with the real future the friends face, of the firing squad and disgrace – not permitted even the consolation of sharing exactly the same fate.

The schoolboy Marius also gains a great friend in Flavian, handsome and highly intelligent, 'prince of the school'; but Flavian is doomed to die young, leaving Marius mourning over his body and alone in the world. The youthful Gaston de Latour enjoys friendship with a trio of gifted boys who have 'detached themselves . . . from the surface of that youthful scholastic world' and who are nicknamed by their comrades 'The Triumvirate'. That reference Pater patently borrowed from his own schooldays, from a 'Triumvirate' at the King's School of which he had once been a part. And although in their ambitions and their appearances the trio Gaston knows – of Jasmin, Amadée and Camille – has scarcely any close connection with Pater and his own two friends, it sounds no less doomed to dispersal: 'Threads to be cut short, one by one, before his eyes, the three would cross and recross, gaily, pathetically . . . divided far asunder afterwards.' Often rearranging the Canterbury scenery, savouring every visual nuance while no doubt forgetting many petty annoyances of school, school-fellows and masters, Pater seems never to have been tempted in any writings to convey anything about the actuality of his days at the King's School or the character of the two friends who had with him made up the triumvirate. Probably because of later events he sealed off the reality and fashioned for Marius – for example – the ideal, proto-Dorian Gray figure of Flavian, beautiful and decadent, an epitome of the pagan world ('. . . the depth of its corruption, and its perfection of form'): the friend Pater himself had failed to find, at school or elsewhere.

Among the new boys at the King's School in the Lent term of 1854 was one slightly younger than Pater, Henry Dombrain, the son of a local hop-grower and wine-merchant. Intense, fiercely intolerant, indifferent to games and at least as profoundly earnest about religion as Pater, Dombrain was an unconventional boy. In itself that was possibly a first bond between them. No nickname for Pater at this period is recorded, but schoolboy shrewdness quickly styled Dombrain 'Archdeacon' – for his authoritarian manner perhaps, no less than for his religious bias.

The two boys became friends. Pater was welcomed in Dombrain's Canterbury home and there he met the extremely High Church vicar, the Reverend Edward Harrison Woodall, of the nearby church of St Margaret's which the Dombrain family attended. The exterior of the church had recently been done over by Gilbert Scott in 'Decorated' Gothic style, an apt expression of Woodall's own tendencies and beliefs, and a style warmly recommended by such reforming ecclesiologistic bodies as the Cambridge Camden Society. Woodall took an interest in Dombrain, and this must have easily extended to Dombrain's new friend, whose religious attitude was then so similar and who was also highly intelligent. Woodall's concern with ritual, the cult of the Virgin, saints' days and so on, must have merely deepened in Pater at this period all the impressions gained at Enfield. To Dombrain and his family, Woodall probably stood for a richer, truer and more fervent Anglican faith, despite dangerous overtones of Roman Catholicism, which the nineteenth century had recovered.

The story of that recovery was not without its shocks, some of them still vibrating in the early 1850s. Matters of faith constantly seemed challenged, and reactions to such challenges were often to be hysterical. On one side lay the threat of rationalism; on the other the far more insidious one of Popery. Newman's dramatic conversion to Roman Catholicism in 1845 had been followed six years later by Manning's. The Camden Society had been preached against on the ominous grounds that *The 'Restoration of Churches' is the Restoration of Popery* (the actual title of a sermon of 1844, published as a pamphlet). Enfield was to feel increasing tremors, with a group of parishioners petitioning Parliament for removal of their vicar because of his innovations smacking of the Church of Rome.

As schoolboys, Pater and Dombrain each found satisfaction in the 'Decorated' observances and ritual practised by Woodall, though also attending services at the cathedral and enjoying Stanley's sermons. Dombrain was committed for life. With Pater it was to prove a phase, rather like the friendship. Woodall unwittingly acted as something of a catalyst when, a very few years later (after Pater had gone up to Oxford), he too was received into the Roman Catholic Church – to the scandal of Canterbury. That this event took place in Paris will have been not the least scandalous aspect in city and cathedral opinion. That it took place formally on 15 August, the feast day of the Assumption of the Virgin, clearly signified Woodall's devotion, though it probably passed largely unnoticed in the shock and dismay of those who had known him. For Dombrain the act consigned Woodall to oblivion. Anything associated with the man was defiling pitch. Almost unbalanced in the violence of his repulsion, he actually altered his choice of Oxford college (Exeter) to avoid going to the same one as had Woodall. In that reaction much is revealed about the man destined to be, in Wright's words, 'a diligent, if rather narrow-minded, clergyman, with a furious antipathy to Radicals and Nonconformists.' Pater believed, Wright on good evidence records, that Woodall had done the right thing, and neither blamed nor pitied him. The attitude of Dombrain appeared to him ridiculous – though its fearsome intolerance might have warned him of how any lapse of his own would be treated.

Between the two of them, even as schoolboys, there was probably never any real temperamental affinity. But Dombrain was at least a companion who shared some of Pater's interests – rare enough – and he arrived at the school just when Pater must have particularly welcomed companionship. Dombrain's prosperous home offered an attractive alternative to the house at Harbledown. Nor was it always the scene of earnest religious conversations. Charades were often performed there, and Pater's unexpected gift of acting and mimicry found an outlet. He had already seen Charles Kean play Hotspur (possibly at the benefit performance of 18 December 1852 at the Princess's Theatre) and never forgot seeing him as Richard II. He developed an ability to imitate him and was to touch (Dean) Stanley to tears by his playing of a scene from *Henry IV* (Part I). Possibly this was at the school Speech Day in August 1857 when in an extract Pater took the part of Hotspur and Dombrain that of Worcester, the third member of their triumvirate playing Northumberland.

Dombrain himself was not always the 'Archdeacon'. He enjoyed telling stories based on local legends or history, and his own family had its romantic historical associations in Huguenot origin. The Dombrains were said to have fled from France in an open boat at the time of Protestant persecution. French ancestry was emphasized by the branch of the family who spelt their name D'Ombrain (re-collected perhaps in the surname 'Deleal' given to Florian's French-descended family in *The Child in the House*) and in that French connection there was a further link between the two boys.

Nevertheless, something stronger and more intimate was probably needed to transform their relationship, and it came in the person of John Rainier McQueen, who arrived at the school in February 1855. McQueen was only eight months younger than Pater. He lived until 1912, not merely surviving into the period when Thomas Wright was working on his biography of Pater but – in contradistinction to Hester and Clara – actively aiding Wright with recollections, letters and poems which testify to the closeness of what seems to have been a quite unsentimental friendship. Everything pointed to its life-long duration. Yet at Oxford, under the influence of Dombrain and in an access of self-righteousness, McQueen was to break the friendship and virtually betray Pater by intervening to prevent his ordination when he realized Pater's doubts about Christianity. Pater never spoke to or saw him again, and never afterwards seems to have mentioned his name. To Wright years later McQueen declared that he still believed he had done his duty. He retained his affection for Pater and indeed developed something of a cult of Pater, preserving his letters and his early manuscripts, reading and annotating books about him, and in some contorted way perhaps attempting unconscious amends in the substantial help he gave Wright. Nobody was to get to know Pater as intimately as had McQueen, but the appalling use he made, at a crucial moment, of that knowledge in itself sufficiently explains why Pater as an adult avoided, doubtless distrusted, intimate friendships.

At the King's School he had been very different, once he had found friends. The haunted pre-adolescent boy, wandering in the house and garden at Enfield, a receptacle for almost heady draughts of bitter-sweet emotion, discovered a less passive and spectator-like role, typified by his acting – and akin more to Hotspur than to Hamlet. And his leading part when the triumvirate publicly played a scene from *Henry IV* accurately represented his place in the group. For the first, though not last, time he realized and relished his ability to hold attention, to charm, amuse and even shock. At school in Enfield he had appeared merely odd. That oddness had hardened by the time he was in mid-school career at Canterbury into being part of his outstanding individuality. Displayed amusingly – as in imitating Dean Stanley or in aptly comparing his schoolfellows to various animals – it probably protected him and even gained him grudging admiration. More important, that individuality when displayed seriously was found capable of stirring interest and affection in other individuals.

At some date about this time, possibly soon after his mother's death, Pater briefly met John Keble (then living as vicar of Hursley, near Winchester) and while he is recorded as having been greatly impressed by Keble's unforced piety and kindness to him, it is also clear that Keble had been no less impressed by the boy. That Pater was talented and might well become a second Keble was the opinion of a relation of the McQueen family, Mary Ann Virginia Gabriel, a composer of popular songs and operettas to whom he had shown some of his early poems. Other members of the McQueen family, especially the grandmother, Mrs Rainier, felt real fondness for him; she shared his hopes of gaining an exhibition at Oxford, and wrote of him in a letter, 'nobody more worthy'. Above all, Pater had the confidence and friendship of McQueen himself, who was to note at the time of their rupture that Pater had for long been 'my constant friend, and in many cases my guide and protector . . .'

Like Dombrain and perhaps like Pater, McQueen was of partly French descent (from the Huguenot family of Rainier). At home he was called René. Like the other two members of the triumvirate, he was profoundly religious, though without High Church inclinations and in later life became Low Church and evangelical. Of the trio, his is the hardest character to grasp, but he appears to have allowed, if not encouraged, Wright to describe him as a quiet, solitary, independent 'and in some respects very singular boy, with strong biases and some extraordinary prejudices.' From all this, he certainly sounds a suitable companion for Pater and Dombrain. His natural independence was bolstered by social status and considerable wealth (at his death in 1912 his estate was valued at over £74,000 gross). His paternal grandfather was the formidable Scottish judge, Robert McQueen, Lord Braxfield, the prototype of Stevenson's Weir in *Weir of Hermiston*, and the family retained property in Scotland, as well as having a country house at Chailey in Sussex. McQueen's father, James, had been posted to Canterbury on the outbreak of the Crimean War as colonel commanding the depots there, and hence the arrival at the King's School of McQueen, along with his younger brother Robert.

McQueen described to Wright his first sight of Pater in the winter of 1855 – with overhanging forehead, brown hair, deep-set mild eyes, a heavy jaw and some malformation of the mouth – and Wright elaborated this, presumably on McQueen's evidence, to emphasize Pater's plain, prematurely whiskered features and hump-back. Yet these physical oddities – odder perhaps to and amid school-boys than among adults – at least drew attention to Pater. McQueen quickly found attractive his highly developed personality, fastidious speech and gentle, charming manners. Pater produced his earlier friend Dombrain. And 'the triumvirate' – a name they owed to their headmaster – was formed.

Disliking organized games of every kind, eager to work hard,

56

yet full of their own diversions and semi-secret allusions, the three boys were not really untypical of any intelligent group in any conventional community. Even their ardent attendance at religious services has its typical aspect. Their jokes and their gifts to each other, their walks in favourite woods around Canterbury (an activity they called, in a word chosen by Pater, 'skirmishing') all expressed their sense of having woven around themselves a screen of almost conspiratorial affinity. Life at school had emphasized that they were different from the majority of their fellows – as probably each had long suspected – but that such differences need not mean total isolation. They were confirmed together. They acted together. In the same form, they competed for, or shared, the same prizes – for classics, for history, for divinity and for English. All three became monitors. They were the school's 'three inseparables': arriving together each morning (there was a corner in Canterbury were Pater waited for the other two to join him) and doubtless leaving together, away 'skirmishing' or visiting each other's houses.

Yet under the outward unity there were traces of distinctions and even of inequality. Viewed in one light, it was Dombrain and McQueen who had the closest affinity, not only in their material circumstances but in being idiosyncratic and eccentric rather than positively talented. And then, though they might interpret Anglicanism in slightly different ways, they remained unshaken in their fundamental beliefs – just as they were to remain friends until Dombrain's death in 1896. Unlike Pater, they were both prosperous if not indeed wealthy; and their parents, unlike his, were alive. Probably it is no accident that while Pater is mentioned as often at Dombrain's house, or as staying with McQueen, there seem few references to their being in contact with Pater's family. He certainly took McQueen to Harbledown, though possibly less to visit his home than to point out the architecture of the church (which McQueen vividly recalled his doing – 'Pater was *always* fond of church architecture, and knew a great deal about it, when quite a lad').

All three boys may have studied intensively, but Pater seems to have lacked McQueen's facility for winning school prizes. To gain a scholarship to Oxford was something important to him not merely academically but financially. Probably that is one reason why he so desperately overworked and exhausted himself to the brink of illness. It was the McQueen family who then stepped in, inviting him to spend part of his summer holidays at their house in Sussex. When he did win his exhibition (worth £60 a year) he also received a gift of money from 'friends' who were almost certainly the McQueen family.

57

Although McQueen may have left the school encumbered with prizes, he apparently had no doubt that Pater's was the truly original and creative mind. Viewed in this light, Pater and McQueen seem to have shared an affinity, partly intellectual and partly emotional, which tended to exclude Dombrain, whose interests were obviously narrower than theirs. Perhaps Dombrain would never have made friends with Pater at all had there not been a common religious fervour to warm the acquaintance. As soon as that cooled in Pater – had reached in fact the point of expiry – Dombrain struck Pater out of his life and memory for ever.

The relationship which grew up between Pater and McQueen, however, could not lightly be overturned and was probably impossible to obliterate by an act of will. McQueen's side of it is, inevitably, the side that is documented, most usefully. But Wright tells a story of Pater late in life meeting by chance a female cousin of McQueen's. She recalled their earlier days together and asked if he had any message for McQueen. Pater hesitated and then replied, 'Yes, give him my love.' It was, Wright states, the last communication between them.

Three aspects of Pater as a schoolboy were fixed in McQueen's mind and tabulated by him: sincere, High Church piety; liveliness and wit; and mental activity – testified to not only by his reading but in his writing, then chiefly verse. Dombrain had realized the first and conceivably responded to the second, but it was almost certainly McQueen who uncovered Pater's attempts at writing, doing so probably by revealing his own. Well before coming to the King's School, he had – like the Brontë children – begun to devise and also draw maps of his own imaginary kingdoms, with names like Argent, Teabert and Dodieland. He continued with these writings during his schooldays – a six-volume history of the empire of Dodieland by 'René el Dodie' was begun in 1855 – and they were read by Pater, who in turn showed McQueen his own early work, encouraged his comments and allowed him to copy some at least of it.

The geography and fauna of Dodieland seem to have interested McQueen far more than its inhabitants, and to have interested Pater, typically, far less. McQueen was using a form of literature to express his determined pleasure in independence, creating his own infantile and capricious microcosm within the real world and carving out a kingdom where he alone ruled. 'I am the King of all Argent,' he is recorded as once having exclaimed when a very young child to a boy who had boasted he was the King of all England. As an adult, McQueen seems to have carried boyhood fiction into fully accomplished fact ('his independence', Wright wrote politely, though perhaps a touch nervously, 'was, and still is, eminently characteristic of him'). He has been described more frankly as opinionated and quarrelsome. Rather unexpectedly, he married; but quite in the imperious tradition of ruling all Argent he later ejected his wife from his house by ordering round a carriage and summarily requiring her to get in and leave him and the premises. After that, her fleeting appearance in his somewhat lengthy will comes as no surprise, nor that it should come ungarnished by the endearments bestowed on 'my dearest Grandmother', beside whose grave he desired to be buried, and on 'my dear Godson', Magnus Rainier Robertson, the son of his butler, who inherited most of his wealth and possessions.

The writings that Pater produced at school and on first going up to Oxford are more interesting for conveying something of his moods and attitudes than for any positive literary merit. That might be the verdict on any writer's prentice efforts, but in Pater's case the distinction is ironically great. All that has survived from the early period of his life is verse. The choice of medium was almost inevitable for emotional statements by somebody young, influenced not only by poets of the recent past like Wordsworth, and by contemporary ones like Tennyson and Arnold (whose first acknowledged volume, including *The Scholar Gypsy*, had been published in 1853), but also by the hymns and religious verse of Keble, Newman and lesser figures.

Nevertheless, judging by what has been published, Pater painfully lacked any spark of poetic instinct or even any feel for the rhythm of verse. Trite language and tired epithets are interspersed with echoes of other writers. Significantly, his break with Christianity coincided with his renunciation of verse as a medium, as it also did with his twenty-first year. He began to appreciate the possibilities of prose. He became a master of it and also its defender. 'You know I give a high place to the literature of prose as a fine art,' he was much later to write to the young Arthur Symons, explaining that the admirable qualities in Symons' verse were those also of imaginative prose (a compliment one could never pay Pater's verse). Within four years of ceasing to attempt poetry, Pater had evolved the highly refined, allusive and utterly personal style of the essay *Diaphaneitè*, with its carefully wrought cadences and chiselled, almost crystalline delicacy: an unstrident yet already potentially stirring instrument in which to express himself.

Apart from class essays and compositions, Pater apparently produced some now lost prose stories while at school. These were very probably semi-religious in tone and he himself may well therefore have destroyed them when he broke with religion. Among the first poems he showed McQueen (or of which McQueen took copies)

59

was one dealing with Saint Elizabeth of Hungary, said to have been suggested by Charles Kingsley's dramatic poem on the subject, first published in 1848 and reprinted in 1851. But Pater had good reason of his own to be attracted to the subject and to try and produce his own version of her story. It must have been with his aunt Elizabeth in mind that he chose it. His stress on the saint's celibacy, piety and charity makes it particularly suitable for her:

> Within her lamp there brightly burned a pure ethereal flame,
> And so she waited till the great Celestial Bridegroom came.

It may even have been written for her birthday in 1855, the first year, that is, of her entire care of the children after Maria Pater's death. The poem may also have made a special appeal to McQueen, since his 'dearest Grandmother' was another Elizabeth (usually known as Eliza).

McQueen, both as boy and as man, was obviously pleased with verse of this kind, including a euphoric jingle, *The Chant of the Celestial Sailors*, tricked out by traditional poetic references to the 'rosy dyes' of dawn, 'matin clouds' and the 'billowy sea'. When Pater was led towards a blacker theme, *Cassandra*, suggested by reading Æschylus, a lament by the doomed Trojan priestess as a captive of the Greeks, McQueen objected to its 'sensuality'. That might seem no more than the attitude of a priggish boy, but nearly half a century later McQueen still stigmatized its 'declension from the high moral and religious, I might say spiritual, tone' of Pater's earlier poems. Yet Cassandra's misery and sense of utter helplessness ('Can'st thou not forgive the error,' she begs the deaf Apollo) clearly reflect Pater's own state at the time. The poem is dated 29 June 1857 and originates, therefore, in the summer term during which Pater's anxiety and application brought him to nervous prostration, if not to near-breakdown. Kind though McQueen might be when he realized Pater's physical state, he perhaps shied away from seeking any underlying cause. A pleasant summer stay at the McQueens' house in Sussex could not lift for long the gloom which Pater, Cassandra-like, foresaw gathering around him. By the following year this had deepened, although on the outside he appeared positively successful.

On 4 August 1858 he celebrated his nineteenth birthday. The next day was the last Speech Day of his school career. His exhibition at Oxford was gained and he had matriculated at Queen's College in June. McQueen was also leaving the school for Oxford, to go to Balliol. Both he and Pater left with prizes (Pater's for Latin scholarship and ecclesiastical history) and with the commendations of the headmaster, though rather differently phrased in each case. McQueen was obviously liked and sincerely regretted: his invariable good conduct, his hard work and what was described as his blameless Christian life brought tears to the eyes of the Reverend George Wallace. If Pater did not move him in the same way, he yet paid scrupulous tribute to Pater's good qualities – including his magnanimity two years before when he had specifically begged for the forgiveness of a boy who had injured him very seriously in a bullying scuffle. Perhaps even a glimmer of humour lightened Wallace's reference to Pater as a monitor: 'I cannot say that you have been an active monitor in suppressing turbulence and punishing the refractory . . .' A tremor of doubt may be detected in his hope that God would preserve Pater 'as a faithful member of that Church in whose principles you have been strictly brought up.' Above all, he openly declared that he would follow Pater's Oxford career, 'with no common interest, for I feel that there is in you that which may redound to your own credit and the honour of the school.'

Amid the assembled families and friends in the solemn surroundings of the Chapter House, it must have been hard for Bessie Pater to restrain her emotions at that valediction. Its nuances were probably lost in a rush of pride and affection. She believed that the orphaned boy, gentle, devout and gifted, would from Oxford pass into the Church. Wallace's words seemed only a confirmation of her sustained faith, which went back to the days at Enfield when her own mother had been alive, in the future of the child now become a young man.

Pater was profoundly agitated, and a good deal more sombre. His state of mind that last summer at Canterbury was indicated by two poems, necessarily Christian rather than classical in their inspiration but with no lightening of the mood of *Cassandra*. *A Chant of the Celestial Sailors when they first put out to sea* is lost, but patently lacked the bouncy tone of the earlier *Chant of the Celestial Sailors*, with at least mentally rougher weather and some uncertainty in their struggles towards their goal. The title of the other poem, *Watchman, what of the night?* in itself conveys the crisis of doubt he was undergoing. While Wallace feared that his religious fervour might carry him towards the dreaded bourne of the Roman Catholic Church, Pater was experiencing a black night of the spirit in which an engulfing horror of death threatened to shake belief altogether:

> Down, down I sink. Oh! let me live in Thee,
> Or deep in hell – it seems so awful not to be.

In the poem, he wants to believe and to find death welcome ('Welcome the hour that lays us in the dust') as bringing with it the revelation of God's purpose.

In reality, the dread of death was not easily exorcized either by night, when he dreamed horribly, or by day. As a quite young child he had been precociously aware of it, sensing something which not even the walled-garden peace of Enfield had been able to exclude, and which led back to Stepney and his father's death. And following the death of his mother and his own growing up, Stepney became an actuality for him. There, in Commercial Road, not far from his father's place of death, and of his own birth, lived John Pendergast, the lawyer who managed the financial side of Maria Pater's estate: Pater visited him more than once and wrote from Oxford to him quite frequently, mingling family news with business.

When Pater rose at his last school Speech Day to deliver his recitation, it was not to assume the brisk *persona* of Harry Hotspur but to read a poem which better than all his own conveyed the complexity of his feelings: Tennyson's *Morte d'Arthur*. Not only does it tell of the passing of an archetypal father-like king but it is drenched in the sadness of farewells and of the dissolution of a noble company, of whom Sir Bedivere alone is left, mourning and apprehensive:

> And I, the last, go forth companionless,
> And the days darken round me, and the years,
> Among new men, strange faces, other minds.

Some of Pater's panic and feelings of extinction must have stemmed from the realization that in leaving school he was about to confront the world truly on his own and virtually 'companionless'.

The house at Harbledown was being given up. Perhaps with some idea of Clara learning German and becoming a governess, his aunt was to settle with his two sisters in Germany, first at Heidelberg. William had presumably joined the army. For somebody as tenaciously attached as Pater to the idea of home, it must have been frightening to experience the dispersal of the family and know that henceforward there would be no household where he of right belonged. Oxford was alien in prospect, and even though McQueen was also going there his was a different college. Beyond Oxford loomed the greater uncertainty of a career: long and fondly anticipated as bathed in a religious light but now made darkly uncertain by Pater's flickering, even expiring, faith.

The King's School, and his schooldays, might seem retrospectively bright and sure, however monotonous.

The idiosyncrasies of the masters had had their charm, if only as subjects for mimicry. Besides, Pater had positively benefited from the teaching of old, portly, poor Mr Fisher who taught English literature and rehearsed the Speech Day recitations. Some of Pater's interest in architecture, and in the visual arts altogether may have been stimulated by the art master, Monsieur L. L. Razé (a Frenchman who had originally stopped at Canterbury on his way to London and remained at the school for many years). In his quite professional pencil drawings are preserved figures like the Reverend George Wallace and the Speech Day occasions in the cathedral Chapter House.

As for the boys, whom Pater faced for the last time when he gave a monitor's farewell address, they might have been in the mass noisy, unsympathetic and insensitive, yet they had had for him a certain animal appeal in their very vigour. Wright ridicules Pater for exhorting them in this address (as recalled presumably by McQueen), 'Be boy-like boys', when he himself had been – at least in Wright's view – utterly unlike the average boy. But high spirits, physical activity and unconscious physical glamour were the boy-like qualities Pater half-envied in them and was in effect urging them to preserve. 'A world of vanity and appetite,' was to be his summing-up of Gaston de Latour's comparable environment of fellow-pages in the household of the Bishop of Chartres, 'yet after all of honesty with itself! . . . They at least were not pre-occupied all day long, and, if they woke in the night, with the fear of death.'

When Pater had teasingly compared the boys to various creatures, it was far from being mere insult therefore, especially from somebody fascinated by animals. Gaston does as Pater had done (the pages reproducing, 'unsuspectingly, the humours of animal nature'), finding one boy 'lithe and cruel like a tiger – it was pleasant to stroke him.' From McQueen, Wright must have learnt how Pater had 'almost adored' Joseph Haydock, a good-looking, aristocratic-looking and violent boy, a rougher version perhaps of his own brother William, who was quite indifferent to him but who possessed all the easy confidence and magnetism Pater lacked. To Haydock's no doubt aggressive demand about what animal he resembled, Pater – according to Wright – had replied, 'A handsome, ferocious, young bull.' McQueen remembered that Haydock seemed pleased; and well he might be, if he appreciated the underlying compliment to his sexuality.

Though Haydock had failed to respond to Pater's frank worship (leaving dreams of what might have been to colour years later the fictions of Marius's friendship with Flavian and Emerald Uthwart's with James), school had brought Pater the more than intellectual bulwark of the triumvirate. Only in that company had he been entirely himself, able to enjoy the absurdities of Mr F.'s aunt in *Little Dorrit* (which he and McQueen read as it appeared monthly) no less than solemnly absorb Hooker's *Ecclesiastical Polity*. For them Canterbury Cathedral had been a spiritual home, in no cliché sense;

they had been stirred by the constant mingling there of surplices and uniforms – all the more in that the Crimean War had been fought and won during their schooldays. But they had also lightheartedly 'skirmished' in the local woods and built themselves a special breakwater in a boyish enough way to satisfy the most conventional sentimentalist; as late as 1860, McQueen's younger brother reported to him at Oxford that he and Dombrain had found the breakwater 'very little injured'.

Without disturbing their friendship, Pater had been able to ridicule McQueen for liking the books of Charlotte Yonge and to shift the mood of a serious discussion of the after-life by mocking McQueen's fondness for unripe fruit: 'One thing is quite certain, in Heaven there won't be any heavenly green apples.' There had been Dombrain's house in which to act charades. There had been the McQueen family, who recognized the friendship and whose letters often referred to 'the Pater' (perhaps a joke of their own); and once when McQueen's mother sent him a pocket perspective glass she warned him that, good though it was, it would not enable him from Canterbury to see Pater at Harbledown.

On 6 August, the day following the Speech Day and two days after Pater's birthday, the triumvirate went for an afternoon skirmish in the familiar woods, their last together as schoolboys. Whatever the previous slight eddying in their relationship, they had never quarrelled. On this occasion McQueen and Dombrain were in particularly cheerful mood; only Pater was unrelaxed, unusually serious and ultimately, untypically, in a rage. He seems to have spoken first of having conquered his religious doubts and then told an extraordinary warning story of a man who had died an atheist in the Jesuit College at Rome. Self-absorption led him to talk next of how, with his Oxford exhibition gained, he was determined to achieve fame. Suddenly he burst out in what seemed violent anger, for which he was the next morning to apologize to his two friends. The incident was attributed by McQueen to nervous exhaustion following on the examinations and the ordeal of Speech Day. And it seems to have been fully forgiven by both him and Dombrain.

What had appeared motiveless anger was no doubt abrupt and total despair, seizing Pater at the very moment he, the leader, should have been sharing the joint mood of exhilaration. He had probably talked himself as much as them into a conviction that his religious beliefs were now firmly fixed and unassailable, and had also tried to strengthen his own hopes for fame in the future. Yet these feelings were fragile under the weight of inescapable, impending facts. His family was dispersing. The only other group of which he formed a part was powerless to help him and was itself losing cohesion, under the pressure of time and change, even while playing for one final afternoon at being the same happy, holy trio of King's School days. He saw further, sensed it would not survive and perhaps felt impelled to destroy what was already dissolving. Misery not anger more likely prompted his eventual outburst – 'The triumvirate is for ever dissolved' – after which he walked off by himself.

Neither the apologies of the next day or the continued friendship of Pater and McQueen during their early terms at Oxford, still less Pater's occasional return visits to Canterbury to stay with Dombrain and his family, could conceal the fact that the sentence had been uttered and was to turn out painfully true.

Four Silent years and godlike aims

IN MARCH 1860, approximately midway through his under-graduate career at Oxford, Pater wrote what was to be one of his last – and one of his best – poems, a sonnet called *Oxford Life*. At first glance, however, it seems to convey little about either Oxford or Pater's life there. Neither the university nor the city figures in it, and apart from a reference to looking south towards Berkshire there is nothing to locate the lines. Its setting is a chilly, windy March day in a countryside of furrowed fields and grey willows, where a single shaft of sunlight on a distant slope helps to bring the rising hills into relief and becomes part of nature's stirring rebuke to the low-spirited spectator, unsure of purpose and sighing for 'a godlike aim thro' all these silent years'.

Yet the mood is certainly not despairing. No crisis of faith is suggested, and indeed Christianity seems replaced by something approaching stoicism. This mood, like the landscape, is very much connected with Pater's experience at Oxford. Even if the years of being an undergraduate were, inevitably, to be silent ones, they were far from being dull or empty. He made new friends, encountered new and often commanding personalities, in life and through voracious reading – adding Goethe, Hegel, Flaubert and Thackeray, among others, to his enthusiasms – and must have increasingly felt that around his own personality hovered the real possibility of achieving significance as a writer. Perhaps he lacked a clear or godlike aim. Perhaps at times the future seemed even more uncertain for him than for his fellow-undergraduates. He was poor, emotionally insecure, personally shy; but intellectually he was bold, and growing bolder.

Oxford itself was full of bold and non-conforming figures, in-cluding the dominant one of Benjamin Jowett (not yet Master of Balliol, and suffering under 'Establishment' suspicion of his religious orthodoxy). By 1860 Pater was, along with his friend Ingram By-water, receiving private tuition from Jowett; and Jowett, so little given to hasty or verbose comments, still less compliments, was to tell them both that he believed they had minds that would come to great distinction. Thus the vague parting hopes expressed for Pater

66

by the Reverend George Wallace received exciting confirmation. Bywater became a distinguished classical scholar and Jowett's successor as Regius Professor of Greek at Oxford. Of Pater as a fellow-undergraduate he later frankly recorded: 'His mind was very much more mature than mine and he completely subjugated me by his verve, and originality of view. . . . His reading was extraordinarily wide . . . and he was full of ability.'

Oxford Life has something of the restless, questioning character of the university climate at the period, at least for young and lively people: the search for worthy aims and the watch for some inspirational gleam to shape and give meaning to existence. Its mood, like its style, had been suggested in poetry by Matthew Arnold's *The Scholar-Gypsy*, which at once deplored the 'strange disease of modern life' and touched the local countryside around Oxford with a glowing allusiveness, compounded partly of skilful use of place-names, it has never since, even today, quite lost. 'Thou waitest for the spark from heaven,' Arnold had apostrophized his wandering Oxford scholar, contrasting the fresh, fatigue-free, undiverted power of his seventeenth-century figment ('Thou hadst *one* aim, *one* business, *one* desire') with the languid doubts, mental fluctuations and unfulfilled resolutions of modern men, 'Of whom each strives, nor knows for what he strives.'

Pater's enthusiasm for Arnold's poem is said by Wright to have been caught initially from McQueen, but the reasons for the attraction of each to it were very different. To McQueen it appealed as the story of a scholar who fled from Oxford and turned gypsy, symbolizing therefore his own unconquerable dislike of the place and his longed-for retreat into not vagrancy but semi-squirearchal state. In Arnold otherwise he had no interest.

Pater had come up to Oxford sharing McQueen's determined aversion. Reunited in a city and an environment alien after Canterbury and school, they had pooled their misery during the early days of their first autumn term. 'He considers me to be the only comfort he has,' McQueen wrote of Pater to his grandmother from Balliol on his first Saturday, while Pater sat opposite him in tears, 'and I certainly know not what I should do without him.' But once the shock of change was absorbed, Pater found a variety of comforts, including the countryside of *The Scholar-Gypsy* and lectures by its author.

Arnold had been elected Professor of Poetry in 1857 and was giving his first, uncompleted course of lectures *On the Modern Element in Literature*, soon interrupted for the series published as *On translating Homer*. John Addington Symonds, a year younger than Pater but his

67

exact contemporary at Oxford (and an acquaintance of McQueen's, being also at Balliol), admiringly noted after hearing one of the latter series, 'A good lecture and full of impudence.' Pater unfortunately kept no journal, but he too attended Arnold's lectures and enjoyed their impudence, as well as appreciating the wide, topical range of Arnold's literary reference and his serious belief in the importance of culture, in addition to responding to the more elegiac notes of his poetry. A last echo of that, a positive ring notably of *Thyrsis* (1866), seems detectable amid the few evocative sentences Pater gives to Oxford in *Emerald Uthwart:* 'when the oars splashed far up the narrow streamlets through the fields on May evenings among the fritil-laries . . .'

When Pater himself as an undergraduate went for excursions with friends in the surrounding countryside, he certainly did not forget its associations with *The Scholar-Gypsy*. Over forty years later, one such friend, Matthew Butterworth Moorhouse, still recalled a long Sunday walk they had once taken together, along with Bywater, and how, after a pub lunch of bread and cheese, as they returned by Bablock Hythe, Pater had quoted the lines:

> Thee at the ferry Oxford riders blithe
> Returning home on summer-nights, have met
> Crossing the stripling Thames at Bab-lock-hithe,

Conversely, echoes of Arnold in Emerald Uthwart's oars splashing up the narrow streamlets are perhaps blended with a fragment of youthful experience remembered, in the undoubtedly memorable Easter vacation occasion (again recalled by Moorhouse) when four Queen's undergraduates took a boat, coxed without any pretence of competence by Pater, up to scholar-gypsy-frequented Godstow:

> . . . through those wide fields of breezy grass
> Where black-wing'd swallows haunt the glittering Thames.

Arnold's poem no doubt played its part in colouring, and thus softening, the Oxford environment for Pater. And its penseroso, pleasurable, semi-melancholy mood must have acquired additional piquancy as it emerged as only one aspect of an author who was publicly showing himself returned to Oxford very much its product: confident, ironic, insouciant and even worldly. Besides, the poet and by no means aged professor – only thirty-five in the year he was elected to the Poetry Chair – were united in speaking with one clearly rational voice, almost daringly free from Christian religious

68

overtones, degrees of theological doubt or sentimental hymn-book phraseology.

There was much in him for Pater to ponder – not least the influence Arnold increasingly exercised. He spoke up for culture, not exactly for its own sake perhaps, and always with a strong ethical basis, but he made it seem the pursuit of any intelligent person. Sanity, grace and light were his beacons; they had blazed with splendour unique, he believed, in fifth-century Greece, and they were certainly badly needed in the Oxford where he lectured. Jowett's experiences of being penalized for his convictions were not unusual. As a young fellow of Oriel, Arnold had caused scandal by his neglect of chapel attendance, but he was – as always – far luckier than his friend Clough, an ex-fellow of the same college, whose provost refused him a reference when he applied for a professorial chair at Sydney, on the grounds that no one could be suitable for such a post who was 'in a state of doubt or difficulty as to his own religious belief.' At Exeter College Dombrain might have been happier than he presumed, since it was there a few years before that the rector had burnt a book, significantly entitled *The Nemesis of Faith,* by one of the fellows, J. A. Froude – obviously disappointed at being unable to include the author in the public bonfire.

Pater had suffered agonies of conscience already as a schoolboy. Being uncertain was for him to become a permanent state of mind, yet *Oxford Life* suggests he was no longer so shaken with guilt and, now older, much less afraid of following where his intellect led. Even if the mood could not be held, at least on 27 March (the day he dated the sonnet) it was almost in Arnold's own *persona* that he seemed to wish to speak. That sere March day and the dull Oxford countryside convey earth's lesson without any intervention by the Deity. Its lesson is of hope, however, for the day is a spring one (amid the dun fields is dimly seen 'A brighter patch of greenness') and the very shape of the partially sunlit Berkshire hills ('Not sleeping but intent') has its hopeful message:

> And that bold outline to the scene imparts
> A spirit and a word for wakeful hearts, . . .

True, Pater calls his a 'poor life' and feels tears starting to his eyes; yet the poem ends with the self-exhortation towards a 'godlike aim' (without a capital 'G') which may be vague but at least suggests a future faced without fear of hell or need for heaven. His attitude in this sonnet can be contrasted with the positively Christian belief expressed in some lines by Moorhouse written at Christmas in the

same year, inculcating the importance of doing one's duty and struggling on, sustained by Christ's presence:

> No lower hope enchains us,
> The love of Christ constrains us,
> Our lives are not our own.

Moorhouse had almost certainly been shown Pater's sonnet. In turn
he showed his verses to Pater, but the lurking divergence in their
views had become too painful. Pater could only shake his head and
say, significantly enough, that Moorhouse's lines conveyed no
meaning to him. Later, he was to pay Moorhouse the dubious, if not
sardonic, compliment of recommending him to write hymns.

Even in the first weeks of his first term, barely settled in at
Queen's, and before he had made any new friends or felt any fresh
influences, Pater had in fact revealed sufficient doubts for Robert
McQueen to write from school to his brother, remarking, 'Pater
seems in a very odd state. Does he still believe in Christianity?' To this
well-meant question there was probably never to be a simple answer.

At another period the matter might anyway have seemed a
private one, the concern solely of the individual's conscience. But
Pater had been born into an age acutely apprehensive about faith –
and almost as unbalanced on the subject of threats to it as later
periods were to be about Communism, homosexuality or pornogra-
phy. As in the case of opposition to those 'dangers', anyone could
presume to be his brother's keeper. Extremes of belief were themselves a threat, at least to established Anglicanism. At their worst they
led to behaviour like the Reverend E. H. Woodall's conversion,
reverberating through Canterbury in the August of 1859; and
danger might lie even in the lighter, camp-followers' fringe concerns
with incense and vestments, percolating down as far as the private
activities of schoolboys at Harrow when John Addington Symonds
was there in the early 1850s ('we . . . donned surplices and tossed
censers, arranged altars in our studies . . . I now inclined to a
farcical ritualism, handling pseudo-sacred vessels in a nightgown
surplice before a pseudo-altar.') By the time Symonds went up to
Balliol and encountered in 1860 very High Church undergraduates,
'redolent of incense', themselves donning sky-blue cassocks, and
buying triptychs with ruby-glass doors to contain ivory crucifixes on
ebony stands, he could scornfully comment to his sister, 'I had
thought the Tractarian humbug had died', going on to indicate the
more typical, new form of fever which Oxford felt was once again
raging particularly in its midst, 'and given way to philosophical cant
of infidelity.'

70

This was the great contagion, detected now in a rationalizing clergyman or classical scholar, earnestly wrestling with Bible problems, and now in a flippant undergraduate. Probably in the former it was the more to be fought, since his example might only too easily sway younger or weaker minds – and where they were to be protected almost any weapons were thought justified. Oxford was, inevitably and bitterly, divided; and it would have taken Voltaire to do justice to its interpretation of Christian tolerance. Christ Church represented the High Church, summed up by Pusey whose opposition to the latitudinarian party represented by Balliol, and in particular Jowett, led him to seek Jowett's suspension from teaching by the university on the grounds it was heretical. When the bishops condemned the book *Essays and Reviews,* to which Jowett himself contributed an essay on 'The Interpretation of Scripture', he wrote pointedly in his diary: 'What is Truth against an *esprit de corps*?'

Regularly, the eloquent, socially successful Bishop of Oxford, Samuel Wilberforce, unkindly known as 'Soapy Sam', rose to preach a sermon which, however varied in chosen text and language, amounted to a thunderous attack on anyone presuming to use his own reason, and a fearsome warning to young men against the slightest doubt or scepticism. (Two of the bishop's brothers, both once clergymen, had succumbed not to scepticism but to Roman Catholicism, as had his only daughter and his son-in-law.) But all Wilberforce's eloquence was powerless to prevent publications and the reading of them. In 1859 appeared Darwin's *The Origin of Species,* early read by Pater and disturbing to his pious friend Moorhouse. In 1860 what seemed 'attack' came from inside the Anglican Church, and from inside Oxford, with the publication of *Essays and Reviews,* a collection of articles by seven liberal Broad churchmen, which was not only condemned by the bishops, but specifically written against and preached against by Wilberforce (to the text, 'For all that He did so many miracles, yet they believed not on Him').

And in the years that followed there were to be plenty of other manifestations to draw public condemnation from Oxford pulpits. Wilberforce's successor as bishop, John Fielder Mackarness, was publicly to imply disapproval of Pater's 'Conclusion' to *The Renaissance.* As late as 1881, Pater's colleague at Brasenose, the Reverend John Wordsworth, who had remonstrated with him over the same book, preached on 'The present unsettlement in belief'. Wordsworth was very much of the Christ Church party; and the resulting sermon reduced Mrs Humphry Ward, a friend of Jowett's and a niece of Arnold's, to intense indignation at its vigorous condemnation of what they and others stood for. Out of that indignation developed seven years afterwards her once-famous novel *Robert Elsmere*. Among the novel's reviewers was Pater, whose mind must have been strangely stirred in reading the history of a personal situation not totally different from his own as an undergraduate.

His urbane review, however, gave hardly a hint of it. 'Robert Elsmere', he wrote, 'was a type of a large class of minds which cannot be sure that the sacred story is true.' Elsmere is also an Anglican clergyman; only after he is ordained, and married to a deeply religious woman, is he assailed by doubts, upon which he gives up orders. 'Of course, a man such as Robert Elsmere came to be', Pater remarks blandly, 'ought not to be a clergyman of the Anglican Church.' Yet he finds it a blot on Elsmere's philosophic pretensions that he is assailed so late, and then deals so suddenly and trenchantly with the problem. Pater, typically, would have expected him to hesitate, 'had he possessed a perfectly philosophic or scientific temper.' There would at that rate scarcely have been a story to *Robert Elsmere*, nor much life in its protagonist, and such claim as it had to be a novel, as opposed to a study of various types of Victorian religious temperament, would have disappeared. Besides, Pater as a young man struggling for mental equilibrium and also a safe, congenial place in the fevered, if not stormy, climate of his under-graduate years cannot have found it so easy to achieve the desired detachment. And indeed all the evidence conveys clearly enough that Pater was soon to direct a good deal of that verve and originality Bywater admired in him against Christianity altogether – in a way that would certainly have horrified Robert Elsmere and did horrify some of Pater's friends.

The process was often painful, as well as erratic – painful prob-ably to Pater as much as to his friends. For one thing, he could hardly have risked in front of his aunt, still convinced of his profound faith and clerical future, those positive jibes about the Christian religion which were part of laying the ghost of his pious childhood and expressed his revulsion from all systems of belief. And then, as he gradually came to feel an intellectual scepticism, the prospect of taking holy orders must have had a distasteful aspect, even if he tried to shrug it off or interpret taking them (as he may well have, to himself) as merely a necessary qualification through which he would be enabled to help his fellow men – almost, perhaps, as a sort of clergyman-cum-simple physician. But intellectual scepticism anyway co-existed with a continuing, now openly aesthetic, delight in the more elaborate types of church service, and a consequent dislike of Low Church ones; and of Pater's friends and acquaintances at Oxford, it is remarkable how many were due to become clergymen, some of them like Moorhouse tolerant and affectionate enough to remain on good terms with him, upsetting though they found his attitude to religion.

Since Pater at this period has to be traced through inadequate references, Thomas Wright's somewhat muddled comments, and the increasingly unsympathetic reactions of McQueen, his exact course is by no means clear. Nor, after all, was he destined to be a 'thinker' or a theologian. Nice points of doctrine – and even the larger ones like the nature of divine revelation and the existence of evil – were never to be the subject of his writings. The very blandness of his references to Robert Elsmere's dilemma points to a mature view that these matters should not excite too much dogmatic emotion or be pored over too intensely; with patently personal application, his review refers to the equally large class of minds who cannot be sure that the 'sacred story' is false and who 'make allowance in their scheme of life for a great possibility.' It is easy to see how Pater as an undergraduate came to feel that amid all the doctrinal storms shaking Oxford no party was right and none escaped being at least faintly ridiculous ('Pater . . .', said Wright about the virulent *Essays and Reviews* controversy, presumably on the evidence of Moorhouse and McQueen, 'expended . . . wit on both parties': a welcome reminder that not every young man of the day at Oxford was earnest, humourless and perpetually the prey of scruples).

The style of Queen's College conveniently and perhaps not accidentally symbolizes the alteration in Pater from the devout schoolboy assiduously attending services in Canterbury Cathedral. Somebody ever-sensitive to his surroundings is not likely to have missed the architectural shift to an environment of cool reason and restrained grandeur, with late seventeenth- and early eighteenth-century chapel, hall and library approached through Hawksmoor's bold, cupola-crowned main gateway. Although such buildings may nowadays be best characterized as 'English baroque', to the Victorians they appeared 'classical', or even 'Renaissance'; in any case, they represent very different ideals from the Gothic style Pater associated with Canterbury and school. All the more must this have been felt at a period when Gothic was admired for its suggestions of shadowy, soaring, spiritual mystery, and the style associated with Wren and his followers largely out of favour, being almost disconcertingly lucid, unadorned and secular-seeming.

It was apparently while staying with Dombrain on a return visit to Canterbury at Christmas 1859 that Pater declared himself 'an enemy to all Gothic darkness', adding that he had come back, 'full of a better taste.' Quite what that was in architectural terms remains

73

unclear. His enmity to Gothic was emotional and proved transitory, once he had shaken off its connection with his own devout boyhood phase (Cologne, Chartres and Amiens were to be among the cathedrals he admired); but the high, luminous coffered prayer-hall interior of the chapel, say, at Queen's (traditionally though wrongly supposed to be by Wren) or the dignified, richly decorated library may well have represented 'better taste', and a calmer, more logical frame of mind, than any amount of 'veined foliage, and thorny fretwork, and shadowy niche, and buttressed pier and fearless height of subtle pinnacle and crested tower', celebrated by Ruskin in discussing the nature of Gothic in the second volume of *The Stones of Venice* (1853).

To claim as much within sight of the crested towers of Canterbury Cathedral, and to still devoutly religious contemporaries like Dombrain and McQueen, may have been part of Pater's teasing challenge. 'Gothic darkness' no doubt meant primarily blind faith in Christianity; but perhaps he also enjoyed rejecting those dogmatic sermons about what is good and bad in architecture which Ruskin had delivered in tones of such moral fervour that by comparison the Thirty-Nine Articles and even the Ten Commandments are robbed of conviction. McQueen testified to how early Pater took an interest in architecture, and it seems that before leaving school he had read at least some Ruskin. It was an influence he could scarcely escape but was bound to react against. He had virtually thrown off the precepts of conventional Christianity; to throw off Ruskin's precepts was less daring, yet only another aspect of denying authority and discovering his own individuality.

For that the physical environment offered by Queen's was congenial. His own rooms – large and high up, facing the library in the second quadrangle – had at first displeased him by their size, but gradually (according to Wright) he became fond of them. They inevitably remained bare and rather cold during Pater's first years, since he lacked the family and financial help available to, for example, a fashionable doctor's son like John Addington Symonds. The earliest surviving letters of Pater date from May 1859 and are repeated requests to the bursar of the King's School for payment of the £30 representing half his annual exhibition money; he had to jog the school's memory again in the following year.

Symonds had an annual income of £350 and could give breakfast parties, intellectual in tone but catering generously for undergraduate appetites with soles, sauces, cutlets, sausages and savoury omelettes. For his rooms his uncle, also a doctor, had provided him with three enormous animal pictures – two of them by Landseer – which were rather too heavily bourgeois for his taste but which he admitted would look well. Pater's rooms were described as looking 'graceless and austere', and even when he was able to improve their Spartan appearance (a term actually applied to them by his acquaintances) he was markedly restrained, especially by mid-Victorian standards.

Wright obtusely implied that this was on account of mere thriftiness and supposed it worth remarking that someone with Pater's aesthetic standards yet lived most of his life in scantily furnished settings. Perhaps limited means were involved, but primarily it was a matter exactly of aesthetics and taste. At least one fellow-don, Humphry Ward, later the art critic of *The Times*, appreciated Pater's intentions a very few years afterwards in his furnishing of his Brasenose rooms and noted the contrast 'to the oaken respectability and heaviness of all other dons' rooms at that day.'

The finely proportioned rooms at Queen's would have been spoilt by stuffing with Victorian knick-knacks; and Pater's omniscient and youthful tutor, William Wolfe Capes, only five years his senior, rather primly but not imperceptively was to describe the final, furnished effect of them as one where 'the decorative features were used with guarded moderation'. In itself that represented a quiet, further rejection of conventional beliefs.

Bywater said that the impression the rooms conveyed was of Bellini's picture of St Jerome in his study and that Pater once spoke of that picture embodying his ideal of a student's room. (This reference is unfortunately baffling, unless Bywater made a slip and meant – as he probably did – Carpaccio, whose memorable *St Augustine in his Study*, in the Scuola di S. Giorgio degli Schiavoni at Venice, for long passed as of St Jerome; and certainly the light-filled study there, with it choice, neatly ordered objects and calm air of humane scholarship, makes Pater's comment immediately understandable.)

In those rooms he worked and entertained his friends – chiefly to tea, judging from McQueen's diary. Bywater had persuaded Moorhouse to call on the freshman who was his junior in terms though not in years; and Pater and Moorhouse established a coterie at Queen's, moving to a table in hall where they could quote Latin and Greek freely without paying the penalty of sconcing (particularly awkward for Moorhouse who had been brought up a total abstainer).

While McQueen perhaps remained Pater's closest friend, at least during their early terms, Pater found more and more congenial companions in his own college. The charm of manner which had won McQueen's grandmother had its effect on other people, and for those who were intelligent Pater's range of reading and originality of outlook must have increased the charm. His reading in English encompassed Berkeley, Hume, Carlyle and John Stuart Mill (whose *On Liberty* was published in 1859), as well as De Quincey, Macaulay, Keats and Scott, interspersed with the human interest story of Mrs Gaskell's recent *Life of Charlotte Brontë* and some mock sparring with Moorhouse over the merits of Browning. It was possibly Pater's study of logic under Capes which prompted him unkindly to declare Browning's poems meaningless, while he teased Moorhouse (who seems to have been unaware of it) by attributing his fondness for them to the fact that he – unlike Pater himself – had been in love.

These were all ways of causing mild astonishment. There was also the rumour that he had had work of his own published; this seems not to have been so, but perhaps Pater did not mind the assumption being made by his new friends. He continued certainly to write and for the first time to write imaginatively in prose. Much of what he read must have coloured his still fluctuating feelings about Christianity and been part of a search for his own 'philosophy'. He seemed, Capes informed Wright, 'more attracted by the thoroughness of German thought than by the clearness and precision of French style . . .' Yet, though this is how he may well have appeared in his essays and to his tutor, privately he was probably drawn already to contemporary French literature, especially Sainte-Beuve and Flaubert; they were the French representatives among the writers whose work he apparently made a regular habit of translating at this period. Flaubert's *Madame Bovary* had been published in 1857, and Flaubert remained fixed in Pater's esteem: 'If all high things have their martyrs,' he was to write in the essay *Style* (1888), 'Gustave Flaubert might perhaps rank as the martyr of literary style.' One of the few occasions later recalled when Pater dropped his normally reticent-courteous social manner of deferring to even crude opinions, and reacted violently, was when someone in his presence disparaged Flaubert.

Flaubert, to whom were soon to be added Gautier and Baudelaire, was one of those writers who appealed to Pater not as a thinker, still less as a moral wrestler with problems of religious doubt, but as an artist. All of them, incidentally, were artists regarded in Victorian England at best dubiously, in so far as there existed any awareness of them. Leading English writers, whether poets or novelists, generally showed no more interest in their truly creative French contemporaries than English painters of the period were to do. As an undergraduate at Oxford Pater was unusual in being aware of such modern French literature – unusual but not unique, since at Balliol Swinburne was both more interested and more knowledgeable, with the advantage of having been in France. Pater might well have found him a more sympathetic companion for literary discussions than any of the earnest, not very exciting, future clergymen who typified his circle, almost his audience, but at this date they did not meet. Swinburne went down in 1860, without bothering about a degree, but not before being glimpsed one day by Pater and McQueen when they were out walking near Headington.

France altogether might stand for one, then still slightly submerged, aspect of Pater's character, a France not just of Gothic cathedrals and picturesque countryside as known to Ruskin or to bourgeois dons during vacation tours, but of sophisticated beliefs in the arts for their own sake. Oxford was the last place to approve of that hedonistic-sounding doctrine. Something lurid and improper continued to be associated with France in English eyes: from French maids to French novels, not to mention the capital city itself, there exuded a sense of unbridled passion which was at once exciting and evil. 'She is a woman of taste and also of strict principle, and objects to having a French person in the house,' was said of a fictional character, the bishop's wife in *Daniel Deronda*; nevertheless, though George Eliot herself might smile at such an attitude, she neither invented nor caricatured it.

By contrast, Germany seemed safe, respectable and intellectual. It represented profound thought rather than mere sensation, even if some of the thought was disturbing, and its academic traditions and its classical scholarship gave it a prestige in English university eyes that France could never possess. Its very language suggested respectability, required hard work to master, and seemed to exclude the faintest possibility of anything frivolous being written in it. Germany too was to exercise an appeal over Pater; what is untypical is his combination of, as it were, French aestheticism and German intellect.

Germany was the first foreign country he knew. He rapidly learnt German in order to read Hegel, according to Bywater; and though he seems always to have disliked speaking any language other than English, the fact of staying with his aunt and sisters in Germany must have increased his facility. Travel revealed to him other cities as well as Heidelberg: Cologne, Mainz, and Worms among them. Echoes of what he felt and saw have now to be caught from the 'imaginary portrait' of Duke Carl of Rosenmold, but were at the time conveyed more personally in letters he wrote to McQueen when travelling, of which only a few phrases survive in Wright's biography.

Also lost (in this case burnt by Pater) is the prose story *Gertrude of Himmelstadt* which he wrote at Heidelberg over the Christmas vacation of 1858. The setting of this, its subject and indeed its language were all inspired by Germany. It may have been based on some local legend connected with an actual castle on the Rhine. When McQueen heard Pater read it during the next term, he noted in his diary: '. . . extremely clever, and on the whole very pretty, but disfigured here and there by the modern Germanized English.' Moorhouse also admired Pater's story; his admiration led him to make a metrical version of it. That survives, but McQueen bluntly said that in the process Moorhouse had totally spoilt and distorted Pater's narrative. With that warning, not much should be deduced from Moorhouse's verses.

The outline of the story concerns at a vague historical date a Fidelio-like heroine, Gertrude, whose young husband goes off to fight the emperor's wars, leaving her behind in his castle with a silver suit of armour he once wore. News comes that he and his men are near defeat, but the next day they are encouraged to victory by the sudden appearance of a figure in silver armour who turns out to be Gertrude. Pater's style was, McQueen later wrote, 'picturesque, graphic and full of colour.' In his diary in 1859 he also noted that the story was 'disfigured . . . by his [Pater's] peculiar ideas in politics, etc., though in a less degree than might have been expected.'

Moorhouse's verses are innocent of a hint of politics of any kind, and it is impossible to know what McQueen detected and disliked – whether conceivably some opinion about Germany, or the role of women or, perhaps more likely, something faintly ethical as well as political about the need to come to the rescue of other people. When Moorhouse produced his rhymed version he appears to have called it, incidentally, *Saint Gertrude of Himmelstadt*, though there is no such saint, and McQueen's diary says nothing of her being so called in Pater's story. What Moorhouse does stress are her unselfish labours and inspiring aid to her neighbours even while she waits anxiously for news of the war ('Many a face downcast and troubled/Caught from her looks a steadfast hope,)' and his verses end with a celebration of woman who, 'clad in the armour of God's own giving', always comes to man's rescue in life's battle. The latter sentiment may suggest the incipient hymn-writer rather than Pater, but the earlier mention of Gertrude's charity recalls, accidentally or not, the deeds of Saint Elizabeth of Hungary, celebrated in Pater's own schoolboy poem.

Something about his story must soon have displeased Pater. It marked perhaps too sentimental a mood, induced by being reunited with three women of his immediate family, or was tinged with some ideas of Christian Socialism which gradually faded. By 1864 at the latest he had burnt all his own poetry, not merely because he recognized its poor quality but because of its overt Christian tone. *Gertrude of Himmelstadt* seems to have gone rather earlier, yet in writing it Pater had paid some sort of tribute to the influence of Germany on him – including its visual influence. A letter of Robert McQueen's to his brother a few weeks after *Gertrude of Himmelstadt* had been read, speaks of Pater's 'German friends' not improving his attitude to Christianity, though it is not clear who these friends can have been. Still less is it clear whether the original Gertrude story had the religious nuance given it by Moorhouse, or whether it was rather a romantically moral tale of true love and bold deeds, with human beings who are good regardless of God.

Tacking emotionally between trying to preserve some faith and rejecting the whole apparatus of belief, Pater was still very much in search of the 'godlike aim' which should give his life purpose. To some extent, his actual homelessness symbolized his state of mind. At least once he seems to have preferred to stay up at Queen's during a short vacation, making his rooms his home. At other times he stayed in London with his second cousin, William Foster Pater, a clerk in the Bank of England. Foster Pater and his family lived in Islington, and his children were approximately of Pater's age; yet although Pater was obviously offered their hospitality, there does not seem to have been any close or lasting relationship, and he is unlikely to have confided his feelings to them. The long vacations he spent in Germany, first at Heidelberg and then presumably at Dresden, where Bessie Pater moved at some point during Pater's undergraduate years. During those summer weeks Pater must have felt it best to let Oxford and problems recede; it was enough to agree that once he had obtained his degree he would be ordained.

This remained his intention, and he stated as much explicitly from Oxford on 8 December 1862, in a letter to Pendergast: 'My friends here advise me to try for a fellowship, but this is uncertain – anyhow I shall take orders in the spring, probably for a London curacy . . .' By then he knew his B.A. result: a second class in *Literæ Humaniores*. To Pendergast he probably said nothing of the disappointment which he felt at missing a first.

Yet just as he was not destined to be a thinker, so he was never to be conventionally a scholar. Apart from other Greek literature he had studied Plato and loved Plato. The last book published in his lifetime would be his lectures on *Plato and Platonism*, but it was typically to be wide-ranging, allusive and almost anti-academic; few scholars and university lecturers on Plato would then have spontaneously enlivened their text with apt mentions of Thackeray, Murillo, Veronese and Raphael's *Ansidei Madonna*. Most likely, the sheer range of Pater's non-curricular reading and interests as an undergraduate affected his preparation and thus his examination results ('the long, pedantic, mechanical discipline . . .' he was later to write of, in considering proposals to found a School of English literature at Oxford, 'which is the necessary accompaniment of a system of examination'). But though he might briefly feel disappointed with a second class degree (especially in contrast to Bywater's first), it did not affect his plans. What did affect them – overturned them drastically – was the action of McQueen.

Five   McQueen does his duty

FOR SOME TIME Pater's awareness of McQueen's existence had probably been growing fainter. Part of the reason lay in his encountering at Oxford other sympathetic acquaintances, some with wider interests and less narrow natures than McQueen's. And then McQueen himself sharply accelerated the process by demanding that Pater should not evolve, expand his personality or be in effect other than the precocious but pious boy of their King's School days.

When it became clear that Pater would not and could not meet these conditions, McQueen was profoundly disturbed. With none of Dombrain's detachment or ruthless self-righteousness, he could 'renounce' Pater only under guidance and by a painful act of will. Just because it was so painful, he perhaps assumed it must be right. Losing any acquaintance in an environment where he felt lonely and depressed would have been hard. To contemplate losing someone he continued to call 'my sole comfort in Oxford' must have been terrible for him. Years later he described himself in a letter to Wright (who did not care to print the remark) as having always been 'one of the loneliest of creatures' – giving a good hint that his repressed temperament had been the cause. He sent Wright an extraordinary poem called *John by the side of John* (written in July 1878), expressing feelings for a 'dear lad' which represents more than some highly-charged but typical Victorian effusion about friendship and seems a tacit confession of homosexuality.

In no sense was Pater a dear lad of his; rather, he as the elder and more dominant, was something of a father-figure, truly 'the Pater' of the McQueen family's joking allusion. He had guided and protected McQueen ('in many cases', the latter noted in his Oxford diary), and now he appeared to have become a dangerous leader, sceptical, mockingly paradoxical and heretical. For McQueen Pater probably never grew faint: if he was no longer a comfort, then he was a torment and a threat. That Pater was undergoing his own acute crises of belief seems never to have been properly appreciated by McQueen, even though the Mephistophelian figure who at times frightened him by a flippant attitude to Christianity was the same person who on other occasions accompanied him to hear a sermon by Pusey. McQueen could explain this, when he considered it some forty years afterwards, only in terms of Pater having been 'an admirable (because unconscious) *actor*' (his italics); and he indicated the depth of his ambivalence, without providing more than superficial analysis, by saying that Pater seemed to him an instance 'of Jekyll and Hyde dualism'. The boy-saint of Canterbury had been taken over by the adult devil of Oxford. Perhaps McQueen felt some sinister attraction still exuding from the baleful combination he postulated, for if his own faith was firm need he have minded Peter's witticisms?

Examples of what Pater actually said at this period are unfortunately largely unrecorded. But perhaps their tone was more disturbing than their content, since he obviously did not so much solemnly debate with either McQueen or Moorhouse as pepper ironically the target of Christianity – and religious systems of all kinds – with the intention of provoking thought. Through Moorhouse there survive a few echoes of Pater's consciously assumed attitude, which he continued to cultivate long after he had ceased being an undergraduate. And even when he had learnt to mute his reactions to topics as controversial as religion, his preferred weapon of comment and criticism remained the paradox. Exercised in mid-Victorian Oxford, it was hardly more effective than pricking pillows with a pin. All that was apparent was that Pater meant to be provocative; what he provoked was to be no re-thinking of received opinions but grave doubts about his moral respectability.

Moorhouse and McQueen were merely pained, puzzled, and even possibly a little dazzled, by the to them infernal squibs which Pater exploded under beliefs they had absorbed as children and which, like children, they simply felt must be true. Using logic late one evening, Pater (along with an unnamed acquaintance) reduced Moorhouse to a night of near-nihilism by proving that if God is everywhere, '*we* could have no existence at all!' After that experience ('I tried to rebut the fallacy, but in vain,' the mature Moorhouse told Wright), it had to be agreed that the three of them would in future discuss only secular matters. On other occasions Pater advanced something still more startling: a defence of religious ceremonies on the grounds of their aesthetic appeal. Moorhouse felt ill at ease in witnessing High Church ritualism, and in an effort to convert Pater to this viewpoint took him to some Low Church services. 'Spectacularly disappointing,' was Pater's comment. As to the sermons preached, they were to be judged entirely, to Moorhouse's amazement, by their language. Anticipating Wilde's Lord Henry Wotton, even down to his languid utterance, Pater observed, 'It doesn't matter what is said as long as it is said beautifully.'

McQueen seems to have been permanently too shocked by Pater's observations to recall any of them for Wright's benefit. Some at least were, according to Wright's account, attacks on the Bible in the manner of Voltaire – in which case they must have been as amusing as effective. But McQueen's sense of humour, once keenly responsive to Pater's caustic and lively tongue, had probably atrophied in the gloom induced by Oxford; and the revelation provided of Pater's reckless-seeming unbelief was itself a terrifying subject, increasing his gloom.

He was Pater's friend, though he must have been well aware of losing something of his special place to Moorhouse and others. Even more was Pater his friend. He struggled with his own feelings and worried over Pater's fluctuations with far too much concern. Every joke or jibe increased his perplexity. He kept his brother Robert regularly informed of the state of Pater's mental health and even consulted their mother about what he should do.

Very probably Pater never realized until it was too late that McQueen had developed a dangerous sense of mission about him. Travelling abroad in his early vacations, he wrote to McQueen. At Oxford they saw each other at first frequently. When McQueen's parents came up to Oxford for Commemoration Day at the end of the summer term of 1859, Pater was naturally included in the party. By that time McQueen had cut Pater off because of his state of supposed heresy, but had been reconciled after a promise that there should be no more jokes about religion. Both of them continued to be friendly with Stanley, a friend of Jowett's and the future Dean of Westminster, who had gone from Canterbury to the Professorship of Ecclesiastical History at Oxford, and whose tolerance and broad sympathies might well have eased McQueen's conscientious dilemma had he cared to be so guided. Something in McQueen may have anticipated Stanley's relaxed, humane and sensible attitude; when eventually he sought guidance it was to be from a High Church source, confirming him in his high-minded but appallingly interfering, as well as insensitive, zeal – a zeal which proved as harmful to Pater as pure spite.

And while Pater remained totally unguarded in what he said to McQueen as to others – enjoying the sense of his opinions dominating and astonishing a much wider audience than at school – McQueen increasingly brooded in isolation over this evidence of a divided, possibly diseased nature. Like a desperate physician determined to establish the cause of some illness, he searched for symptoms in

83

Pater's lightest comments on a cathedral seen abroad or a book read. From every careless or flippant remark he drew ominous conclusions, and by appearing as shocked as he was he did nothing to discourage Pater's behaviour. Shocking McQueen had anyway been one of Pater's pastimes from their schooldays, although it was then chiefly McQueen's literary tastes which he had ridiculed, attacking no figure more sacred than Charlotte Yonge.

Possibly the most puzzling question for McQueen was to decide how serious Pater was. Unfortunately Pater seems to have preferred leaving him mystified, all the more annoyingly for McQueen in that he confided something to other friends. That Pater's attitude to Christianity was not consistent must have been patent enough but he could scarcely be said to be indifferent to it, and for one period, at least at Oxford he identified himself as a Christian Socialist, under the direct influence of F. D. Maurice. This was more than a pose, however it seemed to McQueen, and very far from being an oddity.

Like many a Victorian figure of earnest, unconventional faith, Maurice had been publicly humiliated and punished for his sincerity. His punishment was removal from professorships in divinity and English history-cum-literature at King's College, London. His crime had been to write a serious book *Theological Essays* (1853), which appeared to the principal as tending towards heresy. From 1860 he became vicar of St Peter's, Vere Street, where his intense, prophetic sermons attracted considerable attention. Pater was among those who went to hear him preach, but apparently he found the sermons in themselves nebulous and Maurice's falsetto delivery only too easy a subject for mimicry. Yet Pater must have recognized that Maurice and his ideas were by no means ridiculous. It had been due largely to him that Queen's College in London was founded for the education of women. He had been involved also in the founding of the Working Men's College, of which he became first principal. He was profoundly concerned with the condition of the London poor, and perhaps the most disturbing aspect of his beliefs for contemporaries lay in his denunciation of any political economy based on selfishness.

It may be that something of Pater's sympathy with some of these views tinged the original *Gertrude of Himmelstadt* (and thus would be explained McQueen's otherwise unexplained comment at the time about its author's 'peculiar ideas in politics'). Maurice's concern with the poor might well stir in Pater that instinctive, possibly inherited, tendency to pity; and, at least briefly, it was translated by him into practical terms. He seems to have found at St Thomas's, Beckett Street, and in its vicar, the Reverend Thomas

Chamberlain, a combination of ritualism and philanthropy which satisfied his aesthetic sense and his urge towards active charity. The parish was in a poor, neglected part of Oxford. Inevitably, Chamberlain's crusading energies were resented, and his elaborate ceremonials might seem incongruous, but during a cholera outbreak in the district he proved the depth of his devotion to the sick. Pater may have been drawn more profoundly than he realized to the double image Chamberlain presented of the doctor-priest, reforming, persevering and ministering in an environment only marginally less squalid than that of Stepney. He also joined with friends at Queen's, including Moorhouse, to do charity work for the Oxford Anti-Mendicity Society, which appears to have been an undergraduate venture offering not only prayers but financial aid for the destitute and out-of-work. Pater's interest in this organization was quite likely stimulated by another new friendship he had made, with John Warneford Hoole, the son of a London clergyman, educated at Rugby.

Hoole was two or three years older and had taken his B.A. at Queen's in 1859. He remained to study for a fellowship and probably intended also to be ordained. Wright makes only a passing allusion to him, but calls him a 'very intimate friend', and suggests it was under his influence that Pater's attitude to religion changed. What he fails to make clear is the nature of the change. It scarcely seems to have been in the direction of flippancy, since McQueen recalled that Pater had once solemnly told him that Hoole had formed a theory about the Gospels; and it was Hoole who took charge of a Good Friday meeting of the Anti-Mendicity Society attended by Pater. Rather, Hoole may have been responsible for first interesting Pater altogether in Maurice's concept of Christian Socialism – as repugnant doubtless to McQueen as extremes of Voltairean scepticism. Hoole appears to have worked himself into a state of ill-health while studying for the fellowship; abruptly and prematurely he died.

Other friends Pater made as an undergraduate seem often to have died quite young and either to have been excluded by him from contact with McQueen or – more probably – to have been kept at a distance by McQueen himself, even when they were ex-King's School boys. The tone of Pater's circle is therefore obscure, but there can be no coincidence in so many of these friends becoming clergymen. Pater continued to share the same aim, though only the more profoundly scandalizing McQueen by remarking that it would be fun to be ordained and not believe a single word of what one said. On hearing that remark McQueen protested that if Pater tried to take orders, he would do all he could to prevent it: a protest in which he was merely echoing the words of the Reverend John Bachelor Kearney, a King's School master, present on the same occasion, who continued to take an interest in McQueen, Dombrain and Pater.

Not everything that McQueen learnt of Pater's college existence and visits abroad to his aunts and sisters excited suspicion or required to be earnestly controverted. McQueen not reluctantly missed a term or two at Oxford owing to trouble with his eyes, and thus had no opportunity of immediately checking Pater's description of two of his newly-acquired friends, George Henry Durham and Francis Allston Channing. When Pater described the lanky Durham as ' ten or eleven feet high', even McQueen cannot have smelt heresy in the deviation from truth; of Channing, he recollected Pater saying, 'an American, though a gentleman' (perhaps Pater's quip had actually been the other way round). Durham appears to have become a lawyer; he too died suddenly. Channing also became a lawyer, as well as an M.P. and a baronet. His gentlemanly career culminated in his being created Baron Channing of Wellingborough, and he did not die until 1926. Although he found Pater's life 'unreal', perhaps because it scarcely touched practical matters, he testified to the 'great intensity of thought and feeling' indicated by Pater's conversation which was 'very crisp and clear-cut.'

Most of these friends faded from Pater's life once their undergraduate days were over. Some of them he had perhaps consciously collected because they were good-looking ('All his friends were,' Wright, without probably much exaggeration, reports), just as late in life he liked assembling for his lunch parties what William Rothenstein called 'simple, good-looking youths.' His own presumed plainness continued to bother him and his friends. While McQueen agonized over Pater's soul, the group at Queen's agonized hardly less over his body. It was Moorhouse finally who volunteered to convey the solution that he should grow a moustache – the feature Pater retained for the rest of his life and by which most people remembered him.

If in many ways McQueen felt Pater was gradually being lost to him, and gained by others, there remained one distinction awarded him by Pater, and apparently awarded him alone. What Pater experienced in first travelling to and from Germany – both what he saw and what he felt – was conveyed in letters to McQueen which seem to have been utterly free of the stilted, cautious sentences which Pater later used to almost all his correspondents. Those letters McQueen preserved. Although Wright saw them, he was unable to quote them except in the briefest extracts, since Hester and Clara Pater held the copyright and had in advance refused him permission over any of their brother's letters he might be shown. What happened to these letters after McQueen's death in 1912 is uncertain; they have never been traced and it seems probable that they no longer survive. But the references printed by Wright are sufficient – not unfortunately to make Pater's views and experiences as explicit as would be desirable, but to reveal his use of McQueen as a confidant. Perhaps exactly because McQueen knew his family and his circumstances, it was easier for Pater to confide in him – of all his friends – when the vacations interrupted Oxford life and something of his earlier *persona* had to be resumed.

It is doubtful how far Bessie Pater understood her nephew's state of mind, though she may have sensed his loss of vocation – at least as she had dreamt of it. In some inconsistent and partly inaccurate references Wright implies that she learnt only after Pater had taken his degree that his opinions were changed and that he did not intend to be ordained. But in fact he had not dropped his intention, and it is almost certain that she never saw him again after he took his degree. Only Hester and Clara could have told Wright the truth of these matters, as also the real reason why they remained in Germany year after year ('completing their education,' according to Benson; yet after four years it should certainly have been completed as highly as Pater's; and perhaps rather, in a need for money, they educated others, taught English – or even took in lodgers).

Some hint about such things may conceivably have been contained in Pater's letters to McQueen. He seems to have written to him quite fully from Heidelberg in the summer of 1859, after having gone on excursions with Hester and Clara to Worms and Speyer, looking at the cathedrals with as responsive an eye as ever for architecture, even while typically not failing to notice unusual details of street-lighting, odd conveyances and so on. When the moment came for leaving Heidelberg in the autumn he apparently experienced a mild psychosomatic illness – a sudden fear perhaps of facing Oxford after the security of the summer. 'In perfect loneliness,' he travelled back a day or two afterwards via Mainz, Cologne and Antwerp. He admired the tombs of the archbishops in Mainz Cathedral, enjoyed attending a service in Cologne Cathedral and even more High Mass on Sunday in the cathedral at Antwerp. At Cologne the ceremonial impressed him. At Antwerp it seems to have been Rubens' paintings which made an overwhelming impression; and by attending mass he would have been able to see not only the *Assumption* on the high altar but the two huge triptychs, opened during services, of the *Raising of the Cross* and the *Descent from the Cross*.

The letters provided McQueen with perhaps insufficient evidence about the state of Pater's mind, but they gave him, if he cared to realize it, remarkable evidence about Pater's continuously excited, active visual sense – what he himself would call 'the lust of the eye'. Even through the strict limits imposed by the veto of the Misses Pater, so much is apparent in Wright's précis of a few letters. Some expression of that 'lust', present in Pater from his earliest years, was bound to find its way into his writing, and indeed to become its theme. Travelling stimulated it. He was to write descriptively much more often about France and Italy, but his earliest journeys abroad carried him to his sisters and his aunt in Germany. In writing about 'Romanticism' in 1876 he was to speak of many English readers connecting it with the 'quaint old towns, under the spire of Strasburg or the towers of Heidelberg . . .' Germany may have become invested for him with a little of the character it has in *Imaginary Portraits* for Duke Carl travelling back to his native Rosenmold: ' – the attic windows of the Residence, the storks on the chimneys, the green copper roofs baking in the long, dry German summer. The homeliness of true old Germany! He too felt it, and yearned towards his home.'

None of Pater's gifts, not even the gift of his friendship, could ultimately prevent McQueen from deciding that he must stop seeing someone whose attitude to Christianity diverged totally from his own. Before making that decision he turned to his mother; and the letter she wrote him determined his action (as he recorded in his diary). On the same day that he received it – 21 February 1859 – he wrote a note telling Pater of his decision, and handed it to him at Queen's. A few days later his brother Robert told their grandmother how profoundly grieved McQueen was by Pater's 'religious errors'.

During the earlier weeks of the term, McQueen had been seeing Pater regularly for tea and walks together. The abruptness of his decision, and even its communication in writing, must have added to the shock Pater now felt. And perhaps he felt also that McQueen's decision was too precipitate to be fixed.

McQueen's birthday was on 3 March, and for it Pater sent him a copy of *The Cathedral* by Isaac Williams, a clergyman who had contributed a famous tract, Tract 80, to 'Tracts for the Times', and who also wrote religious poetry. The sub-title of Williams' book was *On the Catholic and Apostolic Church in England,* and the gift's reassuring, reconciliatory significance was enhanced by its being accompanied by a new poem of Pater's, 'To (Joh)N. (Rainie)R. McQuee)N.' Although McQueen eventually lost this poem – rather oddly, when he preserved so much – he rapidly responded to the gesture. He and Pater were reconciled, on the condition apparently that Pater ceased to scoff in his presence at Christianity. By 5 March they had resumed their walks together, and it may well have seemed to them both that their friendship had not suffered. Nevertheless, McQueen had indicated the limits he set on it. Pater had been warned. Whether he realized how seriously McQueen took the matter is uncertain, but perhaps from then onwards he half-unconsciously sought for other more tolerant friends. McQueen became less important to him, though he did not cease to be a problem to McQueen.

In some form the friendship survived into 1860, the year of Pater's twenty-first birthday, itself possibly the occasion for his burning, as he did, the majority of his poems and disposing of his overtly Christian books. McQueen remained sufficiently in contact with him to receive St Augustine's *De civitate dei*, while Moorhouse bought his copy of *The Christian Year* by Keble. On Pater's side, here was adequate declaration of his right to his own views.

What ensued was only in miniature, and restricted merely to two undergraduates, but it reflected a major public Victorian phenomenon which had been experienced often enough in Oxford by 1860: conflict between orthodoxy and the enemy of individual interpretation, identified as speculation, rationalism, agnosticism and ultimately heresy. It had divided even bishops, increased faction in the universities and led to friends denouncing friends – as McQueen was to denounce Pater. The pair of them might almost have posed for some carefully finished narrative picture of the period, *Comrades estranged* or *Two Paths*, at once product and illustration of the social climate which combined harsh morality with uncontrolled sentimentality. *For his own good* could have been McQueen's title for their final *tableau*: two chums, who once knelt together in the same pew as boys, their upraised faces glowing in a purplish ray of light through a stained glass window, now depicted half-turned from each other in a final gesture of farewell in a shadowy college interior of teacups and textbooks, an open Bible dropped heedlessly to the floor and prominent on the tablecloth an unfinished letter with a few sufficiently legible words: 'My Lord Bishop . . . gravest doubts . . . my painful duty . . . erstwhile dear friend . . .'

McQueen's personal farewell to Pater was by no means to be the end of the matter, but their estrangement had become total before the end of 1860. McQueen told Wright in one letter that it took place before the Long Vacation that year, though Wright perhaps heard a fuller version from him orally because in his book he placed it in October and attributed the actual break to the direct influence of Dombrain who had just come up to Oxford. McQueen may well have needed, once again, some outside guidance to bring him to this extreme action; and nobody could have guided him more incisively than

Dombrain. It was actually in Dombrain's rooms at Pembroke (following Wright) that McQueen spoke to Pater for the last time, and it was there that the dissolution of the 'triumvirate' formally took place. At least one ex-King's School boy arriving the following year at Oxford was amazed to hear that the three inseparables had separated for ever.

When in 1862 Pater's B.A. result was known, McQueen broke his two-year silence by a note of congratulations to which Pater responded distantly, alluding to the existence of their friendship, 'in what is now a good many years ago.' McQueen remained baffled, even naively hurt, by this hardly inexplicable pushing back of their intimacy into the past possibly of school. To him it was all recent and vivid; nor had the void he had created for himself in expelling Pater been filled. Suitably, it was at a distance and with no possibility of speaking that they last saw each other, on 11 December 1862, when they both received their degrees from the Vice-Chancellor.

The following day McQueen returned home to Sussex. Shortly afterwards he was alerted by Dombrain that Pater still intended to be ordained – by the Bishop of London, since it was a London curacy which he hoped to obtain. Dombrain had also alerted the Reverend J. B. Kearney at Canterbury, and Kearney at some point apparently wrote to the bishop.

Dombrain himself took no further action, but McQueen believed that Pater might offer himself for ordination before Christmas on one of the Sundays in Advent. In fact, Pater was probably still considering what he should do, and when.

In explanation of his own behaviour McQueen told Wright in December 1903, exactly forty-one years later: 'I could not . . . let an Agnostic be ordained to be an Anglican Deacon.' As usual, however, he needed advice. He wrote therefore to 'a religious acquaintance' of his at Balliol, seeking his opinion and – as far as he recollected – asking if Henry Parry Liddon should be consulted. Liddon was a rising, youngish High Churchman who had just given up being Vice-Principal of St Edmund Hall. Temporarily he had retired to his rooms as a student at Christ Church, where Stanley was also in residence. Back the answer came from McQueen's Balliol friend that he should indeed write to Liddon. This he did. To Wright, McQueen openly confessed that while convinced he was doing the right thing, he guessed how highly Stanley would disapprove of his actions.

Liddon certainly did not. He had a reputation for advising young men in matters of conscience and a manner of reaching, as well as preaching, conclusions which seemed admirably eloquent, firm and sure (though his diaries reveal intense nerves, if not nervousness, underlying the admired manner and the eloquence). Significantly,

Liddon was to decline Stanley's repeated invitation as dean to preach in Westminster Abbey, on the grounds that Stanley had previously allowed F. D. Maurice to preach there. He may have found the case of Pater sad, but Liddon's view was quickly formed, characteristically uncompromising and doubtless crisply expressed: McQueen must himself write to the Bishop of London. Wright glosses the advice, possibly reliably, by adding that Liddon felt that even if McQueen did not prevent Pater's ordination he would have delivered his own soul (a consoling reference to *Ezekiel*, xxiii, 9: 'if thou warn the wicked of his way . . .'). Pater had once not too seriously characterized Liddon at a public gathering as looking 'very saintly and very cruel': an apt prophecy in so far as he was concerned.

McQueen had gained the advice he was seeking. He thereupon wrote to the Bishop of London, objecting to Pater's ordination and referring the Bishop to Kearney for clerical corroboration. He also wrote to Pater, informing him of what he had done. 'To this letter,' he told Wright, '(naturally enough, I dare say) I got no answer.'

The Bishop of London was Archibald Campbell Tait, soon to become Archbishop of Canterbury. He was a shrewd, liberal and balanced Scotsman, with a semi-political flair for steering between extremes of fanaticism in the Church of England. Even in the feverish climate of the day it must have been unusual for a bishop to receive two letters of denunciation about an obscure candidate for ordination who – it emerged – had not so far applied to be ordained. Such was the terse-sounding reply McQueen elicited.

Pater presumably got McQueen's letter and knew what his one-time friend had done. He seems to have been due to spend Christmas that year with Foster Pater's family in Islington; it was there that he heard news as sudden and even more affecting, and yet ironically linking McQueen's action with so much of the past. On 28 December Bessie Pater died at Dresden. Pater apparently set off straightway for Germany. The burial took place in Dresden; and then he returned with Hester and Clara, bereaved, without a home and fearfully uncertain of the future – except that to try for a curacy in London would now be to risk a humiliating rebuff.

McQueen recognized that his action meant losing all chance of regaining Pater's friendship. Nor did he ever again have any communication with Stanley, who almost certainly learnt of his letter. Everything had been carried out at great speed, in great fear, but perhaps none of it had really been necessary. McQueen was left to comfort himself with the words of *Ezekiel*, with an ineradicable affection for Pater and the conviction that what he had done, after all, was only his duty.

Six 'A new and daring philosophy'

IN THE NEW YEAR of 1863 Pater went back to Oxford. He returned to no position, but probably felt that Oxford offered him the best, the safest opportunity for a career. In writing to Pendergast, who was settling the family affairs following Bessie Pater's death, he now gave priority to gaining a fellowship; a curacy had become the alternative to be adopted only if he failed to obtain a college post by the summer. Meanwhile, he lived in lodgings, geographically symbolic of his fringe existence, just off the High Street, and took private pupils to help meet expenses.

This was the sort of life Jowett, for one, did not approve of. 'He talked about fellowships and about staying up at Oxford . . .', John Addington Symonds had noted in the previous autumn, when he too had been living in lodgings while seeking a fellowship. 'He calls it living in a hothouse, and says men get braced in London. . . . To read conscientiously for years on one subject requires peculiar gifts.'

For Pater the atmosphere at first proved chilly rather than overheated. No longer an undergraduate but without any fixed employment, too unsettled to write anything, he must have passed a depressing period, one that stretched out from months into more than a year. He might struggle against what seemed a curse put on him by McQueen, but in vain. Already in January 1863, he tried unsuccessfully to obtain a clerical fellowship at Brasenose. In the summer it was at Trinity that he competed, again for a clerical fellowship – and again unsuccessfully. In telling Pendergast earlier that if he did not shortly get a fellowship he would take a curacy he left the location unspecified, and no longer spoke of London – which is probably significant. He may even have dreamt of some quiet country retreat (with recollections of Keble's pleasant obscurity at Hursley), but seems to have continued to delay over positively offering himself for ordination. By late November he was asking Pendergast to send him 'what remains of my share of my mother's property – I think a little over £30.' Of his plans he said nothing; there was probably nothing to say. The Michaelmas term was ending with Pater scarcely more clear about his prospects – even perhaps less clear – than he had been at the same time in 1862.

In the letter of November to Pendergast he speaks about being soon in London, and presumably he was reunited at Christmas with Hester and Clara, and possibly with William as well. None of them can have felt very settled or sure about the future. The sisters had remained in England, conceivably staying with some branch of the family. In the earlier part of the year Pater had referred to Clara as 'getting better'; whatever illness she had may have come through nursing her aunt, either from emotional exhaustion or from some infection. Although she and Hester went on holiday abroad with Pater the following summer they do not appear to have moved to Oxford and lived with him until 1869. For some of the intervening time they stayed, either with him or alone, at Sidmouth.

As for William, he had left the army by 1864, if not well before, and planned in the autumn of that year to go out to Brazil with one of his Liverpool cousins, possibly with the idea of reverting to the career projected for him as a boy of becoming a merchant. Whatever he hoped for in Brazil seems not to have materialized, though his cousin was living there as a merchant a few years later. In July 1865, a few months after his thirtieth birthday, William at last found an apparently congenial post, one probably little sought for, as assistant medical officer in the lunatic asylum at Fareham. Thus he came to work remarkably close to Alverstoke, the place where his mother had been living immediately before her marriage.

New year 1864 opened for Pater similarly to the previous winter. From London he returned to Oxford. A classical fellowship vacancy – a non-clerical one, as it happened – occurred at Brasenose; Pater and eleven other candidates presented themselves, and on 5 February it was decided to elect him. He moved into college, occupying the two modest rooms on the first floor, with a direct view of the Radcliffe Camera and an oblique one of St Mary's Church, which remained his for the rest of his life. Without any threat or promise of ordination, a fellowship was gained. Pater's career had begun.

And in certain official university ways it had – as a career – already ended. For him there was to be no progress to a professorship, not even the Slade Professorship of Fine Art, and no college preferment. He was never to have a secure, still less a great, reputation as a scholar, or draw huge audiences by his ability as a lecturer. He had been searching, it might seem, merely for a retreat (and the fact that someone personally so quiet and retiring happened to find a home in the traditionally sporting and hearty atmosphere of Brasenose was later frequently to be commented on).

Yet Pater was very far from seeking the unstirring, uncreative existence of the average don, even if he remained unclear about what exactly he would do. He could not foresee the rebuffs of the future, but he may well have guessed that his would not be a conventional academic career, as he must certainly have known that his classical erudition was inferior to, say, Bywater's.

Both emotionally and economically, he needed a place. It was something basically lacking for him since the family had left Enfield and the 'old home'. Brasenose gave him that, with a measure of financial assurance; and in preferring always to keep the narrow rooms first assigned to him as a young and junior fellow, Pater asserted a simple, almost animal-like need for security and stability, what he calls with Jamesian phraseology, in *The Child in the House*, 'the unmistakeable realization of the delightful *chez soi* . . . with the closely-drawn white curtain and the shaded lamp.'

Having realized it, he had a base where he could literally gather his thoughts into creating a distinctive personality and from which he could safely launch that personality through his writings and also, more fitfully, through conversation. As it proved, he rather over-estimated the amount of protection his place gave him. The shaded lamp and the closely drawn curtain sound snug enough for a scholar in his den, but Pater quickly attracted a more glamorous and more dubious reputation, suggestive rather of the magician or the artist as weaver of sensuous spells. Behind the reticent, shy and courteous exterior in the pale green-tinted panelled room was someone playing with moral fire. It was exhilarating, but it was dangerous – how dangerous Pater seemed to be unaware or nonchalantly not to mind. For a few years he probably savoured his increasing reputation. His opinions and his friends were strikingly unconventional; so they had been when he was a schoolboy and an undergraduate, and now as a man he appeared entirely free to say and do what he thought: to be himself.

In electing him a fellow Brasenose had indeed seemed to select on grounds of personality rather than of strict academic accomplishment. Jowett or Capes, Pater's tutor at Queen's, might if consulted have testified to sensing some potential distinction shimmering around him, an incipient halo which in time was to turn lurid. Pater himself could hardly have explained the nature of his own gifts. Certainly he was well-read – far more widely read than was required or expected from a classics don. Possibly his knowledge of German philosophy was, as Wright reports, a factor in his being elected. For the rest, he was patently serious and conscientious, and doubtless eager.

94

Yet as Pater began to be known in the university, it was other qualities which attracted attention – not what he could expound about Hegel or Schelling, or about the classics, but what he propounded about himself and especially the style in which he did it. The rumour gradually grew that, in the words of Humphry Ward (who became an undergraduate at Brasenose in October 1864), Pater had 'a new and daring philosophy of his own, and a wonderful gift of style.' To these qualities, it was supposed, he actually owed his fellowship, though the first is unlikely to have impressed the authorities at Brasenose when looking for a classics tutor, and the second had not been forged at the time of his election.

But rumours of that kind may have served as rationalization of the choice of Pater when it emerged – to the extent of being commented on by his pupils – that his scholarship was occasionally shaky and that his concept of tuition lacked any driving, compulsive, didacticism. More importantly, the rumours testify to how rapidly an essay or two and a few literary articles, published anonymously, gave Pater a reputation in Oxford for novel, challenging ideas, expressed in a novel, seductive way. Perhaps before he quite realized it, or wished it, he was becoming a cult figure, especially among undergraduates. His expression of himself and his views was dubbed a 'philosophy', though it was really a highly personal confession. Under cover of reviews, he revealed intense apprehensions of mortality and no less anxious aspirations towards beauty which had been part of his individual nature since boyhood; and what he reviewed was half drowned in the thrill of his own rich, intoxicating accent. He might duly speak of setting the spirit free by 'any contribution to knowledge', but that was a limp, savourless phrase, no more than the curtest of nods towards the intellect, compared with the singing, urgent words with which he recommended everyone in a melting world to pursue sensation, to catch at 'any exquisite passion . . . stirring of the senses, strange dyes, strange flowers, and curious odours, or work of the artist's hands,' and even, most openly personal of all, 'the face of one's friend'. The more desperately does he urge pursuit, since we are each under the threat of death. We have only the interval of life, the awful brevity of experience, a short day of frost and sun, 'and then we cease to be'. Quietly but firmly, Christianity is there rejected.

The words may have been spoken before, but they could be read for the first time in October 1868, in Pater's anonymous article, ostensibly reviewing three volumes of William Morris's poetry, for the *Westminster Review*. Under his transmuting gaze, fixed where it feels most sympathy and otherwise barely noticing, Morris is

95

absorbed into a medieval atmosphere which might have been compounded by Swinburne and Baudelaire, where 'exotic flowers of sentiment expand, among people of a remote and unaccustomed beauty, somnambulistic, frail, androgynous . . .' Almost autobiographical sounds the reference to 'A passion of which the outlets are sealed, [begetting] a tension of nerve in which the sensible world comes to one with a reinforced brilliance and relief – all redness is turned into blood, all water into tears.'

The final paragraphs of that article no longer deal with Morris or with poetry; they ask what modern philosophy tells about human life. Urged on by an excited momentum, they carry their author up into the pulpit of his own church and turn him preacher of his own profoundly felt gospel in a way he was never so explicitly to be again. It was like a last cry from someone who had suffered sinking and dissolution, 'washed out', as he writes there, 'beyond the bar in a sea at ebb', or has been chilled by premonition of mortal frost and oncoming, final darkness. So little seems left to believe in, but that makes it all the more important to utter and convey the literally saving belief: 'Of this wisdom, the poetic passion, the desire of beauty, the love of art for art's sake has most; for art comes to you professing frankly to give nothing but the highest quality to your moments as they pass, and simply for those moments' sake.'

That quintessence of Pater's creed, with the paragraphs which preceded it, was five years later to become the 'Conclusion' to his first book, *Studies in the History of the Renaissance*. He needed to go on repeating his message; and though in some panic he dropped it as 'misleading' from the second edition, he put it back again for the third and, with very minor modifications, for the fourth, the last to be published during his lifetime, in his penultimate year. Stubbornly he had stated, over a quarter of a century, what was and continued to be his creed. It could not remain new, but it kept about it something of the challenging and daring quality which it had had on first publication.

And although Pater had probably no wish to mould disciples, still less to excite grave scandal or controversy, he did intend to assert his detachment from conventional beliefs by carefully and cogently stating his own. What may have surprised him was how rapidly reactions to those beliefs crystallized. Very far from indifferent, the Oxford of the 1860s and 1870s proved highly susceptible to what he had to say, dividing broadly into a youthful, often undergraduate group, profoundly influenced both by his 'philosophy' and by the manner in which it was conveyed, and an older, more extensive, more established and establishment-minded milieu, where a few might profess to admire Pater's style but where all sniffed, under the skilfully arranged flowers of his prose, the odour of something unhealthy, unmanly, immoral and anti-Christian.

Nor, of course, were they wrong in what they detected. And any disapproval they may have expressed can only have increased Pater's reputation in Oxford for being daring. Yet, like his 'philosophy' itself, this daringness was not something abruptly assumed on obtaining a fellowship, or merely the aggressive pose adopted by an essentially timid man. It was inherent in Pater's increasing awareness of his individuality amid those strong forces of convention (conventional belief, conventional thoughts, conventional morals) which he had been encountering since his schooldays. He had suffered for it, as his experience with McQueen reveals. His originality, his verve, his insight, his ability to stimulate, were the characteristics which those who liked him could not fail to notice. 'Always ready to impart his delightful criticisms and appreciations of art and literature, ancient and modern, which were so helpful and suggestive,' was the suavely sympathetic recollection of the Provost of Eton, Hornby, who had been a don at Brasenose in Pater's very first years there. But Pater's originality was more profound than this, more fiercely felt and to be more forcefully revealed. Even Benson, who knew almost nothing of Pater's earlier, reckless heterodoxy, was able to recognize that under his gentleness of manner lay 'a certain untamed scepticism' and a nature 'not innately humble'.

In time, and after disagreeable experiences, Pater might be led to mask the intensity of his sensations, but his first urge was to express them frankly – express rather than communicate or commend them as such to everyone else. That marked from the beginning how different he was – and meant to be – from Ruskin. He challenged the age by virtually dodging its overt challenge, by declining to preach any unifying message to society, to brace it, scold it, or indeed instruct it at all. Tacitly, he proposed the social divisiveness of each person seeking to cultivate himself and his own sensations. That for him was and had always been the essence of reality.

In taking his place in the social environment of a university he found himself in a climate mentally far more constricting than the mere physical constriction of his two simple rooms at Brasenose. Here was a society consisting entirely of teachers and the taught, created positively for instruction, work, the pursuit of knowledge and some sort of success in the world. Barely, it seemed, had Pater assumed the role of being one of its teachers, with the implied responsibility of influencing young minds, before he began subtly to suggest quite other goals. One undergraduate, Edward Manson, who went up to

97

Brasenose in 1869 and who felt Pater's influence, as well as enjoying the proximity of rooms above his, later summed up the impression Pater conveyed of his theory of life as being, 'Cultivate the art of vivid sensation'. Whether alluring or repelling, the effect of this lightly-dropped doctrine was bound to cause shock. It was the equivalent of finding one's tutor recommending in place of some study of Greek syntax *Mademoiselle de Maupin*. Not without a glance perhaps at the regular, conventional collegiate activity all round him Pater echoed a sentence from his review of Morris's poetry ('Failure is to form habits; for habit is relative to a stereotyped world') in suggesting to Manson and his contemporaries that to form habits was fatal in life. When Humphry Ward, after praising both Pater's personal kindness and the originality of his mind as revealed in the Oxford of the late 1860s, defined his inner world as unlike that of anyone else there, he expressed what many people had noticed. Pater probably met almost as much incomprehension as suspicion; the result increased his isolation and must eventually have been no less disheartening.

As he daily climbed his dark staircase and entered the austerely-furnished rooms which were to remain his for over thirty years, Pater may – at least at first – have felt some sort of pride in that apartness and remoteness from the ideas of the average don. For all his courtesy and kindness, he unmistakably held off from any real intimacy even with someone like Ward with whom he often lunched and walked ('you never felt', Ward recorded in a rather pained way, 'that he was quite at one with you in habits, feelings, preferences'). Pater in effect explained his attitude when, again in the *Westminster* review of Morris, he spoke of experience as being a swarm of impressions reaching an individual in his isolation, 'each mind keeping as a solitary prisoner its own dream of a world.' Humphry Ward, decent, sympathetic, not unintelligent but quite unexciting, reached him, we may guess, only in the form of a faint impression, a friendly far-away buzz, leaving undisturbed Pater's own dream of a world – a universe where the neither frail nor androgynous Ward might have felt bewilderment and alarm.

Like his rooms, Pater outwardly revealed little except a certain choiceness which became in his dress a hint or more of dandyism. Although round-shouldered, he was at this date still slight and 'gracefully made', in the words of the observant Manson. Courteous, charming and reticent, he was yet not afraid to stigmatize the style of, for example, Manson's essays with a series of epithets interesting for confirming by contrast his own standards: popular, rambling, rhetorical and dissolute. Pater clearly liked young Manson, but

Manson was even more explicit than Ward in pronouncing his life to be secluded and self-centred.

It could hardly be otherwise. Pater had only quite recently emerged from the crisis which McQueen precipitated. He had to all intents renounced Christianity (though he must have subscribed, as was necessary, to the Thirty-Nine Articles on taking his M.A. in 1865), and he had been renounced by McQueen.

All his conscious life, back to childhood, he had been under bombardment from visual stimuli which fevered his imagination. Indeed, it was his way (as he says of Florian in *The Child in the House*) of receiving the world. In growing up he had not lost it. Far from finding something with which to quieten it, preferably within a religious system, he was exposed to the sensuous element not only of the arts and of places but of people ('... the face of one's friend'). And there his desire of physical beauty set him, he must rapidly have realized, on the loneliest path of all. A longing, wistful note combines in his work with constant loving allusions to male beauty, and it might almost have been to himself that he alluded in writing of Winckelmann in 1867: 'That his affinity with Hellenism was not merely intellectual, that the subtler threads of temperament were interwoven in it, is proved by his romantic, fervid friendships with young men ... such attachments are nevertheless more susceptible than any others of equal strength of a purely intellectual culture. Of passion, of physical stir, they contain just so much as stimulates the eye...'

Long after Pater's death, Bywater was privately to tell a foreign enquirer that he would notice in the essay on Winckelmann 'a certain sympathy with a certain aspect of Greek life', adding darkly, 'I must tell you that that was not confined to him.' The majority of Pater's contemporaries seem quickly to have noticed and understood this sympathy, which became more and more overt in his later writings, culminating in the baleful, disturbed re-telling of the story of Apollo and Hyacinth in *Apollo in Picardy* (1893). For some people such as Oscar Browning, Pater's daring, apparent declaration in the essay on Winckelmann signalled a welcome addition to the ranks of boy-lovers. He hastened to become acquainted. For others, sooner or later, Pater's marked preference for the company of young and good-looking men, combined no doubt with currents in his work and the nature of several of his friends, was a reason to be highly suspicious. Some of the comment may have remained private gossip spoken and not written, or written only in a diary. But it existed. Sidney Colvin, an early friend of Pater's, is said to have warned at least one young man against knowing him and seems himself to have pointedly stopped knowing Pater. The diary of Mark Pattison, the Rector of Lincoln College, acidly notes taking tea in 1878 at Pater's house, and surveying from one corner Oscar Browning talking in another with '4 feminine looking youths,' to be joined afterwards by Pater, 'attended by 2 more youths of similar appearance.'

Allied to his expression of anti-Christian sentiments, hints of his sexual heterodoxy must have significantly deepened distrust of Pater in influential university circles, better able to digest rationality than homosexuality. The combination was and perhaps remained novel, making him a dangerously pagan figure. And while in his later life and writings he adopted a far more cautious, credulous, even conservative, attitude to Christianity, he could scarcely change his nature. That there was something corrupting about him and his morals was probably the most pervasive and most fundamentally damaging aspect of Pater's Oxford reputation. He appears to have become wearily aware in the end that he would never shake off the shadow so rapidly and negligently acquired by his early frankness.

For a display of that he was not, for all his seclusion, without an audience and not without some reactions. It was in a small Oxford circle, that of the liberal-minded, 'Old Mortality' essay society, that Pater's first heterodox notes were heard, soon after his election to Brasenose. The society had been founded in the mid-1850s by a Balliol undergraduate, John Nichol. Swinburne was among its members and so, almost certainly, had been Pater's friend John Hoole. Its strange title indicated the awareness of at least its founder of the governing fact of human life, asserted probably with deliberately rationalistic, free-thinking overtones, as well as because of its first members' own fragile health.

Exactly when Pater became a member of this society seems uncertain but possibly he was elected in 1863 – during that for him otherwise barren year. On 20 February 1864 he read the society a paper called *Subjective Immortality*. Although this essay as such is totally lost, some echoes of its drift are fortunately caught in the indignant record of one of the other members, a certain S. G. Brooke, whose diary survives. Brooke was sufficiently stirred to prepare and read a paper in riposte, before withdrawing from further attendance.

Probably not since McQueen's anguished denunciations had Pater provoked such sustained fire. Brooke pompously pronounced his essay to be 'one of the most thoroughly infidel productions it has ever been our pain to listen to.' More usefully, he indicated what had really upset him: Pater's concern with self-culture 'upon eminently selfish principles, and, for what to us appeared, a most unsatisfactory end.' This tantalizingly brief reference, taken in conjunction with

100

the essay's title, is enough, however, to suggest that what attenders at the Old Mortality meeting heard from Pater was the first draft of the abruptly added-on concluding paragraphs of his *Westminster Review* article of four years later dealing with William Morris's poetry. What could more aptly be defined as *Subjective Immortality* than the sentences urging everyone to expand the interval of human life, 'in getting as many pulsations as possible into the given time', to pursue high passions ('Only, be sure it is passion, that it does yield you this fruit of a quickened, multiplied consciousness') and to comprehend that of all such passions there is none that gives higher qualities to the moments as they pass than a love of art for art's sake? Those sentences may indeed be summed up as advocating 'self-culture' (which Brooke seems to have equated virtually with self-abuse). Something close to them was very likely enunciated first in Pater's paper of 1864, typically thriftily utilized for the *Westminster Review*, and subsequently placed as the 'Conclusion' to his volume of Renaissance studies. And on the publication of that, S. G. Brooke's indignation could be seen to have been pale and powerless, if prophetic, compared with the thunder which rolled round Pater, never entirely to subside for the remainder of his life.

No doubt Brooke had ceased to attend the 'Old Mortality' meetings before July 1864, by which time Pater had prepared another paper. This is entitled *Diaphaneitè* and is ostensibly no more than a rather cloudy, idealized character study, praising and defining a type of 'clear crystal nature'. Perhaps to someone like Brooke, knowing nothing of what had stimulated Pater to produce this essay, it could have appeared an undisturbing exercise, marred only by one or two references to the sexless beauty of Greek statues and the 'moral sexlessness' of the character being delineated, who had 'a kind of impotence, an ineffectual wholeness of nature, yet with a divine beauty and significance of its own.' Pater himself clearly savoured this phraseology and economically repeated it in reference to Winckelmann in his *Westminster Review* article three years later. It is praise Winckelmann would hardly have wanted, or deserved, but it may have pleased the real subject of *Diaphaneitè*, Charles Lancelot Shadwell, an ex-pupil of Pater's and also a member of 'Old Mortality', who became in 1864 a fellow of Oriel College.

Behind the contrived opacity of the essay's language there can be seen admiration not only of Shadwell's mind ('A magnificent intellectual force is latent within it') but of his appearance ('Perhaps it is nearly always found with a corresponding outward semblance'). According to Wright, whose gossip on the point proves less unreliable than usual, those who knew Shadwell then asserted he had been 'undoubtedly the handsomest man in the University – with a face like those to be seen on the finer Attic coins'. No photograph of the young Shadwell seems traceable, but at the time of his death in 1919 *The Times* declared him to have been, 'in his younger days strikingly handsome, both in figure and feature'.

That Shadwell inspired *Diaphaneitè* was stated first and categorically by Benson. There can be no doubt of the close friendship in the 1860s between Pater and Shadwell. Pater's first journey to Italy was with Shadwell in 1865, and to him was dedicated the fullest result of that visit – *Studies in the History of the Renaissance*. Yet, as so often with Pater, the friendship seems to have cooled in later years, possibly when *The Renaissance* was published, though without apparently any quarrel or positive break. He certainly entertained Shadwell at home in London and late in life wrote an introduction for Shadwell's translation of Dante's *Purgatorio*. And, in turn as it were, Shadwell was to act as Pater's literary executor. It was he, in fact, who first published *Diaphaneitè* (in the volume of *Miscellaneous Studies*, of 1895) when he described it as inserted there, 'with some hesitation . . . as the only specimen known to be preserved of those early essays of Mr Pater's, by which his literary gifts were first made known to the small circle of his Oxford friends.' Although Shadwell would be too circumspect to say so, the preservation of this 'specimen' (dated 'July 1864' and initialled 'W.H.P.') is most likely explicable by the supposition that he, as its subject, had been given the manuscript by Pater, perhaps soon after its completion.

If this paper was actually delivered at a meeting of the 'Old Mortality' – which seems probable – Pater was being as quietly daring about his personal life as he had more obviously been about his philosophy in the paper on *Subjective Immortality*. His wistful, admiring affection is patent for the naturally innocent, guileless, upright, unstruggling character, of conservative tendencies ('Not by it could the progress of the world be achieved'), possibly sitting listening to him in the audience. The diaphanously crystal nature emerges as male and young; and a slightly disingenuous 'often', with its suggestion of generalization, does little to conceal a specific preference: 'Often the presence of this nature is felt like a sweet aroma in early manhood.' At that moment, it seems, all Pater's attraction towards good-looking boys or men, and all his search for the ideal companion, focused on Charles Lancelot Shadwell. In *Diaphaneitè* Shadwell has taken on, already, something of the vagueness of a mythic character. As the portrayal of a real person, the essay would be a failure; but it is hardly intended to be more descriptive of Shadwell than an ode of Pindar's is of the victor he celebrates in the games. And Shadwell may, consciously or not, have been in Pater's mind when he first conceived that passionate litany of sensuous experiences to be grasped and discriminated which became part of the 'Conclusion' to *The Renaissance* and which concludes, after strange dyes, flowers and odours with 'the face of one's friend.'

Perhaps Shadwell never quite understood, or wished to understand, the intensity of Pater's concentration on him. A competent scholar with rather quirky interests and strongly-held views, a lawyer who came from a distinguished legal family (his grandfather, Lancelot Shadwell, had been the last Vice-Chancellor of England), he grew into being almost a caricature of an old-style university don: a bachelor, fond of chess problems and of composing chronograms, devoted to every detail of the history of his college, of which he became provost and a munificent benefactor, dignified, rather forbidding and expecting from his juniors a deference which even pre-1914 undergraduates were no longer accustomed to accord. Whatever his recollections of Pater, he divulged them to no one. He left no memoirs at his death. The crystal man retained his rather baffling innocence and even mystery ('. . . something of an enigma to the younger generation,' remarked *The Times* obituary). Only his continued enthusiasm for Dante seems not quite in character, and not properly allowed for by Pater – though it was most probably the reason why Ravenna, in addition to Florence and Pisa, was singled out by the two friends on their Italian tour of 1865.

For Pater it may have been enough to see Shadwell, to convey something of what encountering him had meant and – a little more intimately – to travel abroad with him, though that seems never to have been repeated. A certain unresponsiveness in Shadwell may ultimately have had its reassuring aspect, keeping him 'harmonized as by distance' (in words used in *Diaphaneitè*) and leaving Pater the more able to admire without any feelings of guilt. In some ways, the character he delineates in *Diaphaneitè* is not unlike that of Emerald Uthwart (he, too, crystalline and passive) and oddly near Pater's concept of Raphael as expressed in a late lecture-article (and indeed already in *Diaphaneitè* also, where he mentions the character's affinity less to Luther or Spinoza than to Raphael).

The appeal of such a nature to him probably lay in its utter difference from his own: simple where he was complex, innocent and untroubled where he was only too aware not merely of death but of ambiguous desires and that 'tension of nerve' he wrote of as arising from frustrated emotions. Above all, he recognized it as physically different from himself, yet as he longed to be: perhaps also as his brother William was and conceivably as he supposed their father to have been. Handsome, healthy, animal-like schoolboys and good-looking if intellectually null undergraduates cannot have done much to satisfy a yearning to give and receive affection. Perhaps Pater dreamt of some real-life modern version not so much of Apollo and Hyacinth as of that medieval French story of Amis and Amile which he was to write of, where the two men, twins in appearance and in adventures, forge 'a friendship pure and generous, pushed to a sort of passionate exaltation, and more than faithful unto death'.

It was a coincidence, which Pater may not have missed, that Shadwell should also be the name of an area close enough to his birthplace to be mentioned as it in several posthumous accounts (e.g. Benson's). Whether or not that accident obscurely played its part, he seems to have made friends quickly with his pupil – among the first of his pupils and one who was only some sixteen months younger than himself. All that survives to document their relationship is a single brief note of Pater's, written on 31 December of (most probably) 1865, giving his temporary London address in Jermyn Street and expressing hopes of seeing Shadwell there before he returns to Oxford. A few months earlier that year they had together been sharing the first impact of Italy: an Italy not only of Dante's tomb and Botticelli's *Birth of Venus* but also, and no less sensuously appealing to Pater, of Tuscan towns, gipsy children and the 'strange grey peaks' of Carrara.

This visit it must have been which inflamed Pater's 'lust of the eye', and encouraged him to begin writing on painters and on the visual arts – a departure from more conventional literary subjects. Something of the delight of that direct experience of Italian cities, landscape and life still vibrates in the essays which he produced at intervals subsequently and which were to be collected into the volume dedicated suitably to Shadwell. At Pisa they must have visited the Campo Santo where the frescoed image of God the Father holding the map of the world, 'as a great target or shield', recurred to Pater when writing about Pico della Mirandola's concept of the world as a limited place. At Ravenna they will have seen Dante's tomb, and what Pater has to say about Dante's poetry in comparison with Michelangelo's is coloured no doubt by conversations with Shadwell. At Florence Pater for the first time encountered and was conquered by the expressive powers of Botticelli's greatest pictures, but he responded also to the cool streets and those darkened churches into which Luca della Robbia's pale blue and white work seemed to have fallen like 'fragments of the milky sky.' He could even compare the loss of della Robbia's savour when his work was moved from its original crumbling walls to what happens in transporting Tuscan

104

wine. And from the angels of Botticelli he was led to recollect fondly the children begging in Apennine villages, on Sundays transformed into choirboys, 'with their thick black hair nicely combed and fair white linen on their sun-burnt throats'.

Never again, perhaps, was Pater to travel abroad in such intelligent and sympathetic company. Certainly, he never dedicated any of his later books to anyone outside his immediate family. The Italian Renaissance and Italy altogether seem to have dwindled as interests; it is doubtful if he travelled more than once in Italy with his sisters, whose preference seems to have been for France. With the possible exception of the essay on *The School of Giorgione* (which may actually have been prepared for the book dedicated to Shadwell) and the special case of *Marius*, he did not return to Italy in a literary sense until as late as 1890, when he published the vivid, semi-travel jottings, *Art Notes in North Italy*, prompted by a visit to the region in the previous summer just after his fiftieth birthday. *Studies in the History of the Renaissance* represented a youthful, effervescent, even reckless period in Pater's life. Consciously or not, its germ lies in the tour of 1865; and in that book, as much as in *Diaphaneitè*, though more subtly, is commemorated his friendship with Shadwell.

To have met and become friendly with Shadwell might be for Pater personally an exciting adventure, lending allure to hot train rides through Italy at the height of the summer and enhancing, say, the climb up to San Miniato at Florence to gaze at the chapel built for the body of the young Cardinal of Portugal, where Pater might respond to all the mingled and for him favourite associations of youth, beauty and mortality, as he was to recall them: 'Rossellino carved his tomb . . . with care for the shapely hands and feet and sacred attire . . . and the tomb of the youthful and princely prelate became the strangest and most beautiful thing in that strange and beautiful place.'

Still, the friendship with Shadwell – even when hymned for a 'small circle' in the sentences of *Diaphaneitè* – was essentially decorous, indeed unremarkable, and given further respectability no doubt by the dignified, reticent character of Shadwell himself. Just at about the same date, however, as this friendship developed, Pater began to come into friendly contact with literary and artistic figures of sometimes shockingly unconventional and utterly unreticent natures, rebels against many tendencies of the age and people with whom he probably felt instinctive sympathy. They too, no less than Pater, had 'new and daring' philosophies – and were often far more outspoken in both preaching and practising them. Their milieu was London not Oxford, though they might have Oxford links; for Pater they represented a larger and more relaxed environment.

Two people in particular seem to have appealed to him not merely as talented but as sharing many of his own private preoccupations and as expressing – unlike, for example, Oscar Browning – in creative art much of those feelings; they were Swinburne and Simeon Solomon. Pater probably met Swinburne through the 'Old Mortality', and it was probably Swinburne who introduced him to the frankly homosexual Solomon, a gifted, sub-Pre-Raphaelite painter whose career was to be destroyed less by his own behaviour than by the period's hysterical condemnation of it. The extent of the prevalent hypocrisy is shown by Swinburne's attitude when Solomon, his close friend, was eventually arrested by the police in a public urinal. Writing loftily of Solomon's 'insanity', he hastened to withdraw the hem of his own rather doubtfully clean garment from someone with whom he had previously shared all his own obsessions with birches and boys being beaten. Swinburne's letters might be full of simple jokes about the Reverend Onan Buggeridge and the diocese of Arseborough, but the breaking in of actuality on his fantasy life proved too much for a previously dormant puritanism. He 'forgot' Solomon, very much as he was later – and probably for allied though unspoken reasons – to deny any real acquaintance with Pater (stating, however, with almost suspicious precision that he had spoken to him only twice, once in London and once in Oxford).

Pater's admiration for Solomon's work, and specifically for a *Bacchus* he exhibited at the Royal Academy in 1867, is recorded by a few words praising the concept of 'a young Hebrew painter', showing 'the god of the bitterness of wine, "of things too sweet",' which occur in his essay *A Study of Dionysus*, published in *The Fortnightly Review* in 1876. On 17 June 1868, Gerard Manley Hopkins noted in his diary that he had that day lunched with Pater in London and afterwards gone (almost certainly with Pater) to Solomon's studio and to the Academy. The following year Solomon in a letter to Swinburne mentions visiting Pater at Oxford. The best testimony to a friendship which no surviving letters document is in the drawing of Pater which Solomon executed at Brasenose, in 1872. Here, with the minimum of idealization, it seems, is an image which Pater could have recognized as at once truthful and agreeable: a sensitive portrayal which manages to convey something of the subject's trim and faintly military appearance, his discreet dandyism and – through those often-praised eloquent eyes – his keen yet half-apprehensive awareness of the world.

A touch of apprehension on Pater's part might enter their friendship when he realized that for Solomon homosexuality was no sublimated, ethereal emotion, but an active force, one excited, incidentally, rather than calmed by association with Swinburne,

Oscar Browning and others. Solomon could depict in words as well as in paint his ideals of beauty (publishing *A Vision of Love revealed in Sleep* (1871) in fake biblical prose but with pulsatingly genuine feelings for naked 'youth transfigured'). He could also attend as an intrigued spectator the notorious trial the same year of a group of transvestites: 'The Queen v. Boulton and Others'. Two years later he himself was the subject of legal proceedings, found guilty and given a suspended sentence. It was with Pater that Swinburne, who happened to be at Oxford, discussed the matter and it is clear from a letter of Swinburne's at the time that Pater felt far greater hope and charity for Solomon that Swinburne even attempted. Pater, Swinburne wrote to a close friend, had seen Solomon's sister and appeared more optimistic that Solomon might be rehabilitated than he himself had 'ventured' to think from the 'horrid version' he had heard. Nor does Pater seem to have turned in horror afterwards from any association with the name. When in 1889, a few days after his fiftieth birthday, he received a drawing of Solomon's from an admirer, the writer and connoisseur, Herbert Horne, he warmly thanked him for 'this beautiful and characteristic drawing . . . so choice a gift.'

Becoming a great friend of Solomon's and willing to go on being one (as Pater seems to have been prepared to do, anyway at first) can have done nothing to allay suspicions about Pater's own morality. And to the daring painter could be added the daring writer, Swinburne, if Swinburne had not so forcefully denied the relationship – thus making odder the testimony of someone like Edward Manson that Swinburne as well as Solomon was among Pater's friends. Certainly Swinburne's factual account of only two meetings is wrong. But his shabby little evasions when deaf, reformed and living at Putney under the genteel tutelage of Watts-Dunton are not of much concern. Over Pater he was to exercise a literary influence which both men recognized. In that way, if not a friend, he was Pater's guide, pointing him towards ambiguous, conventionally unhealthy regions of art and showing him how they might be explored stylistically – in prose rather than poetry.

The degree of Swinburne's daring lay for most of his contemporaries in his poems. Had they read his letters, with their steady allusions to de Sade, childish jokes about Christianity and rather better ones about Queen Victoria putting up 'phallic' stones ('a genuine Priapic erection') in honour of the Prince Consort's virility, they might have been more deeply shocked – or possibly merely amused, recognizing in such topics their own private conversational freedom as opposed to their public respectability.

For Pater, Swinburne was probably not the writer of scurrilous, lively letters or even the extraordinarily vivid, 'quite original, wildly eccentric, astonishingly gifted and convulsively droll' talker who astonished wherever he went and who was recalled by Henry Adams and other assorted guests at house parties given by Monckton Milnes (choosing his more 'shocking' poems to read in the scandalized presence of the Archbishop of York). As for Swinburne the poet, Pater's sole surviving letter to him expresses enjoyment of some of his poems on Gautier, but is remarkably brief, cool and reserved in tone, even allowing for Pater's inhibited style of letter-writing. Indeed, perhaps it was a shared love of Gautier (who died in October 1872), rather than any presumed admiration for Swinburne's poetry as such, that had prompted the exchange. Pater's awareness of not only Gautier but also Flaubert and Baudelaire was quite probably due to Swinburne. That was one debt; how Swinburne wrote about such figures was another.

As early as 1862 *Les Fleurs du Mal* had been reviewed by Swinburne in *The Spectator*. The cadences of his prose style, his choice of alliterative adjectives and his stress on the bizarre elements in Baudelaire might well stir Pater – to read the poet and to write like the reviewer: 'Throughout the chief part of this book,' he would have read, '[Baudelaire] has chosen to dwell mainly upon sad and strange things – the weariness of pain and the bitterness of pleasure – the perverse happiness and wayward sorrow of exceptional people. . . . Failure and sorrow, next to physical beauty and perfection of sound or scent, seem to have an infinite attraction for him.' Not only do such phrases anticipate Pater's style; they seem to come near analyzing much of his own attitude.

And in July 1868, before Pater had published anything specifically on the Renaissance or on the visual arts, Swinburne contributed some 'Notes' on old master drawings at Florence to *The Fortnightly Review*, composed in more elaborately chiselled cadences which seem to have been echoing still in Pater's ear when he invoked the image of *Mona Lisa* (in *The Fortnightly*, in the subsequent year): 'All mysteries of good and evil, all wonders of life and death, lie in their hands or at their feet. They have known the causes of things and are not too happy . . .' Easily could those sentences actually of Swinburne's be sought for in Pater's essay on Leonardo da Vinci. It is hardly surprising that when Swinburne read that essay he found himself agreeing with Rossetti that in it there seemed 'a little spice of my style, as you say.' To *The Fortnightly*'s editor, John Morley, a few weeks after publication of *The Renaissance* in 1873, Swinburne declared that he had felt shy of saying how much he admired and enjoyed Pater's work ever since Pater had owned that the inspiration of his *Fortnightly* essays (of which the book chiefly consisted) came entirely from 'the example of my own work in the same line.'

It was far more than style that influenced Pater. It was the highly subjective – and, where the visual arts were concerned, amateur – approach to works of art, using them to some extent to convey certain moods and emotions, so that what is accreted around the object becomes a reverie. Swinburne responded to, and enjoyed interpreting, the ambiguous work of art, where he might detect extremes of hellish cruelty under divine beauty – as in one Michelangelo drawing of a woman whose 'eyes are full of proud and passionless lust after gold and blood . . . her mouth crueller than a tiger's, colder than a snake's and beautiful beyond a woman's.' She is, in fact, ready to become the typical subject of one of his poems, a sort of steely Faustine-Félise-Dolores figure: a 'mystical rose of the mire' who is (like Dolores) 'alive after infinite changes/And fresh from the kisses of death.'

This mood of an inferior florist's *Fleurs du Mal* – proffering blooms that are not only cut-price but cut off from any real vitality – quickly seems monotonous and silly: almost as silly as the much-admired *Mademoiselle de Maupin* by Gautier which Swinburne, Pater and Wilde all appear to have seriously respected. But in the mingled streams of perversity, playing with sex change, sadism, masochism, homosexuality and hostility to women (so often become hateful, dominating vampires) which Swinburne provided there was – for Pater and doubtless for many other contemporaries – a way of relieving their own obsessions without going through the experiences of, say, Simeon Solomon. At least Swinburne recognized and pro-claimed the ambivalence of the emotions, the erotic appeal of pain, and the human urge towards any intense experience, whether con-ventionally judged good or bad. Nor is what he detected in Michel-angelo's drawings, at least where women are concerned, necessarily unshrewd or the product merely of his own fantasies.

Swinburne, however, was not a young, recently-appointed don at Oxford, who had subscribed to the Thirty-Nine articles and was responsible for instructing undergraduates. He had only to skip away with upper-class insouciance from Oxford, or anywhere else, leaving behind astonished hosts and astonished, scandalized or amused fellow guests. Even Solomon might have claimed from the period some artistic licence – claimed it successfully perhaps had his taste been for women, or had he managed to be more discreet.

Together, Swinburne and Solomon – precociously displaying their talents, though in age very much Pater's contemporaries – might seem to him like a pair of experienced gamblers in an exciting if somewhat dubious casino. Most dons would have shrunk from entry there; but Pater was drawn in exactly because it was here he instinctively belonged. In his own lonely way, he had already experienced it all: scepticism about received morality, the aching desire for sensations, and a painfully intense response to beauty in the visible world. And although Swinburne and Solomon offered encouraging affinities, the corner where he chose to gamble remained an isolated one, while his very presence there was a daring assertion of individuality.

It was not in Pater to emulate the anti-religious flippancy of Swinburne who, writing to Rossetti once at Christmas-time, invented what he called a medieval carol: 'Hark, the herald angels crow/Here's a boy – but not for Joe!' Gravely, yet with far greater risk, did Pater make publicly apparent his opposition to the trammels of any creed which tried to restrict the right to pursue and enjoy all impressions and sensations: 'The theory or idea or system which requires of us the sacrifice of any part of this experience, in consideration of some interest into which we cannot enter, or some abstract morality we have not identified with ourselves, or what is only conventional, has no real claim upon us.' ('Poems by William Morris', *Westminster Review*, 1868.)

When the implications of that sentence were fully absorbed, it became clear that Pater was not content to mouse on quietly cultivating exquisite experiences as might another man his garden or his photographs of the Alps. He intended to jolt society, and for a period at least he went on jolting it not only by what he wrote but by what he said.

Seven The importance of not being earnest

'PERHAPS', Pater wrote in his first piece of published work, a reverie-like essay dealing with Coleridge's prose, which appeared anonymously in the *Westminster Review* of January 1866, 'the chief offence in Coleridge is an excess of seriousness . . .'

The criticism, which he goes on to expand, may seem to have gained a certain retrospective irony, since Pater and his own writings are commonly assumed to suffer from much the same 'offence'. Yet in protesting about this proto-Victorian quality in Coleridge, whom in many other ways he found personally similar and sympathetic, Pater was obviously thinking about himself. Unobtrusively, he marked a distinction not only between his attitude and Coleridge's but between his and general nineteenth-century tendencies to appear, if not to be, intensely serious and intensely earnest.

From the time he was elected a fellow of Brasenose in 1864 up to publication of *Studies in the History of the Renaissance* nine years later, Pater was engaged in carrying out his own programme of cultivating sensations. It was neither arduous nor especially grave. It was a matter of enjoying himself and expressing himself. When *The Renaissance* was published he was, after all, not yet thirty-four. Nothing in his position or circumstances need sadden him. Indeed, these years were probably the most carefree he had ever enjoyed, or would enjoy. Articles by him appeared regularly. Almost without his troubling, his reputation steadily increased. Brasenose made him a college lecturer, though even in lectures on the history of philosophy he preserved an almost disdainful tone ('the novelty . . .', Humphry Ward noted, 'was that [his lectures] rarely mentioned any philosopher's name.'). He became head of a household when late in 1869 he took a house north of the Parks in the newest quarter of Oxford, in Bradmore Road, where Hester and Clara joined him, and where collectively they could reject contemporary standards and establish an exquisitely elegant, artfully devised setting, including the very flowers arranged 'with a simple yet conscious art'.

If no circle exactly gathered around Pater, he must all the same have recognized that groups of people – in London and in Oxford –

were impressed by his writings and appreciative of his conversation. In London he encountered editors of leading 'liberal' magazines, like John Chapman and John Morley, who were eager enough to publish his work. Through Swinburne, presumably, he met Rossetti and then other literary and artistic figures who lived or visited in Chelsea, including Rossetti's friend William Bell Scott, in whose studio he first met Edmund Gosse; with Gosse he quickly established an agreeable if not truly close mutual admiration society which in effect outlasted his death, for Gosse proved practically helpful to Hester and Clara afterwards (and was rewarded by the gift of Pater's last manuscript, the essay on Pascal). In Oxford there were people like the Humphry Wards (Ward married Matthew Arnold's niece, Mary, in April 1872) and the Rector of Lincoln College, Mark Pattison, along with the far more attractive and graceful figure of his far younger wife (Emilia) Francis, an openly unconventional woman in Oxford, artistic, scholarly and an early cigarette-smoker.

In surroundings which he felt sympathetic, and probably when the company was small and familiar, Pater might allow his play of mind to be glimpsed at its freest. Perhaps he still guarded the secret of his own emotional urges, possibly never revealing – even to someone like Simeon Solomon – the intensity of his yearning for the ideal male friend. Or perhaps he carelessly made indiscreet remarks, openly admired some undergraduate's good looks, and prided himself on having misled his hearers in a manner which mingled the amusing with the serious.

The Pattison household was intellectually sceptic and agnostic. There Pater could certainly indulge in hits against Christianity, and in turn hear plenty of caustic criticism about such figures as Pusey and Manning. But his own fireworks in the shape of paradoxes were often meant to throw brief new light on less substantial targets, to provoke and amuse by illuminating the obvious and the conventional in daily life in an unexpected glare. Mark Pattison is traditionally recorded as having protested about this tendency in Pater when there was some discussion of possible travelling companions by peevishly exclaiming, 'I would not travel with Pater for anything! He would say the steamboat was not a steamboat, and that Calais was not Calais!' Pater could do a good imitation of Pattison's tone of voice, and this anecdote – along with others he positively made up about Pattison – is one he himself liked to repeat. In so doing, he helped disseminate his reputation for the paradoxical remark almost as a social trick, whereas more often than not it had for him much deeper significance.

It was all part of his assertion of his own individuality: non-conforming, strongly questioning and quickly stirred to see the ludicrous no less than the beautiful. At school he had been found amusing – at least by McQueen. As an undergraduate, his humour had taken on a sharper edge and become a weapon of scepticism. It remained his way of criticizing society, often without society being aware. Not to be excessively serious was also an aspect of what might be called Pater's moral dandyism – a matter of keeping the mind's furniture as clear and uncluttered as he kept that of his rooms: of injecting a grain of vivacity into otherwise sober conversation, as he enlivened his own dark, formal clothes with the unexpected touch of a fine tie in applegreen silk. It was with basically an aesthetic eye that he scrutinized and often in rejecting ridiculed the conventional beliefs and views of the age – like so many objects arrayed before him about each of which he must privately have asked himself, as he was publicly to do about a song, a picture or even a person (as enunciated in the Preface to *Studies in the History of the Renaissance*), 'What is this . . . to *me*? [his italics] What effect does it really produce on me?'

It is quite true that the sometimes devastating or merely amusing results of answering such questions in the spheres of morality, religion or taste, for example, were largely excluded by Pater from his writings, though here and there more gleams of humour are to be detected than is usually recognized. But they are only faint – and were clearly felt to be faint indeed by those who had enjoyed the occasional direct flash in his conversation.

To some of them it was a friendly, warm, slightly simple humour which he conveyed, the not untypical humour of the scholar-don, learned yet naïve, who took, in his late friend Bussell's phrase, 'a sort of child-like glee in the varying surfaces of things'. Amused, as well as fascinated, by animals, fond of making up stories to divert his sisters about absurdly named members of an imaginary family, enjoying Gilbert and Sullivan's operas, or a farce by Pinero, lightening the demands of daily routine by an attitude of half-grave amusement: such is the humorous character which seemed to be a revelation of the real person behind the books, and which represents truly enough one layer of Pater's complex personality.

Beneath, closer to the essence of his nature, were concealed much more tense, sensitive, and therefore easily exacerbated impulses, some of which were to find expression in a more biting or ironic humour – even a sort of languid flippancy which had in it echoes of Regency dandyism and was only too likely to pain average mid-Victorian society. The paradox became a favourite spoken device of Pater's – his writings are unfortunately devoid utterly of any echoes of its use – since it allowed him to bemuse, often as much as amuse, an audience. His hearers might console themselves, and exonerate him from any too shocking an intent, by saying or supposing that he could not be serious. (Pater might have murmured that he did not mind being serious as long as he was not solemn.) The response of muffling what he had obviously intended as literally sharp criticism was to be perpetuated by Benson who felt it necessary to apologize profusely for Pater's habit: 'it is held by some that he rather presumed on the indulgence of his friends in this respect. . . . The example that he set was somewhat contagious. Those affected by it . . . acquired the superficial conversational method, which consisted in speaking of serious things on social occasions as if they had no seriousness . . . his love of paradox, his recklessness of irony, unquestionably led him to say things which could be unhappily distorted and misapplied . . .'

Much more unhappily, these 'things' have only in a few cases been preserved. That is scarcely surprising, to judge by the nervous attitude still being taken by Benson over a decade after Pater's death. In the 1860s and '70s Pater's reckless ironies must often have been thought best forgotten, if not exactly forgiven – at least in staid university circles. Even the witty criticism he is recorded to have made of George Eliot at an Oxford dinner party was hastily brushed aside by Benson as unserious and 'purely perverse', though at least as a result the remark survives. Stigmatizing George Eliot for producing characters who are practically identical, Pater demanded, 'What is Maggie Tulliver but Tito in petticoats?' This is, in fact, only an inversion, and an economical one, of the more commonplace and laboured criticism that Tito in *Romola* is, in the words of Leslie Stephen, 'to his fingers' ends a woman.' Rather than echo convention to say that George Eliot, being a woman, could not portray men, Pater (reversing the chronological order of the two books) grants that she can create a man and he put the point that, about the heroine of *The Mill on the Floss*, there is something masculine. Pater's spontaneous dinner-table contribution hardly gains from this sort of heavy-handed explication and perhaps the prime purpose of its consciously flippant style of expression was to protest against over-reverent literary discussions (and – probably – against over-reverent Oxford attitudes to George Eliot personally).

In that early essay on Coleridge which is otherwise full of empathy, Pater clearly indicates his own standards while he condemns Coleridge's excess of seriousness as virtually a failure of tact, what he calls a 'misconception of the perfect manner'. Not in the nineteenth century but in the previous one is where Pater finds that best exemplified, as he defines it: 'There is a certain shade of levity and unconcern, the perfect manner of the eighteenth century, which may be thought to mark complete culture in the handling of abstract questions.' Among Pater's English contemporaries Arnold might seem the most obvious – if not, indeed, the only – exponent of this kind of perfect manner, with levity and unconcern passing into a barbed and half-insolent but always urbane tone; and Pater may have had him particularly in mind when composing his Coleridge review in 1868, since that was the year when the first series of Arnold's *Essays in Criticism* was published. Pater was later to speak admiringly of Arnold's manner as being 'delightfully cocksure' and to record hearing him once say how much more he would admire Browning, 'but for his depressing optimism.' As for the eighteenth century, so despised and deeply disapproved of by so many Victorians, its literary ideal of easy accomplished style, accompanied by wit, might seem to live again quite effortlessly in Thackeray's writings (and in a much later essay, significantly on *Style*, Pater was to call *Henry Esmond* 'a perfect fiction').

In one way, it was part of Pater's *ancien régime* interpretation of good manners and good-mannered dissent that nothing should be pushed to extremes and that the sting of criticism should be mitigated by raillery. It avoided argument, as it avoided earnestness. And it allowed him to tolerate foolishness. At the same time, he was practising exactly the same form of discrimination that he applied to a work of art. Humour was itself a sort of acid test, in which many a gross conventional presumption, cliché and superficial opinion became dissolved. 'For the way to perfection', he was to say in writing of Leonardo, but applying it generally, 'is through a series of disgusts.'

Pater seems to have wanted the freedom of travelling lightly, if not positively with levity, unburdened by any luggage of moral preoccupations, political or philosophical systems, or speculations on the nature of art. He had thrown off much of the sad taint of his childhood and was probably less haunted than he had been, or was to be, by the oppressive sense of mortality. For him – at this period, at least – there were no great simple truths. Vitality, pleasure, beauty, and amusement lay in the concrete and the particular. 'Hard and abstract moralities,' he declared in the essay on Coleridge, 'are yielding to a more exact estimate of the subtlety and complexity of our life.' In the same essay he asked, more than rhetorically, who would change 'the colour or curve of a rose-leaf' for Plato's concept of some superior colourless, intangible being, and instanced Goethe's as the type of truly speculative temperament, 'by whom no touch of the world of form, colour and passion was disregarded.'

Presented with the commonplace – as it were, the steamboat to Calais – Pater enjoyed exposing it and diminishing it by the most economical means, whereby it looked just absurd. He never stated his political opinions, though he seems to have been a Liberal. His dislike of Napoleon III, for example, was probably coloured by the enthusiastic hatred of the emperor expressed by Swinburne and Victor Hugo, but his sole recorded reaction was to sigh with exaggerated petulance, 'I hope we shall soon arrive at a time when no one will be so vulgar as to want to go and live at the Tuileries'. In much the same manner he disposed of the conventional fondness for Swiss scenery by declaring that he always shut his eyes when travelling through Switzerland, to avoid seeing those 'horrid pots of blue paint', the lakes.

At each point where Pater and the period at its most conventional collided, a spark was emitted. Some of these sparks were to be a little less ephemeral than others, and a little more serious in their implications. Most were forgotten. But sufficient survive, even if somewhat distorted in recollection, or by the wish to make Pater himself seem absurd, to show how naturally sceptical and challenging his temperament was, crisp, terse and mentally athletic even in being aesthetic.

Literary figures more widely respected than George Eliot might rapidly be exploded – sometimes perhaps the more pleasurably when Pater himself had had a boyhood fondness for them. It was with a touch of real steel, as required when disposing of a rival, that Pater once interrupted a conversation about Ruskin's artistic perceptions to say, impatiently, 'I cannot believe that Ruskin saw more in the Church of St Mark than I do.' When he praised a precocious Eton boy who was able to discuss the merits of Mérimée and Gautier, it was to add that schoolboys with literary tastes were usually fond of commonplace poetry, 'such as Alfred Tennyson's'.

In surveying his ultimately chosen milieu of the university – where, he probably guessed, he would always remain – Pater had at once a target and a forum. And it was there, rather than in London, that what legend he had was gained. His aestheticism might be ridiculed by stories that he appreciated an undergraduates' bonfire at Brasenose because it lit up the spire of St Mary's so beautifully, and enjoyed their high spirits after dinner in hall because he was reminded of playful, well-fed young tigers (panthers, in some versions). Yet in anyway the second of these there is nothing ridiculous – rather, a rejection of the expected response that he would shrink from noise and boisterousness, and an echo of Pater's frank, half-amused envy when a boy of the untarnished, unconscious, physical glamour of his schoolfellows. It was something of the same emotion which led him to intervene in a senior common-room discussion about reforms in university education by protesting that the undergraduate was a child of nature, growing like a wild rose in a hedgerow: 'you want to turn him into a turnip, rob him of all grace and plant him out in rows.' Such laughter as greeted this remark may have been meant at Pater's expense, but in fact he was expressing a protest against stereotypes and uniformity. Nor did he find every undergraduate rose-like or graceful. One of the sleeker and more unctuous he was aptly to compare to a sausage. Even in so doing, he was pursuing his delight in concrete definition.

The idiosyncrasies of other dons were an inevitable subject for appraisal, itself a rather donnish trait, yet the few remarks of Pater's of this kind to survive are recorded as lacking in malice, while being palpable hits in shrewdness. He hardly knew H. A. J. Munro, the scholarly author of a great edition of Lucretius (published in 1864), but when surprise was expressed at Munro's close friendship with someone worldly and convivial Pater declined to share the surprise, remarking, 'I always felt that there was a good deal of the *mahogany-table* element in Munro.' Those present seem to have been struck by the acuteness of the perception. And Arthur Symons recollected what he called a 'beautiful phrase' in which Pater neatly encapsulated a markedly enthusiastic mutual acquaintance; after delaying, meditative 'wells' and 'no doubts' (Symons conveys a flavour of how Pater spoke), he compared him to 'a steam-engine stuck in the mud'. Having related this, Symons went on to state, more categorically than anybody else who knew Pater, how greatly he disliked 'undue earnestness . . . as bad form, which shocked him as much in persons as bad style did in books.'

Perhaps it seemed to him both bad form and bad style to carry the occasional vivacities of relaxed conversation into his own writings. Unlike Wilde, he might have claimed that it was his genius which he had put into his work; and, in fact, his very concept of highly wrought prose, scrupulously laboured over and chiselled into choice and elaborate cadences, made it hard for him to incorporate any hint of the colloquial – still less the flippant or the amusing. Even for irony the mood of his writing is almost too intense.

Perhaps, also, Pater did not have the courage to let his complete *persona* shine naked through his prose. Some secrets found expression in what he wrote – more possibly than he quite realized – but the personality in his writings is itself partly a mask, artful and arranged, more wistfully beautiful than lifelike. Something inhibited Pater from fully revealing to the public who read his books how much witty, cynical or just light-hearted animation lay behind.

Only occasionally, almost slyly, did he hint at traits in his character like his delight in 'those tricks of individuality which we find quite tolerable in persons . . . and with regard to which we are all to some extent humorists' (his essay on Lamb). He could be briefly sardonic with reference to German commentators on Shakespeare, when he was writing on *Love's Labour's Lost*; and in the same essay he lightly but acutely speaks, almost in *propria persona*, of how 'the humorist may observe . . . over all love of playthings, there is almost always hidden an appreciation of something really engaging and delightful.' (It was as a humorist in this sense that he probably regarded the antics of his profoundly-loved cats.)

In his attitude to Christianity there was – in his early work – more animosity than wit. An exception could be made at least about the anecdote originating in Pater's comment (first made in the 1868 review of Morris's poetry) that medieval religion 'was but a beautiful disease or disorder of the senses'. He himself may have fostered the story that an undergraduate's father wrote to him protesting, having heard from his son that Pater described religion as a loathsome disease; after Pater had replied that he doubted if he would have used the word 'loathsome', but might have described religion as a 'beautiful' disease, the parent was entirely reassured.

Although Pater might praise the 'perfect manner' of the eighteenth century, he does not seem to have wanted to emulate such exponents of it as Voltaire and Gibbon except in random conversational remarks. A divergence continued to exist between his style of writing and of speaking. He was not to find – probably did not seek – any context in which to incorporate in prose those paradoxes which, however fitfully, sparkled when he talked around topics of the day, and which so often revealed him as a rebel.

Heterosexual love and marriage scarcely receive any attention in his work, and according to Wright he once acknowledged to a friend that he disapproved of marriage. Not content with this, Wright states that many of his paradoxes 'were pointed against the sex', instancing Pater's subsequent comment in the exchange about marriage: 'Men and women are always pulling different ways. Women won't pull our way. They are so perverse.' The real irony here was quite lost on Wright, as it may well have been on Pater's original interlocutor. If misogyny could be implied on this sort of evidence, Pater was probably wise to indulge his thought-provoking mockery mainly among intimates and to exclude it from what he wrote.

By doing so he left a device lying to hand, to be seized, polished and brandished supremely by Oscar Wilde – both on social occasions and throughout his writings. The paradox, which Pater had quietly

118

enunciated and perhaps had hardly minded seeing fizzle out in the slightly baffled silence of conventional drawing-rooms (after all, he might find a certain piquant if lonely amusement in remaining uncomprehended), now rocketed wherever Wilde appeared – and he appeared everywhere – with astonishing and arresting glitter. For the younger, much bolder and far more compulsively fluent man, Pater must have seemed in possession of a gift he had totally failed to exploit. Much though Wilde admired and paid tribute to Pater's prose, he did not fail to indicate its occasional lack of 'the true rhythmical life of words.'

In turn, Pater recognized in Wilde's prose the very quality markedly absent from his own. 'There is always something of an excellent talker about the writing of Mr Oscar Wilde,' he began his review of *Dorian Gray*. In Wilde's use of the paradox he saw a continuation of 'the brilliant critical work of Matthew Arnold': high and perceptive praise, free from envy though perhaps not untinged with regret. He found space in the same review to praise also Wilde's dialogue, *The Decay of Lying*, for being 'all but unique in its half-humorous, yet wholly convinced, presentment of certain valuable truths of criticism.' Amid the cigarette smoke and the cloud of epigrams sent up by Cyril and Vivian in that dialogue's setting of a Nottinghamshire country house library Pater might discern a bold and successful mingling of two streams in his own personality, no less than in Wilde's. Indeed, the opening of the dialogue – with its lively hits at Nature and Nature's lack of design – might easily have accommodated one of Pater's own spontaneous remarks when out walking on a summer evening heavily scented with meadow-sweet, 'It is the fault of nature in England that she runs too much to excess.'

Even if he had wished, however, he would never have dared to jest in print over a novel like *Robert Elsmere* as does Vivian: '. . . of course a masterpiece – a masterpiece of the *genre ennuyeux*, the one form of literature that the English people seem thoroughly to enjoy.' This leads to Cyril's hardly less devastating defence of it: '. . . as for *Robert Elsmere*, I am quite devoted to it. Not that I can look upon it as a serious work . . . It is simply Arnold's *Literature and Dogma* with the literature left out.'

Pater was in his fiftieth year when *The Decay of Lying* was first published. His own style had undergone subtle permutations, pruned of a good deal of its early luxuriance and singing cadences – just as his character seems to have undergone a similar operation, with toning down publicly and privately of his animus against Christianity. Physically, he was beginning to feel a loss of vitality and to suffer, often painfully, from what he described as gout. People who met him for the first time at this period probably found him faintly dull, rather weary, surprisingly conventional. The verve of mind which had been so much a part of his personality might seem to have dried up and been replaced by gravity and that very earnestness which he had, especially as a young man, positively deplored.

Yet in his response to Wilde's wit and rippling, shimmering verbal exuberance he showed how little he had really changed. Nor was it only in response to Wilde that he could throw off the staidness and semi-timidity with which he had learnt to shroud his true nature. 'My dear audacious Moore,' he significantly began a letter of 1888, thanking George Moore for the gift of his *Confessions of a Young Man*. 'Of course,' he wrote with scrupulous frankness, 'there are many things in the book I don't agree with.' He could only call it a cynical way of looking at the world. But caution and reservations get lost in the rush of praise: 'your originality – your delightful criticisms – your Aristophanic joy . . . – your unfailing liveliness.' Moore was rightly proud of – and frequently printed – this letter from a grudging and self-acknowledged reluctant letter-writer. It is one of the least stilted of all Pater's surviving letters, closing with typically generous wishes, 'for the future success of your most entertaining pen'.

For Moore, even more than for Wilde, Pater was not only the master of modern English prose but, by his status and his manner, as much as by his actual age, a figure removed from the business of living, unlively in conversation ('nor did he even talk about himself', exclaimed the egocentric Moore whose 'even' nicely measures the difference between them) and almost as withdrawn as if he had never lived. 'He never talks about anything that interests him,' Wilde warned Richard Le Gallienne before his first meeting with Pater. The final paradox of Pater himself – outwardly so sober but warmly praising when he read the audacities of Moore and the shrewd wit of Wilde – was left unexplored by these busy men, absorbed in their own activities. They never bothered to talk to people who could have recalled the young Pater, the reckless undergraduate whose remarks upset his friends' faith, the don who was a daring exponent of self-culture in his speech as well as his writings. They never guessed that Pater might have produced *Dialogues* almost as witty as Wilde's and youthful *Confessions* no less satiric and lively than Moore's – and certainly no less audacious, if he had cared to write openly.

When Pater eventually reviewed a book of Moore's, *Modern Painting*, he praised the author for 'the courage of his opinions'. By that late date, 1893, many of those who continued to know Pater were much younger, instinctively respectful if a little disconcerted by his refusal to express or apparently hold opinions of any sort, and probably largely ignorant of the personality who had, some quarter of a century earlier, shocked, as well as impressed, Oxford. Along with his apple-green ties, Pater appeared to have discarded his inconvenient, unconventional and flippantly expressed views. When he reprinted his first published article on Coleridge, he retained the praise of the 'perfect manner' of the eighteenth century but where he had written of that being 'a certain shade of levity and unconcern', he deleted the word 'levity'.

Yet he himself had once practised it. He too had had the courage of his opinions, and held them to the point of creating the flurry of at least one minor social scandal in the calm aesthetic surroundings of his own home in Bradmore Road. It was in the years of deliberate indiscretion, probably not long after *Studies in the History of the Renaissance* had confirmed Pater's reputation as exciting and dubious, that he effectively proclaimed his lack of concern under injudicious pressure from the High Church wife of some unidentified but then well-known professor. A discussion of Christianity, doubtless with a wish to reconvert if not reprove him, at a dinner-party where he was the host, probably epitomized bad form in Pater's eyes. Countering an earnest observation made to him by the professor's wife, he suddenly said that no reasonable person could govern his life by the opinions or actions of a man who had died eighteen centuries ago.

The effect was gratifyingly swift. From wife to husband there must have passed an almost telepathic message, confirming perhaps their lingering suspicion of supping with the devil. There was a marked stir. Before the other guests quite realized what had happened, the professor and his wife were agitatedly hurrying away from the house, leaving Pater master of the field.

It was a notable victory for vivacious repartee. But Pater could not expect to achieve such results on such a topic without causing comment, scandal and some retaliation. For all his delight in mockery and wit, he was probably not emotionally robust enough to stand a sustained war of nerves within his daily environment. In literal terms too, he could not afford it, if he wished to remain as a don at Oxford. He muted statements of his opinion, grew cautious where he had been reckless, doubtful where he had been sure, hastening in himself an ageing of responses which to some people seemed deplorable and to others an improvement. Yet under all the trappings of polite evasion and social negation, and amid, as he grew older, genuine uncertainties and apprehensions, his mind kept its secret independence and that exuberant spark which a reading of George Moore's *Confessions* could turn briefly into a blaze.

As so often with Pater, absorbing into his own personality the personalities he writes of (even when they are historical not fictional), he seems to be describing himself though it is actually the young, witty and provocative Pascal of whom he writes, 'So far, his imposing carriage of himself intellectually might lead us to suspect that the forced humilities of his later years are indirectly a discovery of what seems one leading quality of the natural man in him, a pride that could be quite fierce on occasion.' Nothing – no criticism, derision or antagonism – could rob Pater of a proud sense of his own individuality, and the determination to express something of it through his work.

Eight   Leonardo da Vinci, *c'est moi*

ALTHOUGH during the 1860s Pater was becoming known a little in London, as well as in Oxford, he published nothing at all under his name until 'Notes on Leonardo da Vinci', in *The Fortnightly Review* for November 1869. This was also the first article fully to reveal him as a critic not only of literature but of the visual arts – something Oxford was anyway expecting shortly to learn more about. At the age of fifty Ruskin had been elected first holder of the newly endowed Slade Professorship of Fine Art. The election was made in August 1869, the month of Pater's thirtieth birthday, though Ruskin did not begin a course of lectures until the following year.

Whether or not news of that appointment caused Pater to feel any spurt of irritation and envy, or even prompted an urge to challenge the implied official recognition of Ruskin as *the* English authority on art, he could certainly have found no clearer way to proclaim alternatives to Ruskin's views than by this article. The subject – enigmatic, heterodox in religion and morals, the most profane of painters, as defined by Pater, of sacred pictures – was alien to Ruskin (who never dealt other than briefly with Leonardo throughout his voluminous writings) if not dangerous. A restless artist fascinated by curious beauty, and fond of bizarre landscapes and slightly sinister, unfathomably smiling faces, sometimes of doubtful sex, was too wayward to illustrate 'all right and natural qualities', as could for him even the nudes of Titian and Giorgione. In Leonardo there was a lack also of that 'masculine and universal sympathy' which could palliate such a painter as Rubens in Ruskin's eyes (eyes which seldom failed in perception of painting, whatever peculiar and muddled moral lessons he might afterwards adduce).

In 1869 Ruskin had published a new volume of lectures, *The Queen of the Air*, a study – according to his title page – of the Greek myths of cloud and storm, but threaded through with an extraordinary tissue of disparate, half-started topics, rhetorical questions and dogmatic pronouncements. Among these Pater might have found the most irritating to be Ruskin's treatment of Leonardo – all the more so as he was reading in the same year Arsène Houssaye's *Histoire de*

Léonard de Vinci, an enthusiastic though basically rather thin piece of popularizing by a one-time friend of Baudelaire. At least, with all his faults, Houssaye did not declare – as Ruskin did – that Luini was 'a man ten times greater than Leonardo', or dismiss whole aspects of Leonardo's art with the emotive verdict that he 'depraved his finer instincts by caricature, and remained to the end of his days the slave of an archaic smile'. Those words alone seemed to call for rebuttal by offering a more subtle and sensible exploration of the artist's complex character.

Not only does Pater delight in all the unmasculine mystery, exotic beauty and ambivalence of Leonardo's work, moving closer and closer to the core of it until he fastens rapt on the image of the *Mona Lisa*, but he passes no judgment on it, draws no conclusions, declines utterly to suggest the spectator is better – or worse – for seeing it. Simply, the encounter with the art of this strange personality (that fascinates 'or perhaps half repels') leads – beyond appreciation in an outward sense – to a gradual growing identification with Leonardo. By the end of the essay Pater has been sucked willingly into the whirlpool of another individuality and goes down with it, in the final sentence, even to the grave: '. . . speculating how one who had always been desirous of beauty, but desired it always in such precise and definite forms, as hands or flowers or hair, looked forward now into the vague land, and experienced the last curiosity.'

Use of the imagination in this way was novel enough in England – but novel particularly where the visual arts were concerned. And then the author was no art critic or student of art. He was in the awkward position of being an amateur without completely amateur status, a university don and scholar of the classics not content with gazing at pictures during vacations but who risked writing about them. Nor could he claim Ruskin's private facility as an artist, still less Ruskin's public role of stirring ordinary people to care for the arts. He was not, like Swinburne, a poet with some gift for poetical prose (Ruskin too had begun as a serious poet, winning the Newdigate Prize at Oxford in the year Pater was born).

Yet the ultimate novelty, the most subtle challenge to Ruskin and Ruskin's readers, lay in the style of the 'Notes on Leonardo da Vinci', where what Pater had to say and how he said it are blended into a perfectly calculated, heady mixture, more potent than anything even he ever again managed to concoct. Probably he was to recognize as much and, like any other shrewd artist, to move on stylistically before he began to caricature himself. Besides, he seldom had such an ideal study for his psychological acumen. He must have recognized that this essay required virtually no revision or excision; unusually for him, he made only the very slightest emendations on the occasions it was reprinted (the last time being in 1893). What he had written about the *Mona Lisa* became and has remained his most famous passage, insistently memorable however often it is ridiculed or parodied; it is far more famous than any single passage in Ruskin, and probably still the most famous piece of writing about any picture in the world (a picture itself gaining additional fame thanks to Pater).

Readers of the essay on its first appearance in *The Fortnightly* must have quickly sensed that a new siren voice was singing, low-toned but oddly beguiling, where Ruskin stormed and cajoled, teased, questioned, harangued and, at times rather scornfully, amused. Always in effect addressing a public meeting, and wonderfully adept at varying his manner to hold his audience, Ruskin appeared utterly convinced and totally sure, even in the realm of the abstract. His prose was all argument, and the argument was largely asseveration. Tumbling and flashing by like polished coins in the spate of his sentences about art would come nobility and purity and, especially, truth: words that elsewhere in his prose took on the force of personifications, tramping and wheeling, as if rehearsing some cosmic pageant, obedient to his not entirely coherent cries of command.

Gravely, calmly, with insidious delicacy and constant, probing, verbal discrimination, Pater's phrases noiselessly uncurled – almost like fronds of fern in some shadowy grotto designed by Leonardo. In place of a brilliant, ceaseless stream of language, a near-sluggish, sunken rivulet wound along, penetrating however, and oozing with suggestions of art and beauty as things far stranger than Ruskin supposed, their roots deep down in the conflicting mystery of the individual, and by no means just gifts of God. A wistful awareness of mortality seems hanging over the style, as over its creator; and the most frequent epithets are quite foreign, especially as praise, to Ruskin: curious, capricious, fantastic, languid, exquisite, earth-coloured. Nothing is quite fixed or certain. Leonardo himself hovers behind magic veils; and everything is glimpsed in half-lights, in an atmosphere which is uncannily subaqueous. The very weather enjoyed is subtle and unsure, a matter of the faint light of eclipse or the brief interval 'of falling rain at daybreak'; and the words seem distilled to the point where they might physically be savoured. The prose has been worked at with the refinement and patience of a jeweller setting pale stones by moonlight.

Morally, too, the climate is cloudy. Renaissance Milan glitters briefly, balefully, but with its own glamour: 'a life of exquisite amusements . . . and brilliant sins.' The extremes of beauty and terror described as Leonardo's goals sound close to the writer's own

125

consciousness. Instead of being condemned, Leonardo's grotesques are seen as echoes of nature's grotesqueness, itself sometimes manifested in almost surreal ways – and a few skilfully selected words are sufficient to seize an authentic frisson of panic at nature disfigured in 'the distorting light of evening on lonely roads'.

It was inevitable that the *Mona Lisa* should be enshrined at the centre of such an essay (as inevitable, perhaps, as that Ruskin should never pause over that picture, even in notes on the Louvre, leaving only a single, typical comment on its background rocks). As he approached it, Pater showed that he – like Ruskin – knew how to make adroit use of the Authorized Version. He acknowledged the influence of Swinburne's prose. He had read Gautier, and had responded to the perception and originality of Baudelaire. Casting his net as wide as possible, he brought up all the associations he could assemble, like treasure from the sea, dripping, transmuted and artfully arranged to hang in a series of crystalline, faintly oscillating drops around the head of this masterpiece of ambiguity, decorating and yet piercing it, reaching to the heart of Leonardo's own ambiguity: the image defined from childhood, 'on the fabric of his dreams'. What Pater is analyzing – where he might superficially seem merely rhapsodizing – with every nuance of punctuation as well as vocabulary, wielding the precision instrument of prose, is the meaning of this image to its creator. Leonardo did not so much create it as uncover it. Not its newness but its age, indeed its eternal nature, is the secret of its power. Only familiarity with the opening words of the most famous sentence in the essay has blunted the challenging statement: 'She is older than the rocks among which she sits . . .'

'Why do you not write prose?' Wilde recorded Pater asking him when they first met. 'Prose is so much more difficult' [than poetry]. In publishing this pertinent half-paradox while Pater was alive, Wilde went on to say that at the time (he was then an undergraduate at Oxford) he did not quite understand what Pater really meant. The rhetorical prose of Carlyle and the eloquent prose of Ruskin had seemed to him enthusiastic rather than artful; it was only when he studied Pater's essays on the Renaissance that he understood, so he said, what a self-conscious art prose could be. And Pater's prose was more profoundly conscious of self than perhaps Wilde fully realized.

Artfully enough, and without undue haste, in the five years between writing *Diaphaneitè* and publishing the essay on Leonardo, it had been cultivated by Pater. His philosophy and his style had – as Humphry Ward noted – aroused comment, though in strict bibliographical terms there was no more to record than three anonymous reviews of books by or on Coleridge, Winckelmann and Morris.

In each case, with varying degrees of success or at least relevance, he had practised a combination of empathy and self-expression which gave his style and his approach its unique, hypnotic quality. It was not ideas as such that he wrote about, however finely he might analyze, but personalities. Coleridge and Winckelmann exercised fascination over him – the fascination of being to some extent like himself, or of having become like himself as he writes of them. Much of the wistfulness apparent in Pater's approach to art comes from his awareness of being alone and even lonely. He is seeking there an *alter ego* to relieve the burden of his own nature and accept his affection: an Amis for his Amile, resembling him to the extent of becoming part of him, but with none of the demands, accidents or flaws inherent in a real person. It was very much harder to absorb William Morris in this way: a living figure not basically like Pater at all (and it seems significant that Pater, who quarried most of what mattered to him from this review for the 'Conclusion' to *The Renaissance*, suppressed it in lists of his own work).

But in having Coleridge (Coleridge as man and as prose writer, too) for the subject of his first article, he was able to practise, there still tentatively and vaguely, a form of identification – the more patent parts of which were, significantly, to be struck out when he reprinted an expanded, heavily revised version of it. In 1865, when he was preparing the article, his own recent experiences seemed not so far from what he wrote of Coleridge: 'He left Cambridge without a degree, a Unitarian. Unable to take orders . . . he determined to devote himself to literature. When he left Cambridge there was a prejudice against him which has given rise to certain suspicions.' Like Pater, Coleridge had had a childhood of 'delicacy . . . sensitiveness and passion'. Coleridge's own description of himself, which Pater quotes, might apply to them both when young: driven from life in motion to life 'in thought and sensation'. But then Coleridge's too narrow view of the artist rapidly leads Pater to utter his explanation, and defence, of the artistic gift, defining his own position as if conducting a dialogue with Coleridge. And what he has to say (another passage later dropped) is already sensuously expressed and the core of what he continued to believe: 'What constitutes an artistic gift is first of all a natural susceptibility to moments of strange excitement, in which the colours freshen upon our threadbare world, and the routine of things about us is broken by a novel and happier synthesis.' This – with its visual bias and its wistful sense of life as convention-ridden and drab without art – is part of Pater's biography rather than Coleridge's.

Yet Coleridge attracts him as complex, voluptuous in temperament, charming (even to the stressed physical charm, 'white and delicate skin, the abundant black hair, the full almost animal lips') and, ultimately, as a failure. At the beginning of the essay there is stress on Coleridge's enviable charm and intellectual activity at twenty-five (Pater's age until the August of 1865). At the end Coleridge is seen even more sympathetically, not exactly Pater but sharing all Pater's restless longings, premature weariness, aspirations towards some certainty amid the flux of life – 'for something fixed where all is moving.' He has become the symbol of brilliant unsuccess: the bright star that falls, a sort of Icarus of the intelligence. He is a consolation if Pater – dreaming in his Brasenose rooms – should fail. And though a resonant sentence seems to generalize from Coleridge to the contemporary world, the personal application is detectable beneath: 'More than Childe Harold, more than Werther, more than René himself, Coleridge, by what he did, what he was, and what he failed to do, represents that inexhaustible discontent, languor, and homesickness, the chords of which ring all through our modern literature.'

Perhaps one daring aspect of such writing lay in its naked protest against the 'routine of things', felt the more strongly by someone whose life was hardly as romantically peripatetic as Childe Harold's or as passionate as Werther's. 'I am going to spend the vacation very quietly in Paris with my sisters,' Pater had told Pendergast, the family lawyer, in June 1864; and that is easy to believe. Yet even the quiet tenor of his existence was a process of living; some events, however slight, could not be excluded from it, even if he wished, and its very quietness must have heightened his receptivity. From childhood onwards he had been aware of the small accidents that 'have their consequence' (as he writes in *The Child in the House*; and he had cultivated a sort of passivity, allowing himself 'to be played upon . . . like a musical instrument').

The surface of Paris during the Second Empire, with Napoleon III reigning at the Tuileries, might seem to him opulently vulgar and to be avoided (though it was also the city of Baudelaire, still alive but withdrawn by then to Belgium). Yet this visit probably brought Pater his first direct encounter with the *Mona Lisa*, with other pictures by Leonardo, and with a red chalk drawing, now no longer accepted as by Leonardo himself, of a face of doubtful sex, 'which everyone remembers', he wrote later, 'who has seen the drawings at the Louvre': a head he reproduced in the second edition of *The Renaissance*.

Thus the rather monotonous passage of August days for a tourist in Paris was broken by the stimulation of Leonardo's work. It may well not have occurred as yet to Pater to write about Leonardo, but he is unlikely to have missed the appeal straight away of such a face as that drawn in red chalks, 'with something voluptuous and full in the eyelids and the lips'. In this, as in other faces by Leonardo, he was to find some electric vibration, turning it into a receptacle for mysterious powers, passed 'on to us in a chain of secret influences'. Perhaps he recognized, as he phrased those words, the process of inspiration leading him back to his first sight of what he afterwards described as 'a favourite drawing . . . in the Louvre'. Mingling sensations of fear with beauty, urged on by a terrible curiosity, as Leonardo had been, he may also have gone in Paris for the first time (presumably without Hester and Clara) to the Morgue – which he mentions as sometimes visiting in *The Child in the House*, 'after which visits, those waxen resistless faces would always live with him for many days, making the broadest sunshine sickly.'

For somebody like Dickens, a visit to the Morgue in Paris was inevitable, just part of a characteristically hectic and energetic programme: 'With a dreadful insatiability,' his friend Forster recorded, 'we passed through every variety of sight-seeing, prisons, palaces, theatres, hospitals, the Morgue and the Lazare, as well as the Louvre . . .' For Pater the Morgue and the Louvre sound at first a less likely combination; and yet he himself gave some explanation when he described how, for Florian, 'the fear of death was intensified by the desire of beauty'. Over a beautiful, youthful but dead body he could linger looking freely and unashamed; it prompted a pity which was, as he probably understood, really a suppressed lust. His own imaginary heroes – Sebastian van Storck, Duke Carl, Denys l'Auxerrois, Emerald Uthwart – would be preserved in their beauty by dying young and saved from all those threats of creeping disease, of growing old, of gradual extinction, which haunted their creator.

'He had often dreamt', he was to write of Marius, the most frank and least idealized of his self-portraits, 'he was condemned to die'; and Marius sums up his own uneventful life as something of a *meditatio mortis*. As a child Pater had already begun to question, much as he was to imagine Leonardo questioning, 'how the last impressions of eye and ear might happen to him . . . the scent of the last flower, the soft yellowness of the last morning, the last recognition of some object of affection, hand or voice.' Perhaps he gazed at the bodies in the Morgue, and also at the *Mona Lisa*, until she took on something of their waxen quality: 'like the vampire, she has been dead many times . . .' But in her the terror is finally assuaged by the beauty. Unlike Pater's mother, unlike Leonardo's Duchess Beatrice, painted with 'some presentiment of early death', she dies yet survives. She smiles with the triumphant ultimate knowledge that eluded even Leonardo, for she has 'learned the secrets of the grave'.

In 1864 Pater was not ready to write about, possibly was not able to see into, the picture and himself so profoundly. But an encounter had taken place. It was the start of what for him constituted real experience: the breaking-in on the lonely personality – in essence still the boy secluded in the walled garden at Enfield – of disturbing sensations of beauty that fastened on him in a way that he rightly called 'tyrannous' but which effectively shook him alive. In the person of the disillusioned Marius, Pater was with poignant directness to express in middle age what he had always been seeking: 'We need some imaginative stimulus, some not impossible ideal such as may shape vague hope and transform it into effective desire, to carry us year after year, without disgust, through the routine work which is so large a part of life.'

Under the slow manner and carefully calm exterior of Pater, shared by his sisters and seen doubtless at its most striking when they travelled ('. . . simply impossible to imagine any of the Paters in a crowded railway station, or being jostled about, and losing their luggage,' recorded an acquaintance), a thrilling process of being played on by Leonardo may have already begun on the journey back from Paris in 1864. The Calais steamboat did perhaps cease temporarily for him to be just a steamboat, or disappeared altogether in watching the heave of the sea around it and reflecting on Leonardo's 'solemn effects of moving water' which are traced in the essay through the various pictures by him in the Louvre. And though when Pater came to apply a metaphor to the *Mona Lisa* he echoes, possibly unconsciously, Swinburne's *Félise* ('No diver brings up love again/ Dropped once, my beautiful Félise,/In such cold seas.'), he may have had a marine image of his own in mind in describing her 'as a diver in deep seas'.

In 1865 Pater went to Florence on his Italian tour with Shadwell. He saw what he judged 'the one great picture' Leonardo had left there, the *Head of the Medusa* in the Uffizi which, though actually by Caravaggio, then passed as Leonardo's, seeming to be related to a reference in Vasari. For Pater its associations with his idea of Leonardo were far more important than any question of exact attribution; and while he barely paused in his essay to mention the *Baptism of Christ* in the same gallery, he responded – almost as if in the Morgue – to this head of a corpse, where 'the fascination of corruption penetrates in every touch its exquisitely finished beauty'.

Even into the established quietness of an existence such as his, unexpected tremors from events might occasionally break. Someone so conscious of family and so easily moved to pity, especially where children were concerned, is bound to have been stirred by the news in

January 1866 of the deaths – within three days of each other – of two daughters of his father's cousin, Joseph Pater of Liverpool. On 19 January Annie Clara Pater, aged eight, died, followed on 21 January by her sister, Bessie Adelaide, aged four. The deaths were reported together in *The Times*, and through the girls' very names Pater might find associations enough with his much-loved aunt and his own sister (conceivably Annie Clara's godmother).

Deaths of young children are touched on in *The Child in the House* and in *Gaston de Latour*, but it is in *Marius the Epicurean* that the subject confronts the hero. Once it is the human pagan grief of the Emperor Marcus Aurelius carrying his dying son pressed close to him, 'as if he yearned . . . to be absolutely one with it, in its obscure distress.' Deliberately contrasted with that scene is the Christian household where a child's death is both mourned and hymned. Marius broods over what he has witnessed: 'Dead children, children's graves – [he] had always been half aware of an old superstitious fancy in his mind concerning them; as if in coming near them he came near the failure of some lately-born hope or purpose of his own.'

Amid the associations which the sudden death of Joseph Pater's daughters might set vibrating in Pater were thoughts of his own childhood – and from it even possibly the death of the infant Walter Reginald May, his godmother's only grandson. His recollections of days at Fish Hall with Mrs May were themselves ambiguous, because he later revealed to Arthur Symons that he remembered her in a large cap going out on to the lawn to battle with the surveyors who had come to mark out a railway close by. When this was built the trains terrified him, as did the red flag, 'which meant *blood*'. Just as Enfield had proved powerless to exclude intimations of mortality, so the peaceful country security of Fish Hall was shaken by invasion from an outside world whose angry message seemed, once again, death.

Although Mrs May had apparently receded from Pater's life by the time he was adult, it seems quite likely that they were again in touch, if briefly, during her last years. In the summer of 1867, a few months after the publication of his article on Winckelmann, Pater decided to spend a month or so at Sidmouth, where he had previously stayed with Hester and Clara and where he now tutored Humphry Ward. It was Sidmouth that Mrs May began to visit regularly from 1866 onwards, usually for months at a time. Ward speaks of Pater living in a small house overlooking the sea, and it was in fact in the lodging house she always chose, No. 4, Clifton Place (Clifton Cottage), that he too stayed. That was her address at the time of her death in February 1872; she died from 'total exhaustion' on the beach at

Sidmouth. None of the Pater family is referred to in her will, and it seems an ironic epilogue to the altercations Pater had witnessed in his boyhood that when defining the limits within which her money might be invested she positively permitted 'any incorporated Railway Company or Companies'.

In the essay on Coleridge, Pater had remarked – assuming an urbanity which in later years he might think excessive – that the man of good sense cannot afford 'to be too serious in looking back upon his own childhood'. Yet he had also spoken there, with truer perception, of the complexity of man and how 'remote laws of inheritance' and 'vibrations of long-past acts' reach out to affect a human being in the midst of life. He was then not ready to explore those vibrations as they affected himself or re-enter the world of his own childhood, probably not as yet understanding just how strongly it had conditioned the person he had become. He was much more eager to reveal what he was, what he felt and in what ways he meant to defy convention. In writing on Coleridge he had only tentatively declared himself. An opportunity to be bolder and more explicit was needed; and he soon found it.

John Chapman, the editor of the *Westminster Review*, was partly unconventional and radical himself, and he seems to have encouraged Pater's links with his magazine, giving him plenty of space for his articles and welcoming the prospect of Pater reviewing in it regularly. It was probably Pater who took the initiative in 1866, after the appearance of the essay-review on Coleridge, and proposed a rather similar style article on Winckelmann. A convenient pretext and impetus lay in the publication that year of Otto Jahn's biography of Winckelmann, a figure Pater had certainly known about from reading Goethe and Hegel but whose significance for himself he had perhaps not previously realized.

The life of Winckelmann, closing with his unexpectedly dramatic death, had its own attraction and occasional correspondences, quite apart from any affinity with Pater in temperament. Identifying imaginatively, Pater was able with a single sentence to sketch a solitary childhood unlike his own but conveyed with vicarious sympathy: 'We find him a child in the dusky precinct of a German school, hungrily feeding on a few colourless books.' When it comes to the poor scholar who needed a place in clerical Rome, who yielded to inducements and became an unbelieving Roman Catholic, entering Rome, Pater writes, 'notoriously with the works of Voltaire in his possession', the parallel with Pater's dilemma over ordination could hardly be missed. Artistic excitement, intuition, inspiration – these, 'rather than the contemplative evolution of general principles,' are the characteristics Pater sees in Winckelmann, but surely also in himself. As for the 'romantic, fervent friendships with young men,' Pater almost proudly defends them, not only careless of any imputation that he too must share the same tastes, but virtually inducing the suspicion.

But the final appeal of Winckelmann is found in the removal of another repression felt at the time no less strongly by Pater. Beginning with Winckelmann and Greek art, the second part of the essay becomes Pater's rejection of the cramping conditions of Christianity. Winckelmann and Greece stand for what everyone's spirit needs in 'modern life': freedom. Greek religion is one of gods fleet and fair, white and red – 'not white and red as in Francia's "Golgotha".' Under the light but not misleading cover of aesthetics, Christianity is coldly condemned. 'The worship of sorrow, the crucifixion of the senses, the expectation of the end of the world, are not in themselves principles of artistic rejuvenescence.' The Renaissance is seen coming with all the primal force of spring, and Pater's prose abruptly blazed into a fierce pagan lyricism, sweeping aside wistfulness and timidity: 'true freedom was in the life of the senses and the blood – blood no longer dropping from the hands in sacrifice, as with Angelico, but, as with Titian, burning in the face for desire and love.'

What began with Winckelmann's revolt ends with Pater's. And his are the examples to illustrate the argument, drawn largely from Italian painting and nineteenth-century literature: Holman Hunt, Victor Hugo, Giorgione, Goethe, Keats and Browning, as well as Titian, Francia and Fra Angelico. It is what Pater has read and – especially since travelling in Italy – seen. He it is who comes oddly close to Marx's phraseology in calling the pagan element in all religions 'the anodyne which the religious principle, like one administering opiates to the incurable, has added to the law which makes life sombre for the vast majority of mankind.' In fact, Winckelmann is shown to have missed what Pater is quick to respond to: a sense of the romantic, sometimes mournful, conflict which is as much an aspect of Greek art as the serenity he praised, and strongly characteristic of modern art and life, with its 'passion, and strangeness, and dramatic contrasts . . .'

Seeking for imagination to transfigure 'the meaner world', as he stigmatized it, 'of our common days', Pater could move on from Winckelmann to William Morris with little sense of incongruity – rather, indeed, as shifting the topic but continuing his own train of thought.

Thus, though he savours the colouring, 'intricate and delirious', of the early poems and the simplicity and wonder of the later ones

133

('as of people first waking from the golden age, at fire, snow, wine, the touch of water as one swims, the salt taste of the sea'), he is inhibited from donning Morris's workmanlike clothes or approaching his personality. The general effect of the essay as it concerns Morris is of praise but praise applied from outside and expressed with such conscious verbal refinement that it comes dangerously near outshining the poems under review. In literature Keats, or in painting Botticelli, might have served Pater as well, if not better, for what he is really tracking down is other expressions of his own feeling, 'pensive or passionate, of the shortness of life . . . contrasted with the bloom of the world . . . the desire of beauty quickened by the sense of death.' And so he is carried away from Morris for several pages, to conclude, as he was to go on concluding: 'Not the fruit of experience but experience itself is the end.'

A more mysterious figure than Morris was needed to enshrine that, far more ranging than Winckelmann, though as heterodox sexually, more physically glamorous than Coleridge but sharing something of his brilliant flaws. In Leonardo da Vinci all Pater's conditions were met; and in the *Mona Lisa* he saw summed up 'ten thousand experiences . . . and . . . all modes of thought and life.'

It was as a 'lover of strange souls' that Pater set out to analyze – 'for himself', he pointedly wrote – the strange elements of Leonardo's genius and the impression left on him by his work. He was no longer writing for the *Westminster Review*, turning instead to John Morley's *Fortnightly*, perhaps because it printed its contributors' names (names which included Swinburne, John Addington Symonds, Meredith and Morris). He no longer shrouded his subject with a trailing swathe of his own views. Responding to the pressure – the impression, literally – excited by Leonardo's works, he sank himself totally in that complex personality, at once a handsome prince and a powerful magician, ruling the widest possible kingdom of experience: and he moulded his essay closely to the rhythm of Leonardo's life, all the way from childhood to death, leaving the artist dying but enquiring on the brink of his last experience, going forward to encounter in the final words of the essay 'the last curiosity'.

He was with Leonardo as a child as much as a man. He realized, indeed, that in Leonardo's childhood lay the formative experience which had shaped the personality – realizing it by utilizing his knowledge of himself. 'How indelibly, as we afterwards discover, they affect us,' he was to write of a child's early experiences and feelings, in *The Child in the House*. Things which seem at the time insignificant become 'part of the great chain wherewith we are bound'. And so he analyzed Leonardo's work and tracked back its obsessions with the artist's past – not to intoxicate the reader with some rich Ruskinian evocation of a boyhood in mid-fifteenth century Florence but to lay a confident anatomizing finger, as cool as a scalpel almost, on the seat of Leonardo's imagination. 'Two ideas were especially fixed in him, as reflexes of things which had touched his brain in childhood beyond the measure of other impressions – the smiling of women and the motion of great waters.'

They stand for beauty and terror, for calm and convulsion, for the natural and the monstrous: extremes synthesized supremely in the image of the *Mona Lisa*, painted over again by Pater from the beginning, as if he had been there when it started to take shape on the artist's easel. 'The presence that rose thus beside the water was what in the way of a thousand years man had come to desire.' He recognized that before the painter saw her she had been 'present from the first incorporeal in Leonardo's thought', – and perhaps in his own as well. Older than the rocks . . . the vampire . . . a diver in deep seas, she is also a mother, both pagan and sacred, but one whom maternity has left mysteriously virginal, unchangingly beautiful, self-absorbed and a little languid. Her life is perpetual; she was the image desired of Leonardo's mother into which he had poured himself ('A feeling for maternity is indeed always characteristic of Leonardo . . .') and, as Pater has recreated her, comes to represent the desired image of his.

Effortlessly, he understood Leonardo. He had no need to echo Flaubert's '*c'est moi*' about Emma Bovary, for his identification was inherent from the opening paragraph of the *Notes*. There he writes of how Vasari's first edition of Leonardo's life shows the artist a bold speculator, someone who had little respect for other people's beliefs, himself setting philosophy above Christianity. Vasari softened that outline into something more conventional in the second edition, but Pater prefers the enigma, the genius who can pass unmoved through tragic events, peculiar, solitary and challenging. What is more, a flash of scorn reveals the similarity of their two natures as he stigmatizes the suspicion which attached itself to Leonardo as 'but the time-honoured form in which the world stamps its appreciation of one who has thoughts for himself alone, his high indifferentism, his intolerance of the common form of things'. It was fitting that those words revealing Pater should appear in the first publication which also revealed his name.

Nine   The demoralizing moralizer

IN WRITING about Leonardo da Vinci Pater had discovered not only a personality but also a period in which he could absorb himself. During the three years which followed publication of the *Notes*, he proceeded in a series of essays in *The Fortnightly* to extend his range: moving on first to Botticelli, then to Pico della Mirandola and to Michelangelo's poetry; he also prepared studies on Luca della Robbia and Joachim du Bellay. By the summer of 1872 he had the nucleus of a book which he offered to Macmillan ('I know not how long ago I formed the ambition that *you* should publish what I might write,' he informed Alexander Macmillan twelve years later 'as I glanced over the fascinating list of your publications . . .'). Terms were agreed. In March 1873 *Studies in the History of the Renaissance* was published.

Uneasy in his own century, finding the previous century – for all its virtues or because of them – a little too urbane and prosaic to accommodate his sensuousness, Pater turned back to the Renaissance as providing the ideal climate of culture as he understood it. It possessed the exact blend of visual and literary art which he needed, located for him in Italy and France, two countries stimulating as foreign without being quite alien or inaccessible. Neatly, the period had balanced intellect and imagination. It had been filled by 'special and prominent personalities', as he put it in the Preface, 'with their profound aesthetic charm'. It was, above all, an age of significant freedom, offering a 'life of refined pleasure and action' which as an outbreak of the human spirit could be traced from medieval times: 'the care for physical beauty, the worship of the body, the breaking down of those limits which the religious system of the middle age imposed on the heart and the imagination.'

He might write thus of the past, but he was thinking of the present. His heart and imagination continued to sense and strongly resist all those pressures of his own period to conform which were summed up in the tenets of conventional Christianity. Quietly teaching in his pale-coloured, austere room at Brasenose or quietly walking through the streets of Oxford, returning to the consciously exquisite yet austere setting of the house in Bradmore Road, Pater must easily have seemed the epitome of habit-forming man. Only occasional flashes of exasperated wit or repartee hinted at how violently he rejected almost everything to which the routine of his existence constrained him.

He was attracted to the Renaissance not merely as an escape (though it was that, and allowed him even to escape a – to him – distasteful physical appearance) but as a period of ambiguity mirroring his own ambiguity. Its love of beauty was dignified yet curious, possibly disturbing ultimately, as it is enshrined in Leonardo. Beauty, pleasure, allure, all have their sad or sinister aspect. Leonardo's *St John the Baptist*, with 'delicate brown flesh and woman's hair', becomes like some private temptation of Pater's, a male prostitute inveigling him at a Paris street corner, with a 'treacherous smile that would have us understand something far beyond the outward gesture or circumstance.' Pico della Mirandola is gifted and handsome but dies young, a real-life prototype of one of Pater's imaginary portraits. The colouring of Botticelli's *Birth of Venus* is 'cadaverous, or at least cold', and the face of the goddess is full of sorrow. 'Vague and wayward' are the adjectives to describe the loves of Michelangelo. Even when the surface of his sonnets is calm, Pater writes, 'there is latent a deep delight in carnal form and colour.' The Renaissance attitude to religion, as Pater conceived it, was strangely ambivalent; there was the figure of Pico, 'lying down to rest in the Dominican habit, yet amid thoughts of the older gods', and there was the Madonna as depicted by Botticelli, holding the Christ Child in her arms and yet almost shockingly indifferent, 'neither for God nor for his enemies'.

In such a phrase Pater's own moustached face seems obtruding incongruously through the features of the Madonna. His rather than Botticelli's was the dilemma. That essay suffers perhaps from having been born too close to the shadow of the preceding one on Leonardo. Its tone is oddly apologetic and unsure ('if I have defined aright the temper in which he worked'), even about the subject's status: 'a second-rate painter'. Yet it was the very subjectiveness of Pater's attitude which allowed him to respond to the unconventional appeal of Botticelli – picking up, as it were, the subtle signals emitted from pictures which generations had neglected. Almost certainly he was the first English writer to write an article on Botticelli; he set up the *Birth of Venus* as virtually Botticelli's *Mona Lisa* and gave an impetus to the transformation of in this case a little-known painting into one of the most famous paintings in the world. Well might he correctly claim the priority of his article ('I believe . . . the first notice in English of that old painter') over Ruskin's 'discovery' of Botticelli. Answering the enquiry of a journalist and author in 1881, Pater gently but firmly went on to state that his article 'preceded Mr Ruskin's lectures on the same subject by I believe two years.'

That truth was swept away in the insane rush of Ruskin's egotistic assertion, printed in the 'Epilogue' of 1883 to *Modern Painters*, that he, he alone, had discerned and taught the excellence and supremacy of five great painters, despised until he spoke of them: 'Turner, Tintoret, Luini, Botticelli and Carpaccio.' In fact, Ruskin first spoke publicly of Botticelli at Oxford in the Lent term of 1871. Later editions of *The Renaissance* bore the softest and yet most factual of retorts to this unpleasant and unnecessary boast (unfair, incidentally to several other writers) as it concerned Pater; to the essay on Botticelli was appended the date of its original publication, 1870. And, priority apart, Pater might console himself by refusing to believe – as with the subject of St Mark's church – that Ruskin saw more in Botticelli than he did.

He was not teaching anything, least of all ethics. Nor was he writing a history of the Renaissance. He was selecting from that period a few choice personalities who seemed to speak to him, usually through the medium of their art, as his kindred in subtlety, sophistication and love of beauty. Even if little was actually known of their lives – as with Botticelli and still more with Luca della Robbia – their work bore the impress 'of a personal quality', as he wrote of della Robbia, 'a profound expressiveness . . . the seal on a man's work of what is most inward and peculiar in his moods and manner of apprehension.' To detect that, respond to it and express his response through words was Pater's task. His own life was little different from what he saw as della Robbia's: 'with no adventure and no excitement except what belongs to the trial of new artistic processes, the struggle with new artistic difficulties . . .'

He made the work of both Botticelli and della Robbia part of his own environment. A cast no doubt of a Madonna by della Robbia hung, apparently, in his Brasenose rooms. Two small della Robbia plaques in blue and white decorated the house in Bradmore Road. Mrs Humphry Ward recalled engravings hanging there, 'if I remember right', from Botticelli or Luini, or Mantegna. She also mentions in the drawing-room some of Hester's framed embroidery and an undergraduate visitor of keener aesthetic awareness (D. S. MacColl, an artist and future Keeper of the Tate Gallery and of the Wallace Collection) noticed there a composition of Botticelli's which had been worked in embroidery by Hester.

With Pico della Mirandola it was his personality not his writings that appealed to Pater. The restless quest for a reconciliation between sacred and profane is near enough to Pater's own problems to make

138

Pico sympathetic; and then there is the additional glamour of his appearance ('Mercury as he might have appeared in a painting by Sandro Botticelli or Piero di Cosimo') and his early death. If his thoughts are hardly valuable, still under them Pater finds 'springs . . . of deep and passionate emotion'. Pico himself becomes valuable just for having existed. For all his aspiration, he reached no certainty, adopted no system of knowledge, held no belief – except to believe 'that nothing which has ever interested living men and women can wholly lose its vitality'. And those things are seen as often slight in themselves – no more than dreams, it may be – but given importance exactly because people have been passionate about them.

'A sudden light transfigures a trivial thing,' Pater wrote at the close of the essay on Joachim du Bellay, almost as though continuing this thought, while reflecting on the poem *D'un vanneur de blé aux vents*, and certainly expressing his own passionate attachment to moments of perception heightened by art: 'a weather-vane, a wind-mill, a winnowing flail, the dust in the barn door; a moment, – and the thing has vanished, because it was pure effect; but it leaves a relish behind it, a longing that the accident may happen again.' It was the wistful strain in du Bellay that seems to have attracted Pater to him. After a rather diffuse discussion of the Renaissance in France, the essay finally comes to rest where Pater is happiest, on the in-dividual intimate mood, here du Bellay's nostalgic poems written in Rome: '. . . the sense of loss in passing days, the ennui of a dreamer who has to plunge into the world's affairs, the opposition between life and the ideal, a longing for rest, nostalgia, homesickness –' each cadence is disturbingly intense, bringing the reader, like the writer, back from du Bellay, pining in sixteenth-century Rome for his native *douceur Angevine*, to the Brasenose don isolated in nine-teenth-century Oxford: 'that pre-eminently childish, but so sug-gestive sorrow, as significant of the final regret of all human creatures for the familiar earth and limited sky.'

A similar transitory mood, with more chill overtones, is detected by Pater in Michelangelo's art. His poetry gives an impression 'of something flitting and unfixed, of the houseless and complaining spirit . . .' He himself is seen as lingering on in old age like a *revenant*, 'a ghost . . . in a world too coarse to touch his faint sensibilities too closely.' And the sacristy at San Lorenzo ('I suppose', Pater writes, 'no one would come here for consolation') is a place 'of vague and wistful speculation', where immortality of the soul and existence of any future world grow doubtful under pressure of the process of being disembodied. The formlessness which preceded life threatens to come again – and Pater's prose sinks in one of those moments where he catches a sensation of consciousness extinguished, positively expiring, 'with faint hearing, faint memory, faint power of touch . . .'

In 1871, the year that the essays on Pico della Mirandola and on Michelangelo's poetry were published, Mandell Creighton (a clerical don and later Bishop of London) wrote to his fiancée about Pater, 'in him the ideal of beauty absolutely dominates, and all that does not come under its influence is to him external'. Creighton, himself something of an aesthete, was already friendly with Pater and was preparing his future wife for meeting this unusual Oxford personality, 'You will find him worth a study in that matter'. The Creightons became neighbours and saw a good deal of Pater and his sisters at this period, when Clara was also beginning to emerge as a personality: striking-looking and aesthetically dressed, intelligent and interested not merely in her own education but in the education generally of women.

Yet although it was true, as Creighton pointed out, that 'the ideal of beauty' dominated Pater, the ideal was never secure. Always it was under threat. The aspiration towards it might be intense, the glimpse of it, when a glimpse came, consoling; but all that beauty could do in the end was give brief gleams to the moments as they passed. It could not halt the passage of time or human decay. The fiery vitality even of the Renaissance faltered and grew dim amid the grey tombs at San Lorenzo.

Only when the various essays which went to make up *The Renaissance* were put together could it be fully realized how painfully Pater felt the threat of total annihilation and how desperately he clutched at any fragments of beauty, any moments of pleasure, as the sole way of making life tolerable. The casual historical framework of the book and even the most firmly wrought passages of artistic appreciation are at the close disturbed and set trembling by the apprehensions of a living person, one who finally abandons the pretext of investigating the past and speaks out of and to the present. A strange force has borne author and reader on from the calm, scholarly-connoisseur accents with which the book opens, announcing a study touching 'the chief points' of the Renaissance, which typically prove to be personalities not phenomena, to that hectic, unexpected 'Conclusion' in which nothing is concluded, least of all about the Renaissance, except that all is melting under our feet and that our one chance in the short interval of life is to expand it by 'getting as many pulsations as possible into the given time'.

Pater thought of the contents of the book while it was being prepared for publication as 'so slight . . . unpretending . . . intended . . . for a comparatively small section of readers', and his chief anxiety seems to have been that the final result should look artistic, rather small, printed on rough-edged paper and bound preferably in old-fashioned pasteboard with a paper spine. He pressed Macmillan, vainly, to adopt these proposals, writing rather tartly, 'For a book on art to be bound quite in the ordinary way is, it seems to me, behind the times.'

Nor did he neglect some revision of the contents – notably the essay on Winckelmann. It became if not exactly 'unpretending' at least far less provocative in its near-jibes about Christianity, many of which disappeared altogether. There ceased to be anything as stirring as the remark that the Renaissance had given a freedom to the arts expressed by blood no longer dropping from the hands in sacrifice but, as with Titian, 'burning in the face for desire and love'.

If the eventual appearance of the book was not exactly what Pater had first envisaged, he found it adequately sober in its dark green cloth binding and clear print on imitation wirewove ribbed paper. On the spine his name was given simply as 'W. H. Pater'; on the title page he is styled 'Walter H. Pater', and identified as Fellow of Brasenose College, Oxford. Shadwell was discreetly concealed as the dedicatee with 'To C. L. S.'. At the back of the volume, the publisher took the opportunity to advertise a select number of publications of a vaguely allied kind, scholarly and artistic, and all highly respectable: a new edition of Arnold's *Essays in Criticism*, lectures by the Slade Professor of Fine Art at Cambridge, monographs on Raphael and Dürer, and *Studies in Early French Poetry* by Walter Besant.

Nothing gives a better idea of how Macmillan, and possibly Pater, saw the book and anticipated its reception. But when the essays were collected and read together, there rose from them such urgent and sensuous music of a new kind, celebrating too a view of life equally sensuous and novel, that the tone of the book became more arresting than its contents, with the exception of its 'Conclusion'.

By itself that chapter signalled the book's difference from the work of Walter Besant or the Slade Professor of Fine Art at Cambridge – not to speak of the Slade Professor at Oxford. Few serious books on history, literature or art were likely to close with the admonition that 'To burn always with this hard gem-like flame, to maintain this ecstasy, is success in life.' What had promised to be at worst a harmless browse among byways of the Florentine Renaissance suddenly took on the insidious appeal of some prose *Fleurs du Mal*. Even a visit to Milan might no longer be supposed safe, if the city was still a home of 'brilliant sins'.

Historically, as Mrs Mark Pattison quickly and shrewdly pointed out in reviewing it, the book was deplorably weak and its title a misnomer; and she was scarcely kinder to Pater's art history. Yet she also wrote of his subtle discrimination and exquisite accuracy in choice of words, '. . . they gleam upon the paper with the radiance of jewels'. Symonds, girding himself to review the book, told a friend that Pater's view of life 'gives me the creeps', and he perceived 'a kind of Death clinging to the man', making his music a little faint and sickly. Yet he could not help adding of the music: 'but heavens! how sweet that is!' A review by *The Fortnightly*'s editor, John Morley, in which the philosophy of the 'Conclusion' was prudently said to be 'worth attention', drew criticisms in at least one other periodical, blaming Morley for apparently endorsing Pater's view. From Pater himself it drew a letter of thanks, 'for your explanation of my ethical point of view to which I fancy some readers have given a prominence I did not mean it to have.'

That disengaging, and also somewhat disingenuous, note was sounded too late to check a movement, in Oxford especially, of scandalized reaction to the conclusions of *Studies in the History of the Renaissance*. Pater soon had more evidence than his 'I fancy' would suggest to show that some readers had fixed with positively baleful attention on those eloquent passages in which immortality was implicitly denied, concluding in their turn that he believed 'the only thing worth living for is momentary enjoyment'.

This phrase comes from a long and deeply pained letter he received from the chaplain of Brasenose, John Wordsworth, a great-nephew of the poet, until then a friendly colleague, who had briefly been Pater's pupil. Wordsworth expressed his admiration of 'the beauty of style and the felicity of thought' in the book, but also the grief he felt it had caused to many Oxford contemporaries, as well as his distress over the fact that the 'Conclusion', which he knew had first been published anonymously, was now reprinted 'under your own name as a Fellow of Brasenose . . .' He warned Pater that their difference of opinion would become public and avowed, 'and it may be my duty to oppose you'. Finally, he requested him to give up his share as an examiner in the college's divinity examination.

Perhaps Pater replied. More probably he preferred to remain silent. Wordsworth's hint that he was far from alone in disapproving of the book's tone seems to have been true enough. And the fact was profoundly damaging to Pater. Almost certainly, it was his book that was in the mind of his old tutor, W. W. Capes, who in November 1873 preached a sermon criticizing the new 'humanitarian culture' with its suspicion of habits and its tendency to analyze subtle impulses and evanescent thrills, and its enthusiasm for Hellenism and the Renaissance (polite words to disguise homosexuality and paganism). Pater must have felt the sting of wider public disapproval when in 1874 it was the turn of Brasenose to nominate a university proctor and Wordsworth was appointed, although Pater was the senior man and could normally have expected the nomination. In the following year there came the open attack of the Bishop of Oxford, who quoted a sentence from *The Renaissance* (inevitably from the 'Conclusion') and complained of the effect of such sceptical teaching on the young – always a good device, especially in a university, for stirring up prejudice.

By 1876 the original scandal must have been subsiding, but something of it was probably aroused by the publication of W. H. Mallock's amusing parody, *The New Republic*, a series of conversations which satirized Arnold, Jowett and Ruskin, as well as Pater, who appeared, not very prominently, as the hyper-aesthetic Mr Rose. Languid and dreamy, Mr Rose speaks of everyone – another character comments – 'as if they had no clothes on'. More provocatively, he is found comparing life to the way of decorating the room of a loved one, whether a woman 'or a youth'.

Mallock had only recently ceased to be an undergraduate at Balliol when he wrote his *jeu d'esprit*. He had never met Pater and made fun of his cult of beauty without any implications of its being anti-Christian; indeed, Mr Rose goes occasionally to a ritualistic church service 'when in the weary mood for it'. And although clerical circles sensed and reciprocated Pater's hostility, it was not really the sceptical vein revealed in *The Renaissance* that marked him fatally so much as its compelling theme of enjoyment, experience and release. It seemed a message, particularly to an age that was always looking for messages, and it was set out overtly at the end of the book in a way that suggested it was what Pater had learnt from the Renaissance (though in fact, of course, he had composed the 'message' well before he published anything on the subject). As a message it was not merely shocking but dangerous. Nothing could have summed up more acutely the repugnance Pater had excited, or have more effectively harmed his university reputation, than the pungent characterization of him as a 'demoralizing moralizer', attributed to Jowett.

Jowett had become Master of Balliol in 1870. He was consolidating his hold on the university, and his antagonism was not something to be easily ignored. Although there is no direct evidence that he intervened to affect Pater's career, it seems clear that he strongly disapproved of the tendencies to be detected in *The Renaissance*. In some of the earliest of detailed recollections of Pater (by Gosse and William Sharp, both in 1894) there is mention of a complete estrangement between Jowett and his one-time pupil, and also reported as his is the epigrammatic characterization quoted above. Whomever it was first coined by, it is likely to have gained wide, gleeful currency in Oxford and been at some point passed on to Pater himself.

The book which he had deprecatingly described before publication as slight and unpretending had become notorious. It was read by undergraduates for its style and for its aesthetic philosophy. 'The holy writ of beauty', Wilde was to call it. He read it during his first term as an undergraduate at Oxford in the autumn of 1874, and more than twenty years later, from Reading Gaol, he mused about it as the book 'which has had such a strange influence over my life'.

Pater, wrapped in a personal dream of the Renaissance and concerned to reaffirm his own belief in beauty as the only significant experience, had probably never foreseen the reactions he would provoke. After all, he had published most of the essays before; the 'Conclusion' had been in print, if anonymously, since 1868, so it had had plenty of time to poison the morals of a complete generation of undergraduates. Yet, as his colleague Wordsworth made clear, a book by an identified fellow of a college was a graver matter; perhaps there was even some imputation on Brasenose for harbouring the author. Mrs Humphry Ward recalled how the book stirred and scandalized Oxford, and she may hardly have exaggerated in saying there were 'various attempts at persecution'. The reactions were not the less strong for being only partly explicit. Far more tormenting to Pater no doubt would be gossip and hinted disapproval than some straightforward critical review; and a last echo of what was being said is heard in the words of May Ottley, Clara Pater's pupil, who in 1931 referred to the 'superficial, stupid, cruel and crude misjudgments of those early years'. Pater suffered possibly more than he showed, and he never entirely recovered his confidence.

When a second edition of the book was prepared in 1877, he not only met Mrs Pattison's point by altering the title to *The Renaissance: Studies in art and poetry* but he silently suppressed the 'Conclusion'. In 1888, on the occasion of the third edition, he restored it, but implicitly accepted a semi-Socratic charge of corrupting youth, printing the explanation that he had omitted it in 1877, 'as I conceived it might mislead some of those young men into whose hands it might fall.'

That confession was one indication of how profoundly disturbed he had been. More fundamentally revealing is the fact that after the book's first publication twelve years elapsed – almost to the day – before he published another book.

Ten   A new triumvirate

'W E SAW a great deal that pleased us very much,' Pater reported
to Edmund Gosse in September 1877, describing a 'little
tour in France' made by him with Hester and Clara. 'We all enjoyed
its charming portraiture of Italian things and ways,' he assured Vernon
Lee (Violet Paget) a few years later when she sent him a just-
published ghost-story of hers. 'We hope', he explained in August
1889 to Herbert Horne, 'to leave for the Continent on Monday.' A
few months before his death, after sitting to William Rothenstein for
a portrait drawing, he gave the publisher John Lane the reason why
it could not be reproduced: 'My sisters have seen [it], and think it so
unlike me . . .'

From 1869 up to the very moment of his death, Pater was
rarely to be separated from his sisters, and he was to associate them –
increasingly perhaps – with his life, his friends, his attitudes, and
eventually his writing when in 1885 he dedicated *Marius the Epicurean*
to them. At the time of the scandal surrounding *Studies in the History
of the Renaissance* he must have been particularly glad to have a domestic environment shared with them, away from the daily college
routine of Brasenose and the possibly dubious glances, if not dubious
comments, of his fellow-dons. Nothing, it seems, shook his sisters'
affection or their care of him. And the brief dedication of *Marius* ('To
Hester and Clara') is likely to express his gratitude for fifteen years of
their companionship.

A calm, regular tenor of life, in proximity but keeping decent
reticence between themselves, happened to fit all three – each a
lonely, proud individual – and perhaps in coming together at
Bradmore Road they discovered as adults deeper affinities than they
had ever realized existed when they were children.

After years of separation, they were again united and settled.
Not since Enfield, perhaps, had they enjoyed the security of feeling
they lived in their own home, and the glowing, effectively simple
interior of Bradmore Road may well have captured, consciously or
not, something of the tranquil, austere beauty of the 'old house', at
least as Pater in the person of Florian Deleal recalls it in *The Child in*

the House. Polished wood, a few mirrors, a few flowers, 'a sparing allowance of blue plates and pots' were the objects which furnished the Bradmore Road drawing-room, with 'its pure bright colour', as vividly recollected by Mrs Humphry Ward. The effect sounds rather like that of a Dutch seventeenth-century interior, especially the ideal interior depicted in paintings. 'I see that room always', Mrs Ward wrote, 'with the sun in it . . .' Florian's house is notable for its 'trimness and comely whiteness'; 'there was a cool old parlour', and along one chimney-piece 'old blue-china pots'. The boy loves his home because of the sense he has of the harmony 'between his soul and his physical environment'. The life lived there was 'singularly tranquil and filled with a curious sense of self-possession'. To recover and recreate that existence – before bereavement, dispersal and the process of growing up shook its foundations – might almost have been an aim uniting Pater and his sisters as they fashioned a highly personal setting behind the typical North Oxford semi-Gothic façade of their small house.

The unity of the group they made appears to have struck everyone. It was quietly but distinctly exclusive, detached from the outside world, emphasized by elements of physical similarity, by presumably shared aesthetic tastes and certainly by a shared fondness for animals. The same preference for personal reserve, with avoidance of emotional extremes, noise or intrusion of any kind into the placid, ordered still-life of their lives, seems to have been felt to characterize them all. The exquisiteness of their environment extended to a care for meals and serving of them. When Vernon Lee first went to dinner with them, she wrote afterwards of a 'really beautiful dinner, served with beautiful porcelain and glass'.

And though the situation of two spinsters settling to share a home with their bachelor brother can hardly have been unusual, the very closeness of the relationship – combined with its apparent isolation and detachment from other family ties – made it remarkable. Perhaps rather maliciously, yet truthfully, Vernon Lee reported her Oxford landlady commenting on Pater still living with his sisters in Bradmore Road and adding, 'Mr Pater don't seem to get married, do 'ee, Miss?' Vernon Lee herself had at first meeting found the Misses Pater 'rather gushing old maids', though she drastically revised her opinion of Clara when she got to know her better ('she has a very fine character') and she remained on friendly terms with both sisters long after Pater's death. Mrs Ward wrote many years later that she would never forget 'the exquisiteness' of the Bradmore Road house, 'and the charm of the three people who lived in it.' A strangely poignant anecdote is told by Mary Robinson (a minor poet who was a friend and neighbour of the trio in London) of coming on them unobserved, one snowy evening at Christmas time, in their shadowed drawing-room, totally absorbed in discussion of members of the fantasy family which they had created among themselves.

In this triumvirate, as in that of his schooldays, Pater was the dominant figure. It could scarcely be otherwise. Because of him they lived in Oxford – and it is notable how rapidly and irrevocably Hester and Clara quitted it when he died. Because of him they met and entertained literary and other personalities. It was because of him probably that they travelled so frequently abroad. (When instead they all spent a summer holiday in Cornwall, Pater 'found there not a tithe of the stimulus to one's imagination', he told William Sharp, 'which I have sometimes experienced in quite unrenowned places abroad'.) While he lived, his work and his fame must have been their central concern; and his sudden death only sharpened their slightly aggressive pride in being guardians of his reputation. In the incident over the Rothenstein drawing – not to mention their subsequent attitude to the unfortunate Thomas Wright's project of a *Life* of Pater – a strong proprietorial tone can already be detected. Although Walter and Walter's writings took first place for them, neither of the women seems to have been malleable or easily daunted. Indeed, to meet they were clearly rather formidable and far less able – or far less willing – than Pater to adopt a suave, deferential social manner.

United though the three of them seemed, and basically were, they were individual personalities for all of whom this relationship had elements of refuge: the alternative life offered to unfulfilled private dreams of a warmer, more emotionally satisfying existence. Within the trio itself there lay some imbalance, because Clara was patently the more ardent and intelligent sister, and must have been closer to Pater intellectually if not instinctively as well. Even such career as she had, as a classics tutor at Somerville College, is like a faint echo of his. Yet, from another angle, Clara and Hester shared a conventionally subordinate role simply as being women: appendages of Pater, consciously or not, always having to put him first, just as it was on them in turn that responsibility fell when in 1883 their brother William became seriously ill. As a result, Pater rather blandly explained to Vernon Lee, 'I am afraid my sisters, at all events, will not be able to leave England this summer.' It may well be that neither sister resented this dutiful role, but an impatient acerbity in their outlook and behaviour – very much in contrast to Pater's – suggests some inner dissatisfaction which time was far from softening.

Hester's is the harder character to recover, though she easily outlived her siblings, and her feelings and her opinions are almost as elusive as her appearance. Silence, when a good deal is noted of Clara's distinguished appearance, as well as of her intellectual abilities, seems significant. The only activity of Hester's that is positively praised is her embroidery. The closest any description comes to her in Pater's lifetime seems that of D. S. MacColl who refers to her 'heaviness of face' and her voice as gruffer than Pater's. Even Mary Robinson speaks of her as being 'somewhat sour'; and by the time Henry James went to see her, after Clara's death, her behaviour had degenerated into cantankerousness (she 'glared at him and told him that she hated "horrid" ghost stories about children'). James riposted afterwards, standing on her doorstep, 'She looks *cross*. I suspect she *is* cross. May crossness explain her solitude?'

Like Clara, she dressed in the days at Oxford in aesthetic clothes, of a kind which were then fashionable in young, advanced circles there: simple-looking, smocked, plain in line and usually of plain blues and greens (in reaction to the magentas and puce of middle-class metropolitan taste). Vernon Lee describes her and Clara as appearing once in 'fantastic apple-green Kate Greenaway dresses'. Perhaps it was partly this 'uniform' – allied to their aloof calm – that prompted one contemporary to compare the sisters to the prior and sub-prior of a well-loved religious house. Their combined effect was apparently sufficient to frighten Wilde away from a dinner party when he realized he was due to sit next to them, though it may have been Hester in particular he fled from, since Clara he at least respected.

With none of Pater's friends or acquaintances does Hester seem to have established any relationship – with the exception of Vernon Lee – and nothing is recorded of her having friends of her own. Oxford was perhaps the least suitable of environments for her. She did not, it appears, share any of Clara's interest in educating herself or in higher education for women, and even her slight aesthetic tendencies were probably prompted by her brother and sister. It is difficult to think of her enjoying a conversation with Mrs Pattison, for example, or indeed approving of Mrs Pattison's emancipated behaviour. Her attitude to Pater himself is unclear. What she read of his work she may not have entirely understood, or altogether liked, though *Marius* must have seemed reassuring if she had been perturbed by his previous explicit bias against Christianity.

All that is established about her suggests a narrow, conventional spinster, shy, obscure, sad, perhaps too conscious (like Pater) of lacking physical attraction, overshadowed by a gifted younger brother

148

and sister but following the example of her mother and her spinster aunt in making a home with and for them. Such a woman may more than occasionally have felt excluded, and a little sour about her own situation. When one winter she received an unexpected gift of flowers from Vernon Lee (conceivably for her birthday early in the year) her letter of thanks was at once stiff and affectionate, grateful and surprised, and not without its own mild tremor of aesthetic response: 'They look very Italian with their rich colours in an Indian turquoise vase.'

Hester had probably never been worried by doubts and ambitions for herself. In her all the recessive tendencies of the family were concentrated. She sought no career, least of all the public one of teaching. From her aunt she had probably inherited an uncomplicated but firm religious faith. Unlike Clara's, her mind was not questioning; she escaped therefore the struggle to believe which apparently tormented Clara until the close of her life, and which Pater also endured. When she alone of the trio remained alive, Hester declared that the words inscribed on Pater's tombstone (*In te, domine, speravi*) had been his specific choice, though perhaps her recollection was based on some remark he had once let fall rather than implying any solemn final request, especially as Pater's actual death was so swift, abrupt, and unforeseen. And what to her may have sounded a straightforward pious text, piously chosen, suggests rather the mood of Marius, a cautious, honest, ultimately wistful attitude – Clara's as much as Pater's – in which stress lies on the act of *hoping*. Perhaps there was something more pertinent still about the choice of a quotation from Psalm 31, in which the Psalmist speaks of being 'a reproach . . . especially among my neighbours, and a fear to mine acquaintance . . . For I have heard the slander of many . . . Let the lying lips be put to silence.'

For Clara, the settling with her brother in Oxford stimulated dormant abilities, without perhaps altogether satisfying her. Her character seems to have been complex, with something of Hester's intransigence and much of Pater's sensitivity. Her appearance had possibly a quite close resemblance to her other brother, William; it was certainly striking, even beautiful, and is fortunately preserved by photographs, as well as by a finely-detailed drawing, done in 1870 by the portraitist T. Blake Wirgman. This conveys the 'calm strong face and wonderful eyes' (grey like Pater's and markedly resembling his), described by one of Clara's pupils. It also suggests a keen, highly-bred, nervous-looking refinement: a refinement of dress as well as of appearance and of mind. Recollections of Clara are consistent in emphasizing her strength of will, and her crisp, almost painful truthfulness of speech. At least as shy as Pater and presumably Hester, she seems to have given an impression of powerful emotions held back only with great effort behind a cool, somewhat intimidating manner, enhanced no doubt by her cool physical distinction and carefully chosen costume.

The first effect of Oxford seems to have been to encourage her to teach herself Latin and Greek. She associated with other young and youngish women impatient of being restricted to domesticity, including Mandell Creighton's wife and the newly married Mrs Humphry Ward, and joined a committee to sponsor the 'Oxford Lectures for Ladies' in 1873, an early venture involving members of the university as the lecturers. When a few years later an association was formed there for promoting the higher education of women, with courses of instruction leading to examinations of university standard, she became a member of its committee and began herself to do some teaching. Soon she was involved with Somerville, one of the two newly founded halls of residence established for girls coming to study in Oxford; and during the last year of Pater's life, she was resident tutor of a separate block at Somerville.

In her own inevitably very limited world she had made a reputation, owing a little – though not much – to being Pater's sister. But it seems doubtful whether some of the tributes paid in obituaries after her death to her friendship with Burne-Jones, Morris and Meredith, among others, can be more than kindly, sentimental exaggeration, based possibly on the admiration she may have expressed for these figures, or because they were supposed to have been Pater's own friends. The only contemporary reference which suggests some slightly wider recognition of her is Wilde's, in 1887, when he was considering potential contributors to the magazine *Woman's World*. 'Miss Pater, (sister of the author of *Marius*),' comes at the end of a long list of cultivated women he hoped would write for it. Along with Queen Victoria, whom he ventured to approach in the following year, Clara contributed nothing to *Woman's World*; and there seems no record of Wilde positively asking her.

Nothing is known of her writing anything, though in 1877 Pater, referring to a project Alexander Macmillan had contemplated of having Schnaase's seven-volume *History of Sculpture* translated from the German, ventured 'to recommend one of my sisters', if Macmillan proceeded. Nothing came of the project (the book remains untranslated). It must have been Clara whom Pater designated, and the possibility was being mooted at a date before the association promoting the higher education of women had been founded. She probably hoped for translation work to give her an occupation – and conceivably also a modicum of financial freedom. From Pater's reference

('I fancy I could give [her] some real assistance in the work'), it sounds as if collaboration of a sort was in their minds. And although Clara never collaborated with him, she seems to have acted occasionally as his amanuensis; a portion of the late, unfinished *Gaston de Latour* exists in a manuscript copy presumed to have been made by her.

At Pater's death, she rapidly resigned from Somerville, leaving Oxford to settle with Hester in a small house in Kensington (6, Canning Place, off Gloucester Road). She did not, however, entirely stop teaching; she took one or two pupils for private tuition, among them Virginia Stephen (later Woolf), who read Latin and Greek with her in 1898. Perhaps it was increasing age and ill-health, or recognition of her own limitations, which led her to give up this activity. Although she had managed to learn Greek, she can scarcely have made herself proficient as a serious teacher of it. Virginia Stephen's subsequent Greek tutor found she needed to go back to the beginning, so slovenly (in the tutor's own words) was the approach she had got away with under Clara Pater.

Rather sadly, it seems as if Clara's career – brave though it was in concept – never quite satisfied her or proved very satisfactory. Even her post as resident tutor at Somerville was much less significant than it sounded, closer to the role of matron than to that of an academic, and intended for a much younger, perhaps more extrovert person. May Ottley, a student at Somerville who became a friend of Clara's, was to recognize that it could not have been easy for someone of her age and dominance of character to fit into a subordinate position – still less for someone shy and withdrawn to live in a bustling, vigorous community.

On the surface all was ordered neatness, from her manner and dress to the small, square, yellow room she lived in at Somerville, with its blue curtains and shining brass – sounding like an echo in miniature of Pater's room at Brasenose. Looking wise and severely calm as she sat quietly by the fire, Clara might seem an epitome of the scholastic guide or counsellor, but perhaps she would have welcomed guidance herself. 'Deeply emotional, she disliked and dreaded anything bordering on the sentimental . . .', May Ottley wrote. 'She loved many', Mrs Ward claimed vaguely, 'as they loved her.' Yet it is clear that she repressed her emotions, fearing their force it may be or the paths into which they might lead her (and perhaps in this too she felt affinities with Pater). Her severity must have begun with herself. Not only emotional but intelligent and eager for truth, she was hardly likely to accept conventional religion without scrutiny and then doubts. Pater might have been reflecting on her, as well as himself, when he wrote those words about Pascal: 'the doubts never die, they are only just kept down in a perpetual *agonia.*' May Ottley recorded that for Clara faith was, even to the end, 'a hard fought fight'. And the end was death from cancer in 1910, after some two years or more of illness. She had made her will already in 1898, bequeathing to Hester everything she possessed. Her estate was valued at £50 1s. 8d. She was buried, as Hester was to be, at Oxford beside Pater.

Like Clara, Pater probably shrank from the sentimental and made such shrinking an excuse for repelling intimacy. There was so much he did not tell his sisters (leaving them to assume, for instance, that he had had no desire when young to write) and Benson seems to be thinking of them when he says that even to his intimates Pater was often 'reserved, baffling and mysterious'. Hester, more than Clara, may have found him so; in one of her earlier and less acrimonious letters to Wright she confessed that Pater 'was very reticent even with those nearest to him'.

Yet although he allowed some aspects of his character to elude them – and perhaps never fully realized how much he and Clara could have exchanged confidences – he did not hide from them his acute suffering under criticism. 'Only those nearest to him', Benson writes, with obvious reference to Hester and Clara, 'knew of these dark moods of discouragement.' When his essay on *Style* (first published in 1888) was harshly criticized, he declared his pleasure in writing was gone and that he could never resume work. Benson notes that, but says nothing of what Pater must have undergone at the far more damaging reception of the first edition of *The Renaissance*.

Indeed, it was probably that experience which haunted him and which even the faintest breath of purely literary criticism unpleasantly rekindled. Gosse (not the most subtle of men) thought that Pater quite enjoyed, for example, the notoriety of being 'Mr Rose' in Mallock's parody: it gave him status alongside more famous figures like Huxley, Arnold and Ruskin. And to Gosse Pater doubtless put on a front of amused tolerance at what was certainly an unmalicious joke. Nevertheless, it helped to feed the legend of the 'demoralizing moralizer', whose cult of beauty was hardly more than a sort of weary sensuality. Pater must have come to loathe all the implications, and privately to despair perhaps of ever shaking them off.

Even while Mallock's squib was appearing Pater must have realized that he was not rehabilitated in Oxford eyes. He let his name go forward in 1876 as a candidate for the Professorship of Poetry about to be vacated by Sir Francis Doyle. John Addington Symonds was another candidate, and he and Pater were at once bracketed together as representatives of self-indulgent, pagan 'culture'. A far safer alternative was offered when Principal Shairp of St Andrew's, a Scottish poet and scholar, announced his candidature, supported by Matthew Arnold. Pater prudently withdrew, followed by Symonds. Shairp ('Honest, but dull', reported *The Oxford and Cambridge Undergraduate's Journal*) was elected.

It is not surprising that Pater began to react sharply – in a way that looked to some acquaintances priggish – about anything that might set old suspicions vibrating. When Oscar Browning thought he would be amused by being mentioned as the person who had approved of an Eton boy reading *Mademoiselle de Maupin,* he opened his stern, basically frightened letter of rebuttal with positively Victorian moral fervour: 'I was not at all amused . . . I should greatly disapprove of its being lent to any boy or young man . . . Such statements misrepresent and pain me profoundly.'

Hester and Clara may not always have learnt the reasons, but Pater's pain and discouragement – possibly at times even despair – were not missed by them. In sharing with them, however obliquely, such moments, he probably felt assuaged. Their indignation on his behalf, their belief in him, their admiring companionship must all have brought tranquillity back to the exquisite, austerely luminous drawing-room overlooking the garden at Bradmore Road. The Morris wallpaper, the spindle-legged tables and chairs, the blue plates and the 'Indian turquoise vase' represented peace if not happiness. 'The love of security, of an habitually undisputed standing-ground or sleeping-place', he was to say of Florian, 'came to count . . . afterwards as a salutary principle of restraint in all his wanderings of spirit.'

After publication of *Studies in the History of the Renaissance* Pater had, for a time, little urge to wander, and perhaps not much wish to be alone. What he should write next, whether indeed he could go on writing, must have seemed doubtful. Over a year elapsed before he appeared again in print, with an article in *The Fortnightly* on the eminently safe topic of Wordsworth. Literature altogether, and especially English literature, seems now to have attracted him as a subject on which to write. It can scarcely be an accident that he turned away – in print, at least – from the visual arts. Some curbing of that 'lust of the eye' which was actually among his greatest gifts was perhaps expiation for the too-overt hedonism of his first book. It may even have been something tacitly required by the circumstances of his life with Hester and Clara, where under all the admiration and companionship there was possibly a certain gentle pressure to conform. It may have come as a secret relief to them that in republishing *The Renaissance* he dropped its 'Conclusion'.

Essays on Lamb, Rossetti and Sir Thomas Browne appeared at

intervals during the subsequent years: people partly chosen perhaps because they were idiosyncratic, if not lesser, figures in English literature, having personal meaning for Pater. He had met Rossetti. With Lamb he shared the associations of Enfield. Browne's *Vulgar Errors* he owned an early edition of, but might anyway be stirred by a writer who had been a doctor, who mused so much on death and was master of a freakish yet wonderfully sonorous prose style. And this surprisingly long, sympathetically critical essay is the most successful of the three.

More ambitiously, Pater seems as early as 1875 to have considered preparing a book on Shakespeare. Although nothing came of this project as such, he produced one or two essays typically on the then less familiar plays, beginning with one on *Measure for Measure* which he had had no opportunity to see acted. Youthful memories of what he had seen performed were to come back to him, mingling maybe with recollections of his own boyhood acting experiences. When much later he dealt with the subject of 'Shakespeare's English Kings', it was, perhaps inevitably, on Richard II that he focused. From a distance of over thirty years he recalled the authentic appearance and 'winning pathos' of Charles Kean's performance, and the 'tasteful archaeology' which had re-created Chaucer's London. Kean's *Richard II* had been put on in 1858, during Pater's penultimate year at the King's School. At the Speech Day of 1858, when Pater recited the *Morte d'Arthur*, it was Dombrain who played Richard II in an extract from the great opening scene of Act III.

In *Measure for Measure* what he claimed to see as the main interest was the relation of brother and sister, of Claudio and Isabella, but in fact this relationship meant less to him than the spectacle of Claudio, 'a flowerlike young man', confronting death. It is there that his imagination lingered: 'Set in the horrible blackness of the prison . . . this flower seems the braver.' Over the play hangs the shadow of death, 'blanching the features of youth', and coming capriciously, as Pater recalls it in a momentary recapturing of his Italian travels with Shadwell, as 'in Orcagna's fresco at Pisa'.

So when he wrote of *Love's Labour's Lost*, he felt drawn to the slight, semi-foppish persons of the story: Biron, 'the perfect flower of this manner', and the group generally who possess – he says significantly – 'that winning attractiveness which there is no man but would willingly exercise'. Again death intervenes, 'and Shakespeare strikes a passionate note . . . in the entrance of the messenger, who announces to the princess that the king her father is suddenly dead.' The deposing and dying of Richard II stole virtually the whole of Pater's essay, purportedly on all Shakespeare's English kings. Royal, handsome, flawed, self-pitying and poetic, Richard was bound to become a hero for Pater; he is indeed the very type of Pater's imaginary portraits – a sort of kingly anticipation of Emerald Uthwart, and like him tragically degraded. 'It is as if Shakespeare had had in mind some such inverted rite, like those old ecclesiastical or military ones . . . as in some long, agonising ceremony.' These are the people the world destroys, but part of their glamour lies in that doom.

All the praised 'domestic affections' and 'devotion of his family life', which both Bussell and Shadwell stressed as an essential aspect of Pater, proved no real bulwark against the ceaseless, obsessive conflict of physical beauty and mortality which had once excited him and was gradually saddening him. A quiet trip with Hester and Clara to Brittany or to the châteaux of the Loire, an evening of talk or a select dinner party at Bradmore Road – such things could only briefly keep at bay the sense of isolation and apprehension of the future.

He had violently and notoriously rejected Christianity, but perhaps there was some truth, as there was some comfort, in it. He had proclaimed his belief in a life of sensations, but they passed, leaving him unsatisfied. He had experienced piercing intimations of beauty, depicted things unseen by other people, and evoked them in writing as precisely as he could – in ways that led to his growing fame, to the response of other writers, to the dedication of books to him; and yet he remained perhaps puzzled by his own restless personality.

He was living with Hester and Clara, who had been part of his consciousness from its earliest years. Together they had established a home at least emotionally similar to that of their childhood, and though they might move they probably all three understood that they would never separate until separated by death. In Pater's childhood lay some explanation of the individual he was – had always been. He had searched for it in works of art, found it partly in the *persona* he reconstructed for Coleridge and Winckelmann and Leonardo da Vinci, real figures, nevertheless, who were ultimately far more than his creation. To explain and express his personality, he needed the freedom of a fictional *persona*. Instead of probing the psychology of an existing painted portrait, like the *Mona Lisa*, he would paint in words an 'imaginary' portrait, at once what he was and what he had dreamt of being.

Eleven   'What came of him?'

IN APRIL 1878 Pater sent the editor of *Macmillan's Magazine* an unsolicited piece of prose of an unexpected, even unique kind, so personal that he wished it to appear anonymously. It was called *The House and the Child*.

Rather sporadically, in various periodicals, he had been publishing essays on topics that attracted him, but on none of which did he seem able to settle. He had probably revised that earlier unprinted essay on *The School of Giorgione* which first appeared in *The Fortnightly* in 1877 and which he would later include in editions of *The Renaissance*. There were his articles on English literature. He also turned to a subject he had neglected to write on perhaps because it was so close to his daily teaching: classical Greece. Dealing with the myth of Demeter and Persephone (the subject of two lectures he had given at Birmingham), and on Dionysus, he spoke with the authority of a scholar, but his thoughts drifted again and again into the alluring, dangerous, if not forbidden, territory of the visual arts. When he pondered on the symbolic meaning of Demeter, he mentioned Giotto, Blake, Corot, and even the peasants of Millet. He set Dionysus not only in a classical context but in a Renaissance one, mentioning Titian and Tintoretto's treatment of the god, and also that by early Italian engravers. His Dionysus is the god of water as well as wine, and he suddenly introduces Giorgione's *Fête champêtre* among the associations and 'the sound of the fresh water flowing through the wooden pipes into the houses of Venice'. Old gods are seen retaining a strange vitality; and it may have been while thinking deeply about the implications of the Greek religion that Pater's thoughts first came back to the question of his own beliefs. It is hard not to feel he had himself in mind when he afterwards wrote of Euripides composing the *Bacchae*, 'in that subdued mood . . . in which accustomed ideas, conformable to a sort of common sense regarding the unseen, oftentimes regain what they may have lost, in a man's allegiance.'

The House and the Child was totally unlike anything Pater had produced before. It was the result of a recognition which had probably been increasing in him that childhood is the formative period of the

156

personality: he had strongly hinted as much in writing of Leonardo, and had imaginatively touched in passing on the childhood of Coleridge and of Winckelmann. In examining *Love's Labour's Lost* he had, with a flash of Baudelaire-like insight, referred to the seriousness of play and the real appreciation which lies under children's love of toys.

Now it was his own childhood which he explored, which he perhaps felt urged to explore to release some inhibiting tension in himself. He was in his late thirties – not old, but he may well have felt old when he looked back and wondered how it had all happened, how he had come to be the person he was. It began with a house, that *old house* at Enfield, in which he had grown to full consciousness, and it seemed to end when the family left it, about the time he was twelve, for Canterbury. By then, the elements of his personality had become fixed: the personality which he proceeded to portray under the guise of the romantic sounding, flower-like Florian (a name with a good deal more music in it, he doubtless thought, than existed in Walter), whose French, faintly aristocratic surname of Deleal extends the suggestions of a refined and delicate – almost chivalric – character, a symbolic flower of loyalty or truth.

Like the opening of a fairy tale or medieval story of a saint (and Florian is the name of a Roman soldier saint), the essay begins *in medias res* with precise, almost naïve clarity, possibly in deliberate imitation of Flaubert's method in *La Légende de Saint Julien l'Hospitalier*. That was one of *Trois Contes*, published in 1877; Pater owned a copy and later in 1877 lent it to Wilde.

'As Florian Deleal walked, one hot afternoon, he overtook by the wayside a poor aged man, and, as he seemed weary with the road, helped him on with the burden which he carried, a certain distance.' Florian's charitable action has something saint-like in it, and there is something of the same atmosphere in his being visited that night by a dream, 'like a reward for his pity'. The man has told his story to Florian, and in so doing named the place, 'a little place in the neighbourhood of a great city' where Florian spent his earliest years but to which he has never returned. Florian is no longer young. Almost thirty years have elapsed since he was there, but it and especially the house he had lived in now return in his dream: 'the fashion of its doors, its hearths, its windows, the very scent upon the air of it . . .'

And so, on waking, Florian lies meditating on that environment and on himself as the child he sees 'moving in the house and garden of his dream'. The lineaments of the rooms recur to him in all their trim detail, as if once again he was a boy passing up and down the stairs, marvelling at the little angel faces 'and reedy flutings' which

157

stood out round the fireplace in the children's room, climbing again into the 'wonderland' of the attic and finally out on the flat space of the roof. Over the adult Florian nostalgia sweeps strong as the scent of the lime tree flowers which used to fall on him and his mother as she taught him to read by the window.

Every particle of the visible, sensible world once pressing as so novel on the responsive boy floats again before him, with heightened effect. He recalls all its painful, feverish beauty – as in discovering one evening 'a plumage of tender, crimson fire' in a flowering red hawthorn – and also the stirrings of the awareness of pain itself. The starling caught and caged to be his pet was cried for at night by its young, crying in response; and in the early morning he went down and released it, and saw how it bounded up to its nestlings. Then he felt remorse at how even a small child had power to operate the machine of things which could play 'pain-fugues on the delicate nerve-work of living creatures'. The very flame of the crimson hawthorn pulsed gradually away; in plucking it he had not possessed it, though 'A touch of regret or desire mingled all night with the remembered presence of the red flowers . . .' And thus there seemed for him, already as a child, no real refuge against the creeping fear of mortality. His father had died abroad and might – as he imagined after overhearing the story of a sick woman summoned by a ghost – return to haunt the house, breaking its enchanted air of security.

Florian can never rid himself of that basic fear. In the finest house of the spirit there is yet somewhere a 'chamber of death'. Across the bright carpet or amid the most cheerful company a shadow may abruptly be cast. Powerful as the spell of physical beauty always is for him, it can be dissolved by the intrusive image of a corpse, with the bound chin, the quaint smile, the straight, stiff feet.

In creating and portraying Florian Deleal, Pater had been free to mould his material in a way none of his previous subjects had allowed. He was not even attempting straight autobiography, but something vaguely comparable to certain essays by Lamb (like *Dream-children* and *Mackery End*, the latter about the return to an old house known in childhood) which he must have been re-reading at some time on or before 1878 for his article on Lamb. The exact mixture of real and fanciful was skilfully concocted, and the psychological framework of of the story, with Florian's dream instigated by a chance encounter, carefully devised. The mention of carvings round the fireplace in the 'children's room' suggests a deliberate fusion of fantasy and one or more of the actual rooms with such unusual carving in houses like Great Hadlow Hall in Kent, which he had probably visited as a child. The result is deliberately dreamlike in being allusive and half-

158

mysterious, yet no less dreamlike in its sharply vivid details and utter conviction.

Pater guards himself against saying too much to associate him and Florian on any simple, factual level (and he either suggested or at least welcomed the study being published as an 'imaginary' portrait); but once reborn under a more graceful name, he must have felt the full liberty to depict himself, which was the purpose of writing the piece. Even so, not all was told, and some inhibitions remained.

Florian is confined, in effect, to his house and garden; unlike Pater at Enfield, he does not go to school. Nor is anything said of his fondness for dressing-up as a priest, though he yields easily to 'religious impressions'. The distant death of his father is mentioned but nothing suggests the presence, let alone death, of a grandmother – unless that grim image of the body with 'the bound chin' is Pater's allusion to an event which he was perhaps not yet ready to recall. All these are things which he was to incorporate in the childhood of his later imaginary people – the children of Florian, or at least his brothers. Without this first and most personal portrayal they could not possibly have existed; and it was no doubt in recognition of that fact that Pater made the note to himself, already quoted, about this portrait being 'the germinating, original, source, specimen' of all his imaginative work.

Although there is no need to labour the point that Florian *is* Pater in a way that most of his later imaginary people patently are not, especially in age, Pater himself significantly identifies with Florian at the outset, regardless of age or childhood. Quite unlike all the later people portrayed, Florian is trying to recover the stages of growth of his own personality. His dream of being back once more in the old home is not merely the impetus for an agreeable retrospect; it serves, Pater explicitly says, as 'just the thing needed for the beginning of a certain design he then had in view, the noting, namely, of some things in the story of his spirit – in that process of brain-building by which we are, each one of us, what we are.' Florian wants to understand himself, to grasp – if not indeed to put on paper – an outline of his own history.

Pater was in reality beginning to do that in devising this portrait, which he emphasized to the editor of *Macmillan's Magazine* was 'complete in itself' and not 'the first part of a work of fiction'. Yet it was to be, he also emphasized, the first of a series, 'with some real kind of sequence in them'. He called it a portrait. It was meant, he said, to prompt in its readers the sort of speculation that might be prompted by seeing a painted portrait: 'what came of him?'

That was how Pater felt on first completing it. He obviously

159

thought it privately required some explanation and was at the same time excited, confident, about producing further portraits, possibly of rather similar personalities to be seen at later stages, 'in that process of brain-building'. These might to some extent answer speculations aroused by Florian's portrait, for Pater probably guessed there would be affinities among people created by him who are – however varied their circumstances or appearance – very much reflections of him.

Gradually, too, he may have found himself wanting to answer the question by a more sustained account, which should not stop with the subject's childhood. Instead of prompting speculation about the character's future, it should provide – as it were – a full-length portrait which would carry the story from childhood through adult life and up to the close of life, exorcizing his fear of death by describing the character's death: a complete biography of an imaginary person.

How far Pater had really thought of such an ambitious project when he first conceived the sketch of Florian Deleal is unclear. To begin with, it might have been enough to have completed this evocation of his own childhood and to have expressed so subtly much of what had obsessed him since the days of Enfield and Canterbury, when it had culminated in the poem, *Watchman, what of the night?*, with its desperate cry, 'it seems so awful not to be'.

The editor of *Macmillan's Magazine*, (Sir) George Grove, was an unusually literate musicologist and a polymath, who seems to have been enthusiastic about the essay. At his persuasion Pater agreed to put his name to it, and at some point before its publication in August 1878 its title was changed to the more exact one of *The Child in the House*. Either Grove or Pater gave the piece a heading, 'Imaginary Portraits', and added the number '1' beside its title. Both editor and author certainly expected the series to continue. But by December Pater had to confess that he was not ably to supply another instalment, 'just yet', adding to his letter a disarming paragraph about meaning to read Grove's own article on Beethoven, which he had heard praised and which had appeared in one of the first parts of Grove's *Dictionary of Music and Musicians*.

Over the course of the next decade, under Grove's energetic editorship, his classic *Dictionary* proceeded to completion. But the promised second imaginary portrait by Pater never appeared in *Macmillan's Magazine*, and the sequence remained where it had begun. Pater did send the periodical all four of his later studies (*A Prince of Court Painters*, etc.) published afterwards in the volume entitled *Imaginary Portraits* (1887) but they were not so titled in the magazine and had no link with *The Child in the House*. By the time they began to appear, Grove had anyway ceased to be editor. Readers might well be left wondering what came of the series as well as of Florian.

In fact, Pater had begun – probably about 1878 – and gone a considerable way with a second portrait, positively numbered '2', called *An English Poet*. Although he had pleaded to Grove that his delay was on account of temporary pressure of other work, it looks as if he did not finish or submit this portrait because it dissatisfied him. He left the manuscript among his papers (and it was eventually published by Clara's one-time pupil May Ottley, who with her husband inherited Hester's entire estate).

Whereas the theme of the first 'portrait' had been the recapturing of the sensations of early childhood within a suburban domestic setting (obviously close to the writer's experience), the second portrait's theme is at once more ambitious and more fanciful – and altogether more truly imaginary in many of its incidents. The poet hero (he has no name) is the son of an Englishwoman living rather mournfully with her husband on an isolated Normandy farm. Before his birth the mother has glimpsed a blonde, Apollo-like stranger, whose head resembles an ancient coin dug up on the farm, and emotionally at least the child is Apollo's. The mother, languid after the birth, dies. The orphaned boy is sent to Cumberland and grows up to be a poet.

His childhood is rather mistily described, pierced sometimes with details echoing Florian's sensations (a red honeysuckle in flower replaces the hawthorn as an intimation of beauty), but it extends into his schooldays (when wistfully he fancies 'on the faces of ruddy schoolboys the pressure of their mothers' kisses, and between their lips the milk teeth still'). The brain-building described is meant to show the development of a poet, one doomed probably to early death, but the effect is unfocused and uneasy, in its setting not quite contemporary and yet not clearly historical. The poet is Pater and yet not Pater (who had never been in Cumberland but chose it possibly for its associations with Wordsworth), and this dichotomy flaws the tone of the story. It needed to be resolved by a much better applied artistic discipline.

An English Poet was abandoned, and also abandoned was Pater's proposal, welcomed by Macmillan, for a new volume of his collected essays. The volume was to include *The School of Giorgione*, its first intended title, and the recent studies in English and Greek literature (*Dionysus* was the second title selected). When in November 1878 Pater read the essays in proof he found they contained 'so many inadequacies' that he decided against publication, to Macmillan's surprise and regret. And in 1879 he published nothing; it was the first interruption to annual appearances in print, if only as a reviewer, over the previous eleven years. Although he resumed in 1880, with essays based on his lectures on the beginnings of Greek sculpture, he let the next two years pass silently. In 1883 he partly abandoned Brasenose, resigning his tutorship there and not going abroad during the summer vacation. Again in 1884, nothing by him was published.

It was early in March 1885 that the silence was effectively broken and publicly explained. For the first and last time Pater brought to completion a book – not a collection of revised essays or lectures. Although it was set with scrupulous scholarship in the time of Marcus Aurelius, it was not a contribution to knowledge of the period. It was a sustained portrait of an invented, non-historical figure, a biography in two volumes of a fictional person: *Marius the Epicurean*. And the title page immediately made it clear that this was a story of the Roman world not in terms of characters and romantic adventures (no *Last Days of Pompeii*) but in terms of a mind ('a peculiar type of mind', Pater himself called it in a letter to Vernon Lee). It was about Marius the Epicurean, *His Sensations and Ideas*. In this long-laboured-over book lay many things, not least Pater's answer to the speculations that he had hoped to raise by his portrayal of Florian Deleal. A final, sly, slightly cryptic clue to the nature of the book is given by its Greek epigraph, quoting but not attributing a phrase from Lucian's *Somnus*: 'A winter dream, when the nights are longest.' That comment is put by Lucian into the mouth of someone criticizing his recital of a dream he had as a boy in this autobiographical work concerned with his childhood. It acts as a hint perhaps that though there is plenty of imagination in *Marius* not everything about its central personality should be supposed imaginary. That Lucian himself should appear in the book is only the more apt.

A germ of the work possibly went back to the time that Pater conceived *The Child in the House*, when he first felt the urge to turn away from appreciation of the arts and note instead 'some things in the story of his spirit'. He needed time for what became a major task, the scale of which he may have perceived only as he realized that *An English Poet* was inadequate to continue what *The Child* . . . had begun, and that he must produce not a sequence of short portraits but a single study in depth. That he chose the period of Marcus Aurelius is not surprising. He needed anyway a period when the alternatives of paganism and Christianity co-existed. His interest in Marcus Aurelius, a popular figure in nineteenth-century eyes, may have dated back to reading Arnold's essay on him which had appeared first in the *Victoria Magazine* in November 1863 – that year of anxious hiatus in Pater's life. It was there that Arnold declared that the Aurelian age was 'akin to our own' and Marcus Aurelius 'a man like ourselves.'

Time passed as Pater brooded, wrote, revised, paused and then wrote again. His mind was altering as he wrote on. Like Marius he was undergoing a slow process of almost reluctant discovery, exchanging old reckless certainties for new, more elusive and yet soothing beliefs. In essence it was a shift from sensations to ideas: the progress made by Marius, expressed in the book characteristically by his replacing love for the poetic and pagan Flavian by friendship with the Christian soldier Cornelius. For Marius there comes a day when the purely material world ('the immemorial rocks, the firm marble, the olive gardens, the falling water') seems to become unreal and he apprehends an ideal world, an ideal being and a creator whose existence makes him less lonely and afraid. In place of the flux in which Pater had once felt whirled along – and out of which only fragments of perception could be seized in passing – there comes the hope of 'an abiding-place'. That Pater himself had begun to change was noted by Mrs Humphry Ward about the period *Marius* was in hand. When she, 'reckoning confidently on his sympathy', said she thought orthodoxy must soon break down under so much current attack, he shook his head and looked troubled. He could not agree it was all so simple. He felt there was a mystery, a 'something' inexplicable; and he cited as supernatural a saying that might well have comforted Marius on his solitary way through the world: 'Come unto me, all ye that are weary and heavy laden.'

Outwardly, Pater's life changed little during the years of writing *Marius*. He made new acquaintances, a few warming into real friends like the quirkily clever Vernon Lee and the handsome, golden-haired young poet William Sharp, both of whom learnt something of what he was writing and both of whom dedicated books to him in admiring terms. A letter of Vernon Lee's, written just after her first meeting with Pater in July 1881, speaks of his meditating on spending a vacation near Rome, 'in order to work on his new book on Mythology' – probably a very early reference to *Marius*. By the following summer (when she stayed with the Paters at Oxford in their 'dainty and dapper little house') she knew he was writing 'something . . . in the way of a novel about the time of Marcus Aurelius'. To Sharp Pater referred in November 1882 to work on hand and of his forthcoming visit to Rome, 'where I have never yet been'.

This winter visit was made without his sisters and almost furtively. He seems to have stayed for about a month, spending Christmas there on his own. Hester politely told Vernon Lee afterwards that he had been much obliged by the introductions she gave him, 'and was very sorry he had no time to use any . . . He found he had to give all his time to the galleries and churches and was so tired in the evening . . .' No doubt Pater was tired (he had before leaving complained of the weather 'binding up one's arteries': a premonition of his later gout and lameness), but no doubt also he guarded his privacy. Some of his later letters are quite funny in their social evasions and courteously firm refusals to get too involved. His shyness with strangers, especially abroad, was thought odd by Victorian contemporaries like Mandell Creighton, who recorded that Pater would leave a foreign hotel if a stranger spoke to him. He had come to Rome for a purpose; how seriously he took that purpose is shown by his making the journey in mid-winter and by himself, and staying there so comparatively long.

'Even greater than his curiosity . . .', he wrote of Marius, 'was his eagerness to look out upon Rome itself . . . an oft repeated dream realized at last.' And he was able to insert amid his description of the ancient city an occasional reference to the 'modern visitor', now marvelling like Marius at the noisy strength of Roman throats and now noting in the Capitoline and other museums the family likeness among the Antonines.

Yet although Pater had gone to Rome as part of the discipline *Marius* seemed to require, to make the portrait of the age more authentic, it was in certain ways an irrelevant journey. It is the goal reached at last by Marius towards the end of the first volume, and for him the imperial city and the Emperor – one outwardly so splendid and the other so serene – prove a disillusionment. That is the turning-point of the book, which from then onwards moves gradually away from Rome physically as Marius moves closer to Christianity, retreating first to his own ancestral home, and then, sacrificing himself for Cornelius and conscious of the great hope, that 'hope against hope . . .', into a final *diminuendo* mood of death softened by Christian rites: 'Gentle fingers had applied to hands and feet, to all those old passage-ways of the senses, through which the world had come and gone for him, now so dim and obstructed, a medicinable oil.'

For Pater Rome was no turning-point. Almost certainly he had, from the first, conceived the theme of the book to be how someone came to surrender a life of sensations for a life of ideas, or at least an apprehension of the ideal. The someone was, of course, himself, and for all the care which he takes (especially in the first volume) to set Marius in the Italy of Marcus Aurelius, the setting itself is ultimately irrelevant. By the time Pater wrote the significant chapter 'Second Thoughts' (the second chapter of the second volume), he was virtually

164

confessing as much: 'That age and our own have much in common – many difficulties and hopes. Let the reader pardon me if here and there I seem to passing from Marius to his modern representatives – from Rome, to Paris or London.' And this chapter moves so far from Marius altogether, and from any attempt to retain the historical framework, that it does indeed speak of 'Life in modern London . . . in the heavy glow of summer' and returns to the character of Claudio in *Measure for Measure*. A few chapters later there appear in the text Giotto, Dante, St Francis of Assisi, St Louis of France and even Mantegna.

What the month in Rome probably gave Pater was, ironically enough, not so much the opportunity for absorbing authentic period detail as the opportunity of total, perfect isolation in which to gauge his own state of mind. The toga of Marius is scarcely any longer assumed, and certainly no longer conceals the author once Rome is reached. The second half of the book seems to have been started only after Pater's return from Italy in the new year of 1883. Its tone is far more openly personal than the first part – almost tragically so in the chapter significantly entitled 'Sunt lacrimae rerum', where Marius himself is allowed to speak out from his journal with observations that have a poignant, confessional air. There is the affecting sight of a fine but damaged race-horse being led to slaughter: '. . . and I think the animal knew it.' Several times the 'I' of the journal witnesses minute incidents of family life among the very poor, like the daily spectacle of the bricklayer's small daughter who runs so fondly to welcome her father on his return from work. And incidents like these, the narrator finds, leave him sadly concluding 'that I, for one, have failed in love.' Perhaps that realization – made more resonant in the book at least by the hero's deepening sense of his own loneliness – swept most intensely over Pater during those solitary days spent in Rome.

He came back to England and continued slowly to work on the book. By the summer he talked of hoping to get 'one half of my present chief work' soon completed. It was at this time that, in Sharp's words, he was writing and rewriting the book 'with infinite loving care for every phrase . . .' It was at this time too that William Pater became seriously ill, and was probably thought going to die. Through most of June and July, this illness darkened the Oxford household, taking Hester and Clara away in turn to look after William and leaving Pater himself depressed. Only towards the end of July could Pater record that the account of his brother had been 'of late hopeful'.

A sense of death is never far away in *Marius*. Almost the first thing noted in the opening pages of the hero as a young boy is his feeling about an upright stone, 'still with mouldering garlands about it,' which marks the spot where an aged labourer died. But death hangs even more heavily over the close of the book, not merely over Marius but over the bright figure of the hopeful, handsome, soldierly Cornelius whom he looks on with fraternal affection. It is to save Cornelius from such a possibility that he obscurely intervenes when they are both taken prisoner. 'He had delivered his brother,' Marius muses, as Cornelius goes free and he, Marius, is left in his place, physically weary and utterly dejected, and yet conscious of having almost unexpectedly shown courage ('. . . he felt only satisfaction . . . at the discovery of his possession of "nerve" '). Ill, lonely and worn out, Marius dies; but since he has associated with Christians and in effect given his life for one, his death is accounted by them a sort of martyrdom. And so he dies in a state of grace.

Both Pater and his brother survived the summer of 1883, though William possibly never recovered entirely and had only three more summers to live. Nor need Pater ever have thought in terms of positively sacrificing himself, although he might easily have felt that William's unselfish career made him the more important to humanity. Even the nature of his medical care seems to find a mention when Marius sees the world 'as a hospital for sick persons; many of them sick in mind,' and glimpses a peasant couple bringing an old woman, 'now past work and witless, to place her in a house provided for such afflicted people'. His good looks and his early attraction towards the army give him other affinities with Cornelius (and he may have had a simpler, more firmly held religious faith than Pater's, manifested perhaps during his serious illness).

As Pater laboured on at *Marius*, his identification with his hero grew still closer and more transparent. By the summer of 1884 – a year he kept free of all other writing commitments – he must have been moving towards the end of his task. When Vernon Lee stayed with the Paters for a few days in June, he read to her in the afternoons parts of the book (she shrewdly noted, 'fine, but I think lacking in vitality'). On 4 August that year he celebrated his forty-fifth birthday, approaching the finish of his book at the exact age his father had died.

In its penultimate chapter Marius goes home: back to the old villa, White-Nights, and down into the dusty, now neglected tomb where his family and their servants are buried. He has come back to the point from which he (and the book) set out when he was a grave young boy dutifully visiting the memorials of his family. In the vault he sees the urn of his father – that figure who had always seemed to him a little cold, severe and awe-inspiring. As he looks once more at his urn, 'That hard feeling . . . which had always lingered in his mind with the thought of the father he had scarcely known, melted wholly away . . .' He reads the precise number of his father's years and suddenly reflects, – 'He was of my own present age; no hard old man, but with interests, as he looked round him on the world for the last time, even as mine today!'

That realization is accompanied by a release from inhibition and new warmth of emotion ('. . . a blinding rush of kindness, as if two alienated friends had come to understand each other at last,' is Pater's interesting simile). Completion and publication of the long, arduous task of self-exploration which is *Marius* brought Pater perhaps other reconciliations, as it certainly brought him new assurance. He had traced, with painful honesty, the far from straight path which led from the days of *Studies in the History of the Renaissance* to the close of *Marius*. In doing so, he had actually gone much further back, into the past of his childhood when he had felt – and, above all, had *seen* – the sensuous beauty of the visible world, and had also experienced 'an early boyish ideal of priesthood' (as he describes it in *Marius*). He had told of his youthful love, imagined possibly but none the less desired and passionately conveyed, for a graceful, gifted figure called Flavian, into whose bed Marius gets on the night he is dying, 'to lend him his own warmth'. He had let Flavian (whose name recalls Florian) die young, in fascinated fearful detail, punishing his own sensuousness, it may be, in the mortal fever, coughing and vomiting which humiliate and destroy that beautiful and dearly loved being. And he had carried his own story onwards, even beyond the semi-quiescent, wistful state of mind in which he hoped he believed, calming his Claudio-like horror of death by devising for Marius a gentle, blessed death, a slipping away – as it were – between paganism and Christianity ('neither for God nor for his enemies', might be said also of him), with all the 'passage-ways of the senses' soothed into final oblivion.

In a creative way Pater rapidly displayed what *Marius* had given him. He began writing a varied series of 'imaginary portraits' much more truly imaginary but still in careful historical settings. In sheer literary activity, he seemed re-animated; for the rest of his life no year passed without something by him being published. His fame increased. He was sought out as a reviewer, begged to contribute to new periodicals, invited to lecture. 'Myself overloaded with it [work]', he sighed in 1890. 'I have undertaken to do a great deal during the course of the next few months,' he was explaining to a correspondent in March 1894. 'I have been and am very busy,' he reported to another in mid-May. By August he was dead.

167

Marius had been a success from the first. The reviews were long, very friendly and respectful. A second edition was needed within four months. By the time it was published Pater had taken a significant step, an advance rather than a retreat, symbolizing his new confident mood and perhaps also his wish to disassociate himself from Oxford. He gave up the house in Bradmore Road, though not his fellowship, and moved with Hester and Clara to London.

When a third edition of *The Renaissance* was required (in 1888), he felt sure enough to put back the 'Conclusion', supplementing the footnote about previously having dropped it with the for him almost boastful sentence, 'I have dealt more fully in *Marius the Epicurean* with the thoughts suggested by it.' Characteristically, this statement conceals more than it reveals, but at least it documents the connection between the two books and it suggests how Pater saw *Marius* as something of an apology, as well as an *apologia*, for having published that first daring, even shocking, work.

Of all the reviewers of *Marius* probably only Mrs Ward had known Pater at the period when he had caused scandal in Oxford. Nobody was better placed to understand the personal history which underlay the story of *Marius*, and she began her review by emphasizing the vein of disguised autobiography so often preferred by English writers to memoirs. She mentioned *The Child in the House* as a first attempt at the form, remarking rather sharply, 'it was not disguise enough'. *Marius* she found far more successful and more integrated; she praised its style and its scholarship, though she thought it intellectually weak in its rather aesthetic response to Christianity. And she firmly pointed to its fundamental, confessional basis: 'No one can fail to catch the autobiographical note . . .'

Twelve   At home in London

ON MONDAYS, around 5 p.m., Pater was usually at home to
visitors at 12, Earl's Terrace, the house he had taken in Kensington. When Vernon Lee stayed there in 1886 she thought it 'much
prettier and in better taste' than the Robinsons' house further along
the terrace, 'but it is rather triste'. The discreetly elegant terrace,
almost opposite the grounds of Holland House and set back from the
High Street behind a line of shrubbery and trees, had been built in
the first decade of the nineteenth century, about the same time as
Commercial Road. Few of Pater's visitors commented on the house,
except to find it drab, and its exterior probably seemed to them plain
to the point of meagreness. The severity of the terrace certainly contrasted with the showy and more recent development in and around
Melbury Road where famous artists like Marcus Stone, Watts and
Leighton lived in individually designed, consciously artistic houses.
That Pater had chosen Earl's Terrace was probably ascribed to his
lack of means rather than to any discrimination.

He retained No. 12 until the summer of 1893, the penultimate
year of his life. By then Saturday had been added, or substituted, as
an 'at home' day when acquaintances might take tea with him and
Hester (Clara remaining in residence for considerable periods at
Somerville). Occasionally there were dinner parties, small, quiet and
carefully arranged, 'to meet a few friends', who extended from Vernon
Lee, Edmund Gosse and the poet Arthur Symons to a new generation
of undergraduates including Douglas Ainslie, who had apparently
been introduced to Pater by Wilde. Ainslie was the nephew of Sir
Mountstuart Grant Duff, a Scottish politician and writer for long a
cultivator of Pater's company, and he himself became a diplomat and
writer. He was already writing soon after being an undergraduate at
Exeter College, and his blank verse drama *Escarlamonde* was dutifully
read by Pater in proof ('. . . as you know, the dramatic form of
literature is not what I usually turn to with most readiness . . . a very
sound performance on a novel subject . . . it contains proof of your
capacity for good literary work').

Ainslie might be invited to dinner in brief yet unusually warm
terms: 'Please come and dine . . . and give pleasure to Yours very

truly Walter Pater.' But he was only one of the group of aspirant writers and generally rather minor writers who constituted Pater's circle of visitors. Social life – within his own discreet and firmly defined limits – had no doubt always been part of Pater's concept of an urbane, ordered existence. Space must be given to the relaxing ritual of a walk or some tea and conversation towards the end of the day, and he made a point of never working at all in the evening (according to Bussell's testimony).

Photographs of Pater can give only a slight idea of the figure found by the visitor encouraged to call on an 'at home' day. But at least he was photographed, by Elliott and Fry around 1889. The period was fond of sending and exchanging portrait-photographs of this kind. As an undergraduate, Wilde had sent Pater his photograph; in thanking him for it, Pater explained that he had already obtained a copy from Guggenheim (the Oxford photographer). Although Pater disliked his own appearance, he sent Arthur Symons his photograph (probably the Elliott and Fry one), at Symons' request, and welcomed a photograph of Symons. To a female enquirer for a photograph he wrote with unnecessary caution that he 'believed' Elliott and Fry had one of him. A later enquirer, Arthur Waugh, father of Alec and Evelyn, received one, 'the latest taken', with the comment that Pater never quite liked photographs of himself.

The photograph by Elliott and Fry provides some sort of check on descriptions of Pater, especially in his later years, and also hints at the subdued dandyism which expressed itself in scrupulous neatness, with smart gloves, top hat and gold-topped umbrella – the figure well conveyed in a gentle, clever, uncaricatured sketch by a Brasenose undergraduate. The spotted silk tie apparent in the photograph suggests that though Pater may have modified his taste for bright apple-green ties, as he had modified so much on the surface, he yet continued to indicate by such touches his basic unconventionality. And perhaps the unreliable Thomas Wright was more reliable than usual when he recorded how a youthful admirer of Pater's, Walter Harte, who had gone out to North America, was in the habit of sending him American ties so he might 'cut a jaunty figure'.

Rather heavily built, slightly stooping and beginning noticeably to limp, Pater disconcerted those who expected to meet an aesthete of the willowy kind *Punch* had started to ridicule. His appearance, and especially his large, pale, impassive face and prominent moustache, had for Sharp something Bismarckian about it. Several other people compared his air to that of a retired military man (a compliment Pater would have enjoyed, if he ever heard it). The young Charles Holmes (later director of the National Gallery) noticed and sketched the distinction between Pater's rather lustreless, untidy appearance at Oxford and the figure in 'smart top-hat and black jacket, with stiff clipped moustache, neatly rolled umbrella and dog-skin gloves', to be seen in London. Except for the dreamy look in his grey eyes, wrote Holmes, 'he might have been a retired major in the Rifle Brigade'. Vernon Lee had privately thought him at first meeting like Velazquez' portraits of Philip IV; he looked heavy, shy and dull, she wrote, as well as balder, fatter and uglier than his photograph. When 'Michael Field' (the pen-name adopted by Katharine Bradley and her niece Emma Cooper, joint authors of books of somewhat advanced lyric poetry) first called at Earl's Terrace on a Monday afternoon in July 1889, a few days before Pater's fiftieth birthday, they encountered a serious, quiet man, with 'constantly kind eyes', which Miss Cooper described as 'blue'. Most observers continued to comment on Pater's eyes and on their unusual light grey or grey-green colour.

To George Moore Pater merely had 'small eyes that shifted quickly', and his whole appearance as conveyed by Moore – furtive, uncouth and very ugly ('like a figure moulded out of lead') – underlines Moore's disappointment at Pater's reticence, disinclination for a good Irish gossip and his total failure to respond to Moore's idea of a great writer. Possibly, though such a thought is not likely to have occurred to Moore, Pater was no less disappointed with him – both physically and mentally. A less brash approach was anyway needed to charm Pater into animation, whereupon he exercised his own charm. The leaden figure described by Moore came to life, and even the admittedly plain, heavy face was lightened. A visit by the sympathetic undergraduate Lionel Johnson to Pater in Kensington, in 1889, revealed his host as in 'radiant spirits and most delightful'; and Johnson, in reporting this visit to a friend, added, 'London transfigures him'.

Similarly, Arthur Symons, whose work Pater enthusiastically admired and reviewed, came to discover Pater in middle age in the role of 'almost bustling' cicerone at Oxford and as a simple, affectionate man in his London home: picking up the great black Persian cat found on the way upstairs after dinner and in a 'perfectly natural way' kissing it and setting it down again carefully. This was the cat, he told Symons on another occasion, that had torn up the essay on Baudelaire presented to him by Paul Bourget, 'and as Baudelaire was such a lover of cats I thought she might have spared him!'

George Moore's misunderstandings about Pater extended to sending him a copy of his consciously realistic novel *A Mere Accident* (the accident being the rape of a girl by a tramp on the Sussex downs), in the expectation he would review it in *The Guardian*, an Anglican newspaper where, more suitably, Pater reviewed such work as *Robert Elsmere* and Symons' book on Browning. Pater's reply declining survives only in Moore's paraphrase, but even in that his bewilderment over the purpose of such a book is very clear (as Moore admitted). Pater had read Zola, and perhaps was less shocked by the novel than by the request— and also by the incongruous choice of place to review it.

Whatever is mildly comic about his relations with Moore broadens into near-farce with the replacement of Moore by Frank Harris, an unexpected admirer of Pater's prose, who sent him in 1891 his *Modern Idyll*, a short story dealing with a Baptist preacher tempted into sin by the flirtatious young wife of a middle-aged deacon. In a letter showing no indication of gulping over the strong meat of this, Pater wrote back praising the story's 'freshness, reality and proportion', and telling Harris to write more. This Harris later did. He assembled a series of *Contemporary Portraits*, based with varying degrees of authenticity on his acquaintance with eminent figures – among them Wagner, Tennyson, Wilde, Moore, Carlyle, Hardy, Maupassant and Browning – whom he had, or believed he had, met. Pater appears in the second volume of this series, published in 1919 and thus, technically, available to be read in old age by Hester, whose temper would not have been improved had she done so.

The quiet dinner at 12, Earl's Terrace to which Pater is said to have invited Harris may very well have taken place. To Harris (living in Park Lane, thanks to his wife's money, and entertaining peers, poets and at least one royal duke) the occasion would have been as sombre and drab as he describes the setting as being: 'The house might have belonged to a grocer.' That the grave, low-voiced conversation of Pater and his sisters, 'two colourless spinsters', subdued even Harris seems equally probable – certainly rather more convincing than the scenes of Harris in turn entertaining Pater with champagne, vintage port and a description of the body of a little cabaret dancer he had known in Montmartre (finer than any statue, and thus a victory for Harris and life over Pater and art). Pater, according to Harris, replied that he had often enjoyed seeing the undergraduates bathing in the river at Oxford.

In moving his household to London Pater had probably been drawn to the opportunity of making fresh acquaintances, if not quite as fresh as Harris, and – above all – of breaking the monotonous routine of life in Oxford. One thing Hester and Clara did say, Harris reported, was that they 'liked London best'. The publication of *Marius the Epicurean* had not only helped to rehabilitate Pater; it had consolidated his reputation as a literary figure. And yet the year of its successful reception, and re-printing, was the year of a further rebuff at Oxford, following Ruskin's final resignation of the Slade Professorship. Pater let his name go forward for election, perhaps hopeful of having no competitors within the university. He would have been in many ways the ideal successor to Ruskin, which he had already proved unofficially to be. Vernon Lee thought he deserved to be elected, but felt certain he would not be; and she was right. (Sir) Hubert von Herkomer, a German-born Associate of the Royal Academy who had founded the Herkomer School of Art, was elected, 'very absurdly', Vernon Lee remarked. He remained Slade Professor for the rest of Pater's life.

After such an Oxford experience, Pater might be the more glad to escape to London. What he in fact established was a pattern of convenient flitting between the two cities, providing him with – among other things – the occasion for avoiding social engagements by the excuse of leaving one place for the other. His letters seem often to have been written at the moment of departure: off to London . . . about to leave London . . . I must be in London . . . I am leaving for Oxford . . . unexpectedly have to leave tomorrow morning . . . one of my flying visits . . . in haste. And gradually over the years the refrain of haste loses any suggestion of evasiveness and becomes the total truth. The increasing burden of work, with perhaps a sense of diminishing energy, made the double life of London and Oxford too much. At the beginning of 1893 Pater was ill ('. . . able to read and write very little,' he told Katharine Bradley and her niece), and by the summer he had decided to give up 12, Earl's Terrace and settle once again in Oxford.

Nevertheless, the activity of the London years is itself a testimony to the exhilaration Pater must have felt, shuttling between the capital and Oxford with a freedom he had not had during the previous twenty years of his fellowship. In breaking routine, he had given himself the exact amount of liberty he required, without losing touch with friends and acquaintances (themselves often kept apart by him).

At the same time, he perhaps surprised himself by the ingenious twitches on the various literary lines he held in his hand – especially where reviews of his own books were concerned. Each new publication probably stirred, however irrationally, apprehensions of undergoing the trauma associated with first publication of *The Renaissance*. He also learnt how to be discouragingly diffuse when, for example, Herbert Horne wrote of their meeting in Italy since both were going to be there at the same period ('Our programme is a little uncertain and may become more so in execution'). Books kept arriving at Earl's Terrace, and it is hard not to think that Pater sometimes smiled as he devised subtly truthful acknowledgments. He was grateful to receive the homage of a volume of perceptive essays by Coventry Patmore, whom he did not know, but less at ease with an offering from 'Michael Field': 'a sterling piece of literary work. I feel, however, that I don't deserve this handsome present.' When Lady Dilke (as Mrs Pattison had become soon after Mark Pattison's death) sent him her stories collected as *The Shrine of Love* the polished opacity of his short response was positively oriental: '. . . I suppose nothing really better can be said of a book . . . than that it is what it was meant to be; and this book seems to be all yourself.' To the American playwright Clyde Fitch, who had coyly dedicated to him a story in a children's book, he wrote that the dedication was more 'than I deserve' (probably a politely veiled indication that Fitch should not do it again).

Faintly lionized by the Boston poet and journalist Mrs Louise Chandler Moulton, who had intimations of founding a salon during her summers in London, Pater skilfully evaded capture by a variety of soft apologies. Other, more distinguished figures – like Sargent and Henry James – he might meet at tea in London houses, but seems never to have sought to become friendly with. Wilde, with whom he had been friendly enough during Wilde's last year as an undergraduate, appears not to have been asked to Earl's Terrace, though in January 1890 Pater wrote vaguely of having hoped to be able to call at Tite Street ('It seems an age since we met'). Pater had then just published *Appreciations*. Wilde had just been listed as a contributor to a new weekly *The Speaker*, and Pater gave a broad hint that he hoped Wilde would review *Appreciations* in it. A few weeks later he had to write Wilde a letter of warm thanks for 'your pleasantly written, genial, sensible, criticism in the Speaker', but no more was said of visiting each other. Mrs Moulton, who had sent Pater her poems (*In a Garden of Dreams*), was also owed a letter, though she did not receive one until she too had, unprompted, reviewed *Appreciations* most favourably in the Boston *Sunday Herald*.

At first, at least, London seems to have stimulated Pater to more creative activities. He had been settled in Earl's Terrace only a month or two when he revealed the release – and the confidence – he had gained from completing *Marius* by publishing the first of a new kind of imaginary portrait: *A Prince of Court Painters*, with the explanatory sub-title, 'Extracts from an old French Journal'. This was probably prompted in part by the presumed family descent from Jean-Baptiste Pater, Watteau's sole pupil, and in its attempt to portray the character of Watteau it was far from imaginary. Twenty years earlier Pater might have been inclined simply to write an essay on Watteau (as he had on Leonardo), mingling the facts of his life with deductions from his pictures.

Watteau is briefly mentioned in *The Child in the House* (where already he is 'the old court-painter'), though his pictures were not to be seen in English public collections in Pater's lifetime – with the exception of the Dulwich gallery, where hung *Les Plaisirs du Bal*. According to Thomas Wright, it was a visit to Dulwich which inspired Pater to write on Watteau, and this may have some element of truth in it. It is not necessary, however, to follow Wright when he states that Pater first visited Dulwich in the company of Richard Jackson, an eccentric figure who had, presumably, met Pater occasionally and who claimed to be the original of Marius, as well as one of Pater's closest friends (a claim Wright naïvely accepted, turning the garrulous, egotistic Jackson into a sort of secondary hero of his biography).

Among the freedoms Pater enjoyed through living in London was that of being able to visit not only churches but art galleries. Some of his later series of proposed though never completed imaginary portraits were to deal with people portrayed in pictures in the National Gallery (like Moroni's *Tailor*, for instance): pictures which had prompted in him the question of who were the people in them or what happened to them. About that picture he conjectured that the father might tell the story of the portrait; the 'Tailor' himself was intended to die of heart disease. In the year he took 12, Earl's Terrace the National Gallery acquired Raphael's *Ansidei Madonna*, a picture he was to pick out and particularly commend in lecturing in 1892 on Raphael. And his *Art Notes in North Italy* (first published in 1890) are almost as full of comment on the National Gallery's representation of Moretto and Romanino as on such painters' work in North Italy.

He need not, of course, have waited to go to Dulwich until he had a house in London. Yet a definite return – virtually a rush – of interest in painting altogether seems to follow the move from Oxford: a reward perhaps after the long and somewhat punishing labour of producing *Marius*, though rather a bitter one for the rejected candidate as Slade Professor of Art. While writing *Marius* he had described it as 'an Imaginary Portrait', and it was in a rather similar type of framework that he chose to set Watteau, seen from within his own period; and the device of a journal in the first person may possibly have developed from the tentative use of the journal kept by Marius. Watteau becomes a portrait painted in her journal by Jean-Baptiste Pater's sister (herself painted by Watteau in the course of the account, in a portrait that symbolically remains unfinished).

Through the journal quietly beats the pulse of her unrequited, barely explicit love for Watteau, thought of in Paris while she passes her lonely days in provincial Valenciennes: 'With myself,' she muses, 'how to get through time becomes sometimes the question – unavoidably.' For Watteau time is passing more rapidly, feverishly and restlessly. In his pictures she senses a storm brooding over the windless lawns and glades where the masquerade figures gracefully recline; and the pictures themselves represent something transient and ungraspable, even by the painter, 'that impossible or forbidden world which the mason's boy saw through the closed gateway of the enchanted garden . . . his dream of a better world than the real one.' Watteau is dying, she knows. Then, Watteau is dead. Her journal ends with the words, 'He was always a seeker after something in the world that is there in no satisfying measure, or not at all.'

In that sentence Pater memorably assimilates all his own wistful longings and Watteau's (Watteau momentarily becoming almost another Marius); but by adopting the device of the girl's journal he can also express his admiration of and attraction towards such a person, talented, physically glamorous (his first success gives him a Florian or Claudio-like air, 'the bloom of a flower'), prematurely dead and yet preserved in this way from age and decay. Jean-Baptiste Pater's sister's epitaph on Watteau serves as her own: she was seeking in him something that would always elude her (had he stayed in Valenciennes, she reflects, it would have been better for him, 'as it might have been better for me!'), and the conclusion must be that she will never marry, never leave Valenciennes, no longer bother perhaps to keep that journal which had afforded her 'an escape from vain regrets, angers, impatience'.

Although a picture or pictures by Watteau (as also reading about him) may have prompted Pater to produce this 'portrait' – a double portrait, really – his aim was obviously to create a personality rather than discuss Watteau's paintings. And though the later imaginary portraits may positively be suggested by pictures, and are thick with the associations raised by pictures and other works of art, he moved away from real characters (whether painters or not) to the total freedom of imaginary people, young, handsome and doomed: figments which took away a little from that inner loneliness which even an agreeable, busy life divided between Oxford and London could not disguise.

In May 1886 he published the first of these quite 'free' studies, *Sebastian van Storck*, set in seventeenth-century Holland. In October there followed *Denys l'Auxerrois*, a story of medieval Auxerre. The next year he published *Duke Carl of Rosenmold*, a study of the dawn of French enlightenment in eighteenth-century Germany, and followed this up almost immediately by collecting the four studies in volume form as *Imaginary Portraits*.

For all the variety of vividly evoked historical settings, and the different types of mind apparently represented, Sebastian, Denys and Carl are strangely similar, each 'restless, romantic, eccentric' (in words applied to Carl and true additionally of Pater's Watteau). All die unexpectedly in youth, mysteriously if not monstrously.

Sebastian is first seen through a series of winter pictures, skating over a frozen water-meadow and portrayed in boyhood with furred muff (a portrait said to be by Isaac van Ostade but conceivably suggested by a Van Oost portrait of a boy with a muff acquired by the National Gallery in 1883). He rejects the bride he is expected to marry, detaches himself from the world to study the truth of things, however bleak, and dies during a flood, perhaps having given his life for a child found asleep, 'swaddled warmly in his heavy furs'. Like Watteau he is consumptive, and a doctor attempts to comfort his mother, 'by remarking that in any case he must certainly have died ere many years were passed . . .'

What is frozen and repressed in the pensive Sebastian flames out provocatively in the blonde and god-like Denys, 'a flaxen and flowery creature', noticed in a fragment of stained glass by the narrator visiting a *bric-à-brac* shop in Auxerre on a wet afternoon. This Dionysian figure, found also in some tapestries and mentioned in notes in the local priest's library, was born of a mother killed ('as it seemed') by a stroke of lightning; he leads the people of Auxerre in joyful processions, cultivates the vine and protects animals. Yet he suffers, grows melancholy, almost mad. The populace begins to hate and fear him. He is to lead one final pageant through the town, playing the part of Winter, but in putting on the rough clothes he pricks his lip. The trickle of blood excites the spectators who hunt him down in horrible reality. He is torn to pieces, and little shreds of his flesh are stuck in the men's caps, fixed by long hairpins borrowed from the women.

Denys is too alluring to live – so alluring that he must die savagely, dismembered by the very people who once worshipped him. Pater kills him off with a relish recalling the death of Flavian in *Marius*, and anticipating the death of Hyacinth in *Apollo in Picardy*. And, if not his death, the post-mortem operation on the body of Emerald Uthwart seems part of the same fascinated disgust, the stifling of desire by an emphasis on death. Pater of course had long before written about Dionysus and about *The Bacchae*, and

177

probably understood the ambiguous appeal for him in the story; the tortured, suffering Dionysus (the other aspect of the honey-pale, half-effeminate, beautiful god) had already been discussed by him. Nor could he fail to hint at the immortality of his Denys (whose heart alone remained to be buried). The image dismembered is fondly imagined as still wandering on certain days through the town. 'I seemed . . . to have met Denys l'Auxerrois in the streets,' are the closing words.

Between this portrait's publication and that of Duke Carl, a real death intervened. Very early in 1887 William Pater's heart disease became serious. On 4 January he made his will at Stafford and probably shortly afterwards moved down to Hastings where Hester and Clara took it in turns to nurse him. By March it was obvious that he had to resign his post at Stafford. He moved to lodgings in Paddington (at 12, Oxford Terrace) and died there, of dropsy as well as heart disease, on Sunday 24 April, aged fifty-two. 'To the last', Pater reported to a Liverpool cousin, 'he was hopeful and cheerful in moments of relief.' To Gosse, who had invited him to Cambridge for a visit in mid-May, he wrote more frankly of William's 'long and trying illness', confessing that he did not yet feel in the mood for visits. Gosse perhaps heard some details from Pater of William's character; only he among those who left memoirs of Pater referred to him, and he notes William's sole aesthetic trait as a marked pleasure in being surrounded by 'pretty objects'.

Duke Carl starts as a skeleton, unearthed – with that of the country girl he planned to marry – at the beginning of the nineteenth century. A century before, she and the enlightened 'sanguine, floridly handsome' young Duke had disappeared, while a foreign army was crossing the neutral territory of his little duchy of Rosenmold. His disappearance was perhaps the more mysterious since he had once before disappeared, pretended to be dead so as to go travelling and had, disguised, followed his own ceremonious funeral procession, with its empty coffin, into the ducal burial vaults ('. . . the faded glories of the immense coroneted coffins, the oldest shedding their velvet tatters around them'). As his grandfather's heir, he plays at French culture, longs to travel as far as Italy, but is brought back by news of the old Duke's death. He crosses Germany much perhaps as Pater had once crossed it when his aunt suddenly died: 'With a real grief at his heart he hastened now over the ground which lay between him and the bed of death . . .' The hopes of his own reign, the prospect of marrying the girl he loves, happiness, are swept away in a storm by night, merging with the storming alien army which – it seems – trampled the lovers to death as they sheltered waiting for the priest who would marry them. Carl does not survive to see the Enlightenment in Germany; that is left to others, like Goethe and Herder 'coming well within the natural limits of Carl's lifetime', to introduce.

Painter, philosopher, god and prince: taken together, the four portraits might almost have been of one family executed by Rubens (Duke Carl's favourite artist) as he is there described painting 'privileged young people who could never grow old'. Unlike Marius, these people have only the slightest links with Pater's own life, but each of them is intensely coloured by what he had felt, suffered and dreamt. They are all wonderfully gifted by nature; they have high aspirations; but they fail and die. In the imaginary gallery where their portraits hang, there lies the bar of that familiar shadow, from out of which their youthful features gleam only the more brightly and poignantly. Even in sleepy, peaceful, semi-rustic Rosenmold there are inescapable hints of death: village church bells break the afternoon air with their tolling, and down in the grand-ducal vault the vigorous Rubensian young Carl finds an array of dropping crape and cobwebs. 'The lad, with his full red lips and open blue eyes, coming as with a great cup in his hand to life's feast, revolted from the like of that, as from suffocation.'

The death of his brother William, half-feared perhaps for some time, saddened Pater more probably than it shocked him. He had lived longer than either their father or their uncle, but he was scarcely old (he had very likely celebrated his fifty-second birthday during the last stage of his illness). Neither Pater nor his sisters had seen much of him, except when he was ill, since they were children. He had come close to them in London only when he was dying. His hopes and his aspirations had perhaps never been very clear to them, apart from his early wish to join the army. And now his death made further knowledge impossible.

It interrupted the pleasant London existence Pater had built up for himself, and though it did not disturb his literary activity it left at Earl's Terrace a wake of 'much trouble', as Pater described it in declining Gosse's invitation to Cambridge. A month afterwards *Imaginary Portraits* was published, and it was on mourning paper that Pater informed Sharp that a copy had been sent directly to him, adding a sentence of explanation at the end of the letter, 'We lost my poor Brother about four weeks since.'

Suitable as it would have been, *Imaginary Portraits* was published too soon for Pater to make it any memorial to William, and it appeared with no dedication. The following year a third edition of *The Renaissance* was published, as well as several reviews, including that of *Robert Elsmere*. In the summer there began to appear in *Macmillan's Magazine* the first chapters of Pater's new and full-length 'portrait', *Gaston de Latour*, which he later described accurately enough as 'a sort of Marius in France in the 16th century'. In December 1888 he published the elaborate essay on *Style*, which reads like a sustained if oblique defence, a proud one, of the vehicle of prose ('the characteristic art of the nineteenth century'), with unexpectedly moral overtones in defining how good art becomes great art: 'if it be devoted further to the increase of men's happiness, to the redemption of the oppressed, or the enlargement of our sympathies with each other . . .'

That essay became the first and most prominently advertised chapter of his next book, a collection of articles and reviews, *Appreciations: with an essay on Style*, published in 1889, a year when he declared himself 'already so full of work, promised elsewhere, and partly begun' that he could undertake no further commissions for books. The importance he attached to the essay is indicated by the proposed first title for the new volume: *On Style/With other studies in literature*. The title, though probably none of the contents, was changed, and the book was published with an unexpectedly full and solemn dedication: 'To the memory of my brother/William Thompson Pater/who quitted a useful and happy life/Sunday April 24 1887/Requiem eternam dona ei Domine/et lux perpetua luceat ei.' William Pater had written nothing and, publicly, had done nothing; but by this dedication his existence was, as it were, proclaimed (not concealed, like Shadwell's, under initials) and his relationship to the author openly declared. Perhaps, too, his death healed a temperamental breach existing between the boys since childhood. His skill had been in medicine, not art, and yet the exact nature of his career might have been in Pater's mind when he wrote those phrases about the increase of men's happiness and redemption of the oppressed.

Appreciations contained nothing that, in one form or another, could not have been read before, but even the reviews not prompted by Pater or written by such friends as Sharp (who appears to have reviewed it twice) were highly favourable. It was by a perhaps rather typical quirk of reviewing that this volume (with its essays on Wordsworth, Shakespeare, Lamb, Browne and Rossetti) should be greeted almost as a revelation of Pater's abilities. Wilde had the perceptive courage to call the essay on *Style* the least successful, but he also recognized how Pater stood 'almost alone' as a certain kind of artist in prose. And amid much other praise, the poet William Watson, whom he had never met, stated in his review that Pater was 'beyond rivalry the subtlest artist in contemporary English prose.' Abruptly, it seems, the truth of these claims was widely recognized. At the age of fifty, unobtrusively yet definitely, Pater had become famous.

Thirteen   A degree of fame

BY THE TIME Pater became famous the last decade of the nineteenth century had begun. If he could now be saluted as the 'subtlest artist' in contemporary prose it might seem partly because some obvious, older rivals had disappeared. Arnold had died in 1888. Newman died in 1890. Ruskin had broken down irrevocably in 1889, leaving *Praeterita* splendid, flawed and unfinished, with himself in the last sentence for ever poised entering Siena through a sunset darkening into night – only too tragically apt a description of his own state.

But the deepening recognition of Pater's status was due to less simple causes. The century in which he had so often felt ill at ease was itself very gradually altering, shrugging off – or having tugged off – some of the earnest conventions in which it had wrapped itself, and which had weighed so heavily on him. The process was slow, erratic and not widespread. Whistler, Wilde, Beardsley and *The Yellow Book* might, in different ways, typify new artistic attitudes in England, but controversy, resentment, if not pure hatred, lay very near the surface over which such phenomena danced. Wilde, in particular, might have been warned by the hysterical tones of some reviews of *Dorian Gray* ('Dulness and dirt . . .': *The Daily Chronicle*; '. . . if he can write for none but outlawed noblemen and perverted telegraph-boys': *The Scot's Observer*) that the society he seemed born to charm was not profoundly changed from that which had been scandalized by Swinburne and suspicious of Pater. Indeed, it may have felt basically less secure, more flooded with 'French filth' and infiltrated by aesthetes; a line would have to be drawn, and it was virtually inevitable that it should be drawn – like a sword from a scabbard – at the most successful figure of the period, its jester-artist-prince and then victim, Wilde.

Yet though the implications of modern art, of all kinds, might be attacked, there were also people to defend it. Whistler had, after all, won his legal battle with Ruskin: that was far more significant, ultimately, than the derisory damages. By ridiculing aestheticism, *Punch* had helped to popularize it and give it a meaning, however muddled. Gilbert and Sullivan's *Patience* (1881) was a satire which could only be effective if there was a trend to satirize. By the 1890s there had come into being a sufficient audience for the view that art existed for its own sake. To those people the scandal and ridicule which had followed *Studies in the History of the Renaissance* on first publication must have seemed nearly incomprehensible. Its 'Conclusion' was for them the obvious conclusion. Time had almost robbed of being daring its doctrine of pursuing sensation, cultivating beauty and esteeming art regardless of morals. All that could be done was to give the doctrine new piquancy by pithy and witty re-statement – as Wilde was to do in the aphorisms forming the preface to *Dorian Gray* when published in 1891 as a book. *The Renaissance*, however, was still in demand; and the fourth edition, of 1893, was the largest printing of all (2,000). It was then to be read by undergraduates and others scarcely born when it had first appeared. 'In those days', Richard Le Gallienne was to declare in his autobiographical *The Romantic '90s*, 'we were all going around quoting the famous description, or rather re-creation, of the Mona Lisa . . . and we were all exhorting each other . . . to maintain that ecstasy which is the true success of life.' When in 1896 Beardsley sent André Raffalovich a list of books he was without but wanted, it was headed by *The Renaissance*.

Pater had described it, before its first publication, as 'unpretending'. He had assumed he was addressing 'a comparatively small section of readers'. And though the book's reception had not been entirely hostile, it had been somewhat puzzled. The author had been left feeling rather isolated, as well as uneasy. His jewelled, faintly drugged style was really too heady and enclosed for those used to Ruskin's vigour and vigorous praise of God's natural world of bright clouds and high Alps and wild flowers. But by the 1890s the patent artifice of Pater's style, no less than its lingering over the stranger aspects of art, was part of its appeal. It replaced the banality of nature by a vision of something far more recondite, more tantalizing and more truly artistic because created by man. Pater's prose itself came to be seen as 'art', regardless of what it conveyed. 'Who . . . cares', Wilde makes Gilbert ask in *The Critic as Artist*, 'whether Mr Pater has put into the portrait of Monna Lisa something that Leonardo never dreamed of?' And he goes on to answer the question by saying that Pater's criticism 'treats the work of art simply as a starting point for a new creation'.

Much of the most open homage to Pater came from Wilde, with all his characteristic generosity, tinged perhaps with the realization not only of what he owed Pater but that Pater would never claim it. Pater's work had made its own contribution, after all, to the ostensibly more sympathetic climate where Wilde exotically bloomed. And it might have seemed that the period was now set to welcome Pater as its uncrowned king (even, where Wilde was concerned, its king-maker) and that at last – in the last decade of the nineteenth century – he would feel at home.

No doubt this could have happened, despite Pater's natural reticence and then his sudden death. Ironically, however, the decade more often found him not concocting perfect and poisonous paragraphs à la Wilde – and still less paradoxes – but on his knees in Brasenose chapel. He was drifting back into something of the mood of his early childhood piety. Almost certainly, he could not entirely recapture that, any more than he could – or would – quieten the instincts which flared up in *Apollo in Picardy* where by night the naked Hyacinth and Apollo play a doomed game of the discus.

In attending church services, in London as in Oxford, he experienced something aesthetic, doubtless, yet something calming, making him feel less weary (the word he frequently used, repeating to himself Blake's 'Ah, sunflower, weary of time'). Before giving a lecture in London at Toynbee Hall he had gone into a local church just to compose his mind, but to the vicar of the Italianate high Anglican Church of the Holy Redeemer at Clerkenwell he wrote of finding its Sunday morning services 'very touching and attractive, very winning', though he hastened to add that he knew they had greater significance than that for the vicar, 'and others'. He thought of the church, he had said earlier in the letter, as a help to the people who lived around: 'Religion, I sometimes think, is the only way in which poetry can really reach the hard-worked poor.'

His friendship with Frederick Bussell seems, accidentally or not, to date from the time Bussell became chaplain at Brasenose, in 1891, at the age of twenty-nine. In preaching on Pater Bussell necessarily stressed 'the student of deep religious feeling' (admitting that such a picture was different from that formed by some people from passages in Pater's writings), and, though he presented a drastically over-simplified view, this is clearly how Pater appeared to him. They saw each other almost daily in those last few years, entertained each other or together entertained undergraduates. Probably no one was by then as close to Pater as Bussell. His testimony is not unexpected: it confirms, if a little too exclusively, the seriousness of Pater's search for peace and assurance.

Twenty years earlier it had been the chaplain of Brasenose (John Wordsworth, Bishop of Salisbury by the 1890s) who had thought it his painful duty to remonstrate with Pater's expressed scepticism:

184

'that no fixed principles either of religion or morality can be regarded as certain.' Bussell declared that the Pater he knew was 'never happier' than when discussing some of the cardinal mysteries of the faith, 'and I well recall how he would reprove any symptom of a rationalizing spirit'. And yet Pater left the 'Conclusion' to *The Renaissance* remarkedly unchanged. All still melts under our feet; we are still urged to grasp at any exquisite passion or any stirring of the senses, strange dyes, strange colours and curious odours amid the awful brevity of our experience: 'What we have to do is to be for ever curiously testing new opinions and courting new impressions, never acquiescing in a facile orthodoxy . . .'

Only to their author, perhaps, had these sentences lost their power to excite. To be greeted as the singer of that particular song had become not distasteful but positively disturbing: it revived too many memories and set in motion again anxieties which lay dormant.

'Hopelessly prudish' was the indignant comment of one half of 'Michael Field', Miss Bradley, on learning in 1890 that for the second edition of *Appreciations*, Pater was dropping his essay on *Aesthetic Poetry* (a revised version of the 1868 review of Morris's poetry) because it had offended pious people: 'Deplorable!' Pater admitted as much to Lionel Johnson, though he gave a slightly satiric edge to his explanation, saying, as reported in inverted commas by Johnson, that he had suppressed it because 'there were things in it which some people, pious souls! thought profane, yes! profane'. (Possibly Bussell, already a fellow of Brasenose, was among these.)

There remained a core of apprehension in Pater which was beginning to seem nearly absurd in the decade most prepared to admire him, though in fact he had a truer, keener sense than Wilde of what society would tolerate. He himself drew back, politely but distinctly, from *Dorian Gray*, even while finding ways of praising parts of it; and soon afterwards he appears to have drawn back altogether from Wilde. D. S. MacColl noted how even in 1893 Pater still seemed conscious of 'disapproval and suspicion'. He was cautious about recommending his pupils to read Flaubert (*Salammbô* he called 'a *very* wicked book'); and a more well-disposed undergraduate than MacColl, or one less irritated by Pater's attitude, remarked on the 'playful conservatism' apparent in his last years.

Very probably it was this aspect of Pater which amused Wilde, neither reluctant nor timid himself, and genuinely unable to follow the complex process by which Pater appeared to be retreating rather than advancing while his position as a literary artist and an influence became more patent. A letter of Lionel Johnson's (written from Oxford early in 1890) conveys Wilde's all-conquering charm on someone who had never met him before and also something of Wilde's reactions to Pater whom he must have known Johnson greatly admired. It was Pater he had come to Oxford to see, but he also called on Johnson, whose poems he had read, rousing him from bed at mid-day and begging him to get up: 'Which I did . . . He discoursed, with infinite flippancy, of everyone . . . laughed at Pater: and consumed all my cigarettes. I am in love with him.'

Invited early in 1894 to be a contributor to *The Yellow Book*'s first number, Pater excused himself on the convincing ground of being already over-committed to work, though he let his name appear among future contributors and he wished the new magazine success ('Kindly tell Mr Harland this'). Death prevented any contribution arriving from him. The contributors to the first number were typically heterogeneous in a period of aesthetic confusion (Beardsley, Leighton and Sickert; James, Beerbohm and Arthur Symons), and the effect not particularly 'decadent'. But Pater's failure to be included in *The Yellow Book* has a certain symbolic appropriateness. He might not have cared much for Beerbohm's *Defence of Cosmetics* ('. . . we are ripe for a new era of artifice') or Symon's poem *Stella Maris*, about a street-walker ('The Juliet of a night . . .'). Indeed, his previous enthusiasm for Symons and his work seems to have waned markedly by this period; he had reverted to addressing him in letters as 'Mr Symons', a nuance of distancing which must have been deliberate. At a given point in his acquaintance with, for example, Sharp, Pater began to write to him simply by his surname explaining, 'I think we have known each other long enough to drop the "Mr".'

A final irony for the mutual attitudes of Pater and the period arose from his genuine modesty. Absorbed in the tasks he had taken on, and determined most likely to sink as much as possible of his being in work (he was fond of Balzac's saying, 'Le travail est la loi de l'art comme celle de la vie'), he did not properly understand that he had become famous. When the young Bernard Berenson, just arrived in Oxford from Harvard, no doubt having read American editions of Pater, asked if he could attend his lectures, Pater declined – with courtesy but obviously in confused surprise: they were not public lectures – not really lectures at all, just informal instruction to the undergraduates of Brasenose, and anyway the course was coming to an end. Berenson seems to have remained conscious all his life of having received a snub.

In November 1890 Pater gave a rare public lecture. He was

chosen as the second lecturer in an annual series on foreign literature at the Taylor Institution in Oxford, and he took Prosper Mérimée as his subject. Later lecturers included Paul Bourget and Mallarmé. As always on such occasions, Pater read his lecture – and read it in a low, monotonous voice. To his strong dislike of appearing and speaking in public, however, was added something unexpected in the size of the audience. It was too large for the room; he seemed, an acquaintance in that audience noted, surprised, overwhelmed and frightened: 'I don't think he knew how much of a celebrity he was . . .' Perhaps he might have gained a hint of some sort just a month previously, when he was parodied in the *Cornhill* magazine, in the company of Kipling, Ruskin and Tolstoy, company rather lowered in tone, at least by today's standards, through the inclusion also of R. D. Blackmore. All were the work of Barrie Pain, though they appeared anonymously; that on 'our dear Pater' Wilde described as 'clever and horrid'.

The Mérimée lecture was repeated a week later in London and then printed in the *Fortnightly*. It was Pater's most sustained treatment of a near contemporary French writer (Mérimée had died in 1870) and at first sight a less obvious choice than Flaubert, Baudelaire, Hugo, Gautier or even Stendhal. Books about Mérimée, and volumes of his letters, had followed his death, and Pater probably began to read him seriously when he was planning *Gaston*, for which Mérimée's *Chronique du Règne de Charles IX* was clearly relevant, along with Dumas and Balzac. It is significantly praised in Pater's lecture ('an escape from the tame circumstances of contemporary life into an impassioned past').

Charles IX himself irrupts into the countrified childhood of Gaston: a sinister, elegant, slightly deranged figure, who arrives from hunting to the sound of horns one night. The silver flambeaux that light him to his apartment reveal him not merely with bloodied hands but '*steeped* in blood' (Pater's italics) from the animals he has slain. He seems scarcely human. 'He was very pale, like some cunning Italian work in wax or ivory . . . endued by magic or crafty mechanism with vivacious movement.' Part of the story of Gaston was to be his attraction first towards the court of the Valois at Paris (rather as Marius had been drawn to Rome) and then his disillusionment with its corrupt atmosphere, especially under Henri III. Beauty and horror are summed up in the hideous relic of her executed lover's head kept by the graceful *grande amoureuse* Marguerite de Navarre on an altar in her oratory; and this atmosphere becomes even more eerie with an extended description of the public torture of a youthful murderer.

Pater's audiences knew nothing of those later scenes (which still remain unpublished). Publication of *Gaston* had stopped after five chapters, with the hero barely entered 'the hotly-coloured world of Paris'. But even in the early description of Charles IX there is some indication of what drew him to Mérimée, the exquisitely polished, steely stylist who created 'the exquisitely cruel story' of *Matteo Falcone*, '. . . perhaps the cruellest story in the world'. The dispassionate-seeming cruelty in Mérimée's art fascinated Pater. And however low-toned the delivery of his lecture, the words are animated with such thrilling imaginative response that it eventually becomes revealing as well as rather frightening. Mérimée's style is praised for its simplicity and detachment, the more effective since its subject-matter is frequently shocking in its exotic colourfulness, like 'some harshly dyed oriental carpet from the sumptuous floor of the Kremlin, on which blood had fallen'. Romantic violence, energetic passions, terror without pity, and everywhere the promise or presence of bloodshed: 'it is', Pater said, 'as if there were nothing to tell of this world but various forms of hatred, and a love that is like lunacy'. He compares the polish of Mérimée's style to a stiletto, and quotes half-fascinated his dry observation, made 'as if with regret', that assassination is no longer a part of our manners. In Mérimée's hero Bernard de Mergy (from the *Chronique*) he admires amid his tears and blushes the sentiment of deadly steel: 'it is a part of his very sex'.

And when he is telling how Mérimée records 'All the grotesque accidents of violent death . . . with visual exactness, and no pains to relieve them,' he seems to anticipate incidents of his own late stories, *Emerald Uthwart* and *Apollo in Picardy*, as well as that unpublished chapter of *Gaston de Latour*. Even into the somewhat slack lecture on Raphael, delivered at Oxford in August 1892, there comes an abrupt spurt of excitement when the Baglioni of Perugia flash across the scene like characters from a Mérimée tale, with their complete expression of certain tendencies of the age, 'veiling crime – crime it might seem, for its own sake, a whole octave of fantastic crime – not merely under brilliant fashions and comely persons . . .'

In most ways Pater had not changed and could not change, even if he half wished to. He remained the boy whose nature he had described more than once and expressed yet again in Gaston: 'A nature, instinctively religious . . . But what would be the relation of this religious sensibility to sensibilities of another kind . . . the imaginative heat, that might one day enter into dangerous rivalry with simple old-fashioned faith . . .'

188

If he was now consciously striving to recover 'simple old-fashioned faith', almost as a course in tranquillity, and to give his personality a cool, docile surface, still there burnt underneath a hot imagination unaffected by age or fame and about to blaze out fiercely in the story of *Apollo in Picardy* and the imaginary portrait of *Emerald Uthwart*. Had Bussell looked at these, he might have glanced a little more sharply at his friend with his quiet manner, gentle humour and faintly guarded talk of sermons, chapel-going and cats. But then Pater, in turn, would not have found so much solace in Bussell had he probed and questioned.

Bussell was perhaps something of a Shadwell re-born. He was young, reserved, religious and scholarly ('with something like genius for classical literature,' Pater wrote, 'especially for the early Christian theology and late Pagan philosophy'). His slightly saturnine, faintly military appearance was very much part of his appeal. 'Just the look I think so fine in him', Pater declared on receiving the likeness of Bussell sketched by William Rothenstein, 'and have not seen in his photographs.'

While Pater thought Bussell 'a little too reluctant' to write for the general public, he himself was increasingly – it seemed – occupied with lectures, articles and reviews. He was turning his lectures on Plato into a volume intended to interest 'a larger number' of young students than had attended the original lectures. And amid a diversity of tasks undertaken or mooted, he found time in 1892 to contribute an introduction to a translation of part of Dante's *Purgatorio* by Shadwell – an interesting coming-together publicly (almost a 'reconciliation') of the two friends twenty-seven years after their visit to Italy.

'Exclusively personal and solitary' had once been Pater's description to Sharp of what his kind of literary work must be. Not even the constant companionship of Bussell could alter that, and in fact it left Pater free to re-enter – after the pleasant country walk or the playful conversation – the cell of his own imagination where a new, stirring life began.

He still felt the urge to people his solitariness by imaginary characters, often more physically glamorous than himself but with mental affinities to him. Probably about this period he sketched *Tibalt the Albigense* and *S. Gaudioso the Second*, beginning with the re-creation of their childhoods and then finding it hard to continue once that significant stage was reached. It was the childhood and youth of Gaston de Latour that he saw most powerfully. With that captured, the book slackened and advanced only fitfully; and probably Pater felt that he was losing any concept of Gaston's individuality under too heavy a rain of impressions. Like Marius, Gaston was to withdraw eventually from the over-luscious, sinister and exotic capital city and return to his old country home, dying at the age of forty-two. But the similarity of the progression – regardless of the very different setting – probably worried Pater, and the effort of bringing *Gaston* to its conclusion became too much.

Yet he had thought of it, at least when he began, as the second part (*Marius* being the first) of a trilogy. The third part would have been set in England, 'probably' – Pater's own adverb – at the end of the eighteenth century. 'An English Poet' was possibly connected in his mind with this third portion. England had not been the setting for any published imaginary portrait, except that of Florian Deleal. Pater had preferred to transmute his own environment and sensations into the two countries which had visually stimulated him most: Italy and France. Gaston going on a frosty winter day to serve in the household of the Bishop of Chartres was obviously Pater going down to the King's School at Canterbury, and the 'triple flower' of Jasmin, Amadée and Camille (future soldier, lawyer and poet) reflected loosely Pater's triumvirate at school. Gaston himself, grave, sensuous and orphaned, sounds like Marius and derives, of course, from Pater. In place of a widowed mother, he has aged grandparents. The echoes of *Marius* are particularly strong at the opening of the book, where Pater's sense of religious dedication in the Enfield days becomes Gaston's positive tonsuring as the first step in his taking holy orders. In fact, Gaston was in character really too close to Marius to make for any novelty, and that realization also may have discouraged Pater from continuing the portrayal. A fresh and more direct impetus – almost an emotional shock – was needed.

On 30 July 1891 Pater revisited the King's School. It was the annual Speech Day and Robert Ottley, May Ottley's husband, was the Anniversary preacher. Perhaps some slight consciousness of his own fame, or curiosity after the lapse of so many years, encouraged Pater to return. What he saw and felt was too vivid to be expressed in any fanciful historical terms, or transposed very far out of its actual setting. He began – and this time completed – a last imaginary portrait, *Emerald Uthwart*.

It is the story of a Sussex boy, born late in the eighteenth century, who goes to school and Oxford, then joins the army with his schoolboy friend James Stokes. Obscurely they disobey orders while fighting abroad, are court-martialled and sentenced to be shot. Stokes is executed, but Uthwart is reprieved, though cashiered. He wanders home in disgrace and dies just after the news that the

190

incident has been re-examined and he has been exonerated. A surgeon's journal ('August – th, 18 – ') serves as postscript to the story; it tells of how, assisted by Uthwart's mother, he operated on the corpse in the coffin, to remove a musket-ball. 'I was struck by the great beauty of the organic developments . . . the wind ruffled the fair hair a little; the lips were still red. I shall not forget it.'

The prime visual stimulus for *Emerald Uthwart* clearly came from the summer day's visit to Canterbury: at once familiar and yet changed to the eye of a middle-aged man. The 'old ecclesiastical city' (though not named), the 'hop-gardens', the Gothic cathedral and the adjoining school do not disguise but rather identify the location – as if Pater wanted this time to come nearer than before to real autobiography. But the sight of Canterbury had stimulated far more than memories of himself at school. It stirred recollections of his family, carrying him back beyond Enfield and Stepney to the days when the Paters lived in Buckinghamshire. And other recollections, memories, fears and aspirations wove themselves into the richly, frankly morbid tissue of *Emerald Uthwart*, as literature presided over by Mérimée and Edgar Allan Poe but shaped ultimately by Pater into the fullest expression of what had for so long haunted him.

By calling his hero 'Uthwart' he revealed, possibly without realizing, how deep in childhood the associations lay. He may vaguely have remembered hearing the name Uthwatt mentioned when he was a boy, perhaps not understanding that this family existed (and still exists). Their estates were at Great Linford, a village in Buckinghamshire not far from Weston where his own family came from. In the small church at Great Linford there is still the Uthwatt chapel; and though the family tree shows no 'Emerald' it does have two early nineteenth-century Uthwatts called Edolphe and Eusebius.

Emerald Uthwart's family is an old one, but without a distinguished history ('Sunday after Sunday, [he] reads, wondering, the solitary memorial of one soldierly member of his race . . . who had *not* died here at home, in his bed'). And though Emerald – handsome, passive and due to die young – escapes from the envelope of Pater into the usual imaginary ideal, he is from the first sufficiently similar to have his birthday in August and to be brought up in an old house called Chase Lodge. Of the children he alone goes to school (some of his brothers being 'placed already in the world') and feels resentment accordingly as if 'sent *ablactatus a matre*'. William Pater's youthful apprenticeship to a merchant seems among the things here recalled, and the situation of the family after Maria

Pater's death in Emerald's sense of 'brief holidays' where 'he rejoins his people, anywhere, anyhow, in a sort of hurry and makeshift.'

These were experiences Pater had not given to his earlier heroes and which had probably been sealed away at the time, to be released by the visit to Canterbury. For Emerald school means not only the beautiful, blackened, semi-monastic building and the cathedral rising beside it but fervent friendship with the prefect James Stokes (a sort of combined Flavian-Cornelius figure). Together they leave for Oxford, bracketed as 'Victors' of the school, but quickly enlist when war breaks out – joining their regiment in Flanders. Already the army was a presence in the city of their schooldays, 'where a military garrison had been established in the suburbs for centuries past, and there were always sons of its officers in the school.' McQueen thus obliquely enters the story, with an echo of Canterbury during the Crimean War ('soldiers mingling in the crowd which filled the unchanged, gabled streets'). But in Emerald's ambition to be a soldier it is once again William Pater who seems indicated (as perhaps also by Emerald's extreme good looks).

The 'portrait' opens not with any painting but with an epitaph, that in the local church, telling of Emerald's death at twenty-six at his place of birth, Chase Lodge, Sussex (the county where McQueen's family had their country house in which Pater had once stayed). Emerald's appears to have been an uneventful brief life, from his epitaph; the story's purpose is to show how misleading that assumption is.

Emerald is judged to have broken the code of the society he has chosen to join. His submissive character makes him easily follow James Stokes, after they go to Flanders, in 'an act of thoughtless bravery, almost the sole irregular or undisciplined act of Uthwart's life' (they have left their posts to raid an enemy town and seize a flag on their own initiative). Their act of heroism proves one of folly. A court martial finds them guilty. They are sentenced to death, and an eye-witness describes in precise detail how Stokes kneels down on his coffin before the firing squad execute him. Emerald also witnesses the public scene, and then – reprieved – endures the humiliation of having his sword snapped over his head, and his epaulettes and buttons torn off. He is left to wander the Flemish countryside ('actually came round again to the scene of his disgrace . . . wept then as never before in his life') and finally returns home on a flawless July afternoon ill and dying.

This circling back to the home recalls *Marius* and *Gaston* (as planned) but Pater had never allowed any of his imaginary heroes to suffer such an ordeal as Emerald Uthwart's. Nor does he seem punishing Emerald just for his charm and beauty; he is too closely identified with him for that, and it is more likely that Emerald goes through something symbolizing what Pater had been through when he recklessly published *Studies in the History of the Renaissance*. Oxford came near to rejecting him – did in official ways reject him – but he survived. The period had, however, at almost the same date, claimed a victim in his friend Simeon Solomon, utterly disgraced and punished for 'sins' of which Pater was merely suspected. Solomon was, to all intents, dead, while Pater lived on and gradually grew more respectable. Yet the ordeal of being *condemned* to die was a haunting one: it is exactly what Marius is said to have 'often' dreamt of, and his dreams come horribly true for Emerald Uthwart.

Emerald is fated to die young, but it is an essential aspect of his story that he does not die in disgrace. He survives long enough to savour with new intensity the physical beauty of the summer days that are his last: he, 'the lover of roses' (Mallock's 'Mr Rose' suggests itself), is dying in the season of his own birthday and 'as the breath of the infinite world came about him, he clung all the faster to the beloved finite things . . .' And he survives long enough to learn that over the incident of his reckless act there has been 'a revision or reversal of judgement'. The matter has been re-opened; it is discussed in Parliament and the newspapers, and a speaker who cites Emerald and James Stokes as '*pessimi exempli*' is decisively controverted. 'As happens with our countrymen', Pater remarks, 'they repent.' Cleared of the original charge, the dying Emerald receives the offer of a commission. The letter lies beside him on his sickbed; it is the token of his rehabilitation and he has it buried with him. 'It was as if there was nothing more that could be said.'

Emerald Uthwart was published, in two parts, in June and July 1892. By then it was less a prophecy than a summing-up of Pater's emotional experience (not apparent in any simple epitaph-like record of the facts of his existence). He was to return to live at Oxford in the following year – in a final move which probably had for him some connotations of returning home. Respect as well as fame was gathering around him. When at the beginning of 1893 he published *Plato and Platonism* it was the occasion for Jowett, himself to die in the autumn of the year, to congratulate him, and some sort of reconciliation apparently took place. The 'demoralizing moralizer' was certainly absent from that easy, vivacious rather than languorous or wistful book where Plato is compared with Thackeray (he 'would have been an excellent writer of fiction').

Yet Pater still refused to conform to the restrictive role just of

193

lecturer-don, seeing pupils, setting essays and giving scholarly lectures to be turned into books. *Emerald Uthwart* has no connection with that brisk, outward, university world; it is personal, indiscreet and at the end poignantly lonely, as if its author gazed at his own tombstone as he buried Emerald: 'What did it matter – the gifts, the good fortune, its terrible withdrawal, the long agony? Emerald Uthwart would have been all but a centenarian today.'

In describing the ordeal of Emerald and James Stokes facing the firing-squad Pater had adopted a Mérimée-like tone. Something would-be dry and factual was also needed for the 'Postscript', though the actual scene of the macabre opeation on the corpse suggests the atmosphere of a story by Poe. Pater could not leave Emerald in death. To justify his lingering over the coffin, enjoying the handsome face laid among the flowers (recollection of visits to the Morgue in Paris and the cemetery in Munich), he adopted his father's and the family profession: he assumed the *persona* of a surgeon. At last, he overcame an inhibition, did not merely look at but actually dared to touch the flesh, 'still almost as firm as that of a living person', of someone desirable though dead.

It was a confession, barely disguised, that might seem to separate him finally from most of his fellow-men. He had brought himself to make it, knowing that the longing was unappeasable. It had existed as far back as the days at Enfield, perhaps when he had reached out to touch the bowl of autumnal fruit and been stung by a wasp, and when he thought of young boys like himself, 'fallen into incurable sickness . . . early dead . . . cut off from golden summer days . . .'

'Solitary' was how Peter had described his work to Sharp, and it was the word which summed up the tenor of his life. He had felt it as a child, known it as a man, and could hardly feel it much softened by his sisters, his friends or his degree of fame. Perhaps, after all, it was what he wanted. Once asked a typical Victorian parlour-game question – 'If not a man, what would you like to be?' – Pater answered that he would like to be a carp swimming for ever in the green waters of some royal château.

Fourteen   'He was always a seeker . . .'

PATER was probably installed, with Hester and Clara, at their new Oxford home, 64, St Giles', by 4 August 1893, his fifty-fourth and, as it proved, last birthday.

The house was destroyed in the 1920s to make way for the Dominican priory of Blackfriars, but judging from a photograph it was rather similar in style to Earl's Terrace, with simple but handsome proportions, large casement windows and discreetly plain front door: strongly suggestive of the preceding century, in contrast to the Gothic of Bradmore Road. Although Pater entertained at 64, St Giles' and could offer to put up a friend like Gosse, there seems no record of how exactly it was furnished. Pater must have had a study there and it was there presumably that his last cats, Tony and Molly, were to be seen seated on his writing-desk.

From St Giles' it was only a short walk to Brasenose, where he kept the rooms he had first moved into on his election as junior fellow in 1864. That was the setting in which most people recalled him after his death. Over the years the small sitting-room might have changed colour (recollected as blue by some, as white by others) but the simple furnishings – the one easy chair, the small bookcase, the china bowl filled with dried rose petals – seem to have remained much the same. Pater encouraged visitors and signalled his accessibility by never closing the outer door of the room. There he sat, relaxed, friendly, almost inviting interruption; he was quick to get up and leave the easy chair to any visitor, while he went and perched on the window seat. In this room his pupils read or discussed their essays, or he talked on various topics like Plato and Platonism, 'in a deep and curiously balanced voice'. He liked to be listened to and not have his every word noted down, a pupil afterwards recollected, admitting that in his group there had been a division between those who tried to hold Pater's eye as they listened and those who wrote down as much as possible, hoping not to be detected.

And occasionally, to single visitors, Pater talked – more personally – about his interests, his tastes or things he had noticed. He declared his admiration of Newman; he spoke of how impressed he was by the blueness of the sea in Devon; he praised the interior of St Philip's Church behind the London Hospital (close to his Stepney birthplace). About art (that subject Bussell declined to discuss with him), he said, 'I have never had to surrender any of my first opinions . . . I think.' He went on to add, tantalizingly, 'but I have found that I have come to admire things which I did not once, especially in the case of some forms of rococo.'

So much for what might be learnt in casual conversation. What he was writing, even what he was reading, was probably not spoken of except in a general way. The threads of temperamental affinity which connected him to minor, literary figures like André Raffalovich and Count Stanislaus Eric Stenbock could perhaps hardly be concealed, but acquaintance with them seems to have been kept very private. Possibly he did not actually know Stenbock, though he certainly owned a copy of Stenbock's poems, *The Shadow of Death*, published in 1893. Stenbock, summed up by W. B. Yeats as a 'scholar, connoisseur, drunkard, poet, pervert, most charming of men', had befriended Simeon Solomon in the 1880s. His poems celebrate an obsessive dream ('But I have only one dream – I and he') which was bound to attract Pater. Stenbock also published a volume of bizarre short stories, *Studies of Death* (in 1894), and must have read such a 'portrait' as Pater's *Apollo in Picardy* with at least as much fondness for the theme as for the style.

Although Pater had returned to Oxford to live in an odour of near-respectability, and now appeared swimming with a sort of contentment in the calm waters of the university, he still cultivated his fantasy existence and still propounded his original assertion of the individual's right of judgment in artistic matters. Into the middle of his essay on the cathedral at Amiens (the fruit of a last late summer holiday in France in 1893, published in March 1894) he put that question which he called 'the salt of all aesthetic study', and which had first been put by him thirty years before: 'What, precisely what, is this to *me*?'

It was the question which, less obviously, he must have asked himself as he was stimulated by some beautiful face in a picture (like that of Romanino's St Gaudioso) or by such a story as that of Apollo and Hyacinth. And he continued to assert his right to create his own answer.

In the chapter on Lacedaemon in *Plato and Platonism* he had touched briefly on the Spartan festival of the *Hyacinthia*, celebrating 'the death of the hapless lad . . . greatly beloved of the god, who had slain him by sad accident as they played at quoits together delightfully.' The references are neutral and scholarly – as detached in tone as the subsequent brief mention of Spartan warriors as 'the beloved and the lover, side by side . . .' on the battlefield. No parent was likely to write anxiously to Pater or the Brasenose authorities as a result of these anodyne and no more than obligatory statements of historical fact. And this consciously austere tone is, suitably, the tone of the whole book, which ends with a recommendation to love the intellectually astringent, well-drilled, patiently achieved 'dry beauty' which Plato himself recommends and is shown to have – against the instincts of his temperament – achieved.

This view of Plato recalls Marius, Gaston de Latour and Pater himself in middle age. As so often, he comes near to describing his own state of mind when he analyzes the personality about whom he is writing (and for him Plato is a personality before he is a philosopher). The 'persistent hold of sensible things' on Plato suggests one affinity, and identification goes further in a sentence of almost autobiographical emphasis: 'Austere as he seems, and on well-considered principle really is, his temperance or austerity, aesthetically so winning, is attained only by the chastisement, the control, of a variously interested, a richly sensuous nature.'

For Pater the story of Apollo and Hyacinth had a resonance far too profound to be contained by cursory reference in an expository, semi-pedagogic book which – whether he quite intended it or not – signalled his return to the academic milieu of Oxford and partial acceptance of its standards. 'Austere as he seems . . .' in *Plato and Platonism*, he had also to give expression to the richly sensuous nature which was there so firmly controlled.

The book was published in February 1893. By July Pater was telling friends of his plans to settle again in Oxford during the summer and then go abroad before the new term began. 'Abroad' meant France with Hester and Clara: it was to be their final holiday together. They travelled as far as Vézelay, but also spent some time in Picardy, notably at Amiens (and probably also visiting Beauvais). By the early autumn he could report that he had returned from France with his mind 'rather full just now' of the 'fine old churches' which he had been studying.

At some point probably between publication of *Plato and Platonism* and the holiday in France Pater completed *Apollo in Picardy*, the last piece of purely imaginative work which he published. It was printed in the American-European periodical *Harper's New Monthly Magazine* in November 1893, and may possibly have been written – or at least finished – as the result of a direct commission. No record survives to explain the circumstances or the choice

197

of periodical (where Pater had never appeared before), but the story is as free and fantasy-filled as *Emerald Uthwart* and hardly less horribly macabre than that of *Denys l'Auxerrois*. Once again, it is about a pagan god returned in medieval times, Brother Apollyon, who is at once beautiful and sinister, destroying the lives of a prior and novice who have left their community to recuperate in a valley of Picardy. The French countryside, monasticism, and its buildings, the juxtaposition of extreme beauty and death, religion, pity, cruelty and madness – all Pater's dreams, nightmares as well as wish-fulfilments, find expression here. And all culminates in a re-telling of the death of Hyacinth which would certainly have marred the cool, rational mood of *Plato and Platonism*, as shockingly as a real blood-stain on its title-page. While Pater was demurely travelling through Picardy with his sisters, admiring cathedrals and small medieval towns and the autumnal landscape, he must already have created this wild and ultimately despairing cry, set in that region, against the destructive, tyrannous spell of beauty. That disturbing power overturns – as the story shows – religious faith and drives men mad.

Prior Saint-Jean, dedicated from childhood to the monastic life, destined apparently to write a profound treatise and due soon to become abbot of his monastery, discovers the beautiful sleeping figure, golden-haired and white-limbed, who calls himself Brother Apollyon. Mysteriously powerful music comes from Apollyon's tarnished harp, his sole possession apart from a bow which he teaches the use of to the young novice Hyacinth ('pet of the community', with 'rebellious masses of . . . black hair, with blue in the depths of it') who learns to shed blood. Apollyon attracts the rare animals and birds, but wantonly slays them, breaks their backs and leaves them pierced with arrows. His knowledge amazes the prior and then drives him distracted. And finally, after Hyacinth has found a discus dug up in making a grave, he and Apollyon strip naked on a stormy night to play the game that kills him as the wind, perhaps, sends the discus flying from Apollo's hand to crush in his skull: 'The last drops of the blood of Hyacinth still trickled through the thick masses of dark hair . . .'

The god goes free. The prior is suspected of murder and becomes deranged. His monastery intervenes and withdraws him, no longer prior but simply a brother, to their own community. What remains of his life passes – almost like that of Ruskin – in a peaceful, protected but vacant contemplation ('He never again set pen' to his confused, unfinished treatise). He gazes longingly towards the valley where Hyacinth died and where blue flowers now bloom. Eventually, it is agreed he may return there; but the permission arrives

198

too late. Standing up and gazing out, amid preparations for his journey, Brother Saint-Jean has died.

The end is really more disillusioning than that of *Emerald Uthwart*, but no less a confession. The failure of the monk Saint-Jean to keep his sanity comes from his leaving, unwillingly, the cloistered environment of the monastery where he was bred. There he was destined for great things: he is obedient, talented and pious. He had never left it before ('busy and satisfied through youth and early manhood'), and he goes apprehensively – as Pater had gone out into the world from his pious, cloistered childhood. 'The seductive person of this mysterious being', the beautiful slayer Apollo, had in some way haunted him too. The monk clearly, if unconsciously, loves the novice whom Apollo slays; he is suspected of murder, 'in a fit of mania, induced by dissolute living . . .' Pater had been suspected of scarcely lesser crimes. No more than the wretched witless monk could he recover his earlier untroubled faith, itself as a bulwark frail against sensuous, indeed sexual desires.

Something of the hopelessness which haunts that story lingers around the ostensibly more straightforward essay, *The Age of Athletic Prizemen*, which Pater had finished just about the time *Apollo in Picardy* was published. It was one in a fitful series of studies of Greek sculpture which he never lived to complete, and which Shadwell was to assemble very soon after his death. When Pater writes of the *Discobolus*, he almost inevitably thinks of it in connection with the incident of Apollo and Hyacinth. Less overt though actually closer in feeling is the sense he conveys of a faint melancholy passing across the very statues he most admires, 'even with the veritable prince of that world of antique bronze and marble, the *Discobolus at rest* of the Vatican.' Their perfect physical beauty – for all that it is fixed in unchanging material – only reminds him that in life it could never have been fixed, was always on the verge of fading or being slightly chilled by the dawning of thought, awakening sensations and perhaps the stirring of awareness of pain. One of the 'very pleasantest human likenesses' he finds is of Trypho, son of Eutychus, which he knew well from the British Museum: 'With all the suppleness, the delicate muscularity, of the flower of his youth, his handsome face . . .' For Pater Trypho has almost ceased to be a statue, yet he understands that this image came from a cemetery, 'a son it was hard to leave in it at nineteen or twenty', and that the boy vividly portrayed as emerging from the tomb was commemorated in this way exactly because he no longer lived.

Like both Apollo and Hyacinth, like Romanino's St Gaudioso and Shakespeare's Claudio, he represents the essence of beauty which continued to elude Pater. All these are similar to the faces glimpsed in his childhood, the faces that Florian Deleal felt activating in him 'the lust of the eye' which was to lead him so far. And in writing that, at the age of not quite forty, Pater had already sighed, 'Could he have foreseen the weariness of the way!'

By the time *The Age of Athletic Prizemen* appeared in print in 1894 (in the *Contemporary Review*) Pater had experienced not only that accustomed weariness but – more alarmingly and untypically – a bout of quite serious physical illness. He had returned to Oxford to work as busily as ever. Letters had accumulated, and the actual move to the new house was fatiguing, emotionally perhaps as much as practically: it was a return with something final about it, almost a retreat from London, which may have slightly depressed Hester and Clara. Pater had found his summer visit to France had stimulated that old, boyhood fondness for architecture; he began a new series of essays, *Some Great Churches of France*, though only those on Amiens and Vézelay were written. Indeed, new projects probably seemed more tempting to him than old ones, especially if they were comparatively short. *Gaston de Latour* was left on one side, perhaps in the recognition that it would never be finished.

As Christmas 1893 approached, Pater became ill. It was a period which may always have made him and his sisters feel the sort of loneliness Mary Robinson had become aware of when she stumbled on the three of them evoking a ridiculous imaginary family. Christmas may have recalled – at least for Hester and Clara – that Christmas of 1862 at Dresden when their aunt had died. And the first Christmas again at Oxford, away from the friendliness of the Robinson family as neighbours in Earl's Terrace, might well seem particularly lonely.

On 17 December Pater told a correspondent that he was confined to the house with bronchitis. By 4 January he was better, though obviously not totally fit, and spoke of having been 'laid up with a very disagreeable attack of influenza, or something of the sort'. However, with the beginning of the new term, he had recovered to the extent of being overwhelmed by work and perhaps found that state mentally reassuring. He submitted his essay on Amiens to the *Nineteenth Century* and was pleased by the approval of the editor, James Knowles, who was an architect.

Pater had published hardly anything on architecture, despite his strong response to it, perhaps because he felt, reluctantly, the prestige of Ruskin's writings on the subject. In writing about Amiens he began, in a tacit rejection of Ruskin, by asserting the secular character of the cathedral; even the carving (the subject of Ruskin's

Bible of Amiens) is interpreted as secular, 'free' in spirit, human and personal. And the prose style seems deliberately calm, unluxuriant, presenting an impression of the building unfolding as if being walked through by someone sober yet sensitive. Finally, even Amiens is tinged with wistfulness. The cathedral is seen brooding over a bare, sad countryside, offering in its cliffs of quarried and carved stone some sort of hope to existence which apparently ends 'in a sparely built coffin under the flinty soil, and grey, driving sea-winds'. In much the same way, in writing about Vézelay a month or two later, Pater leaves it on a half-melancholy, regretful note despite all his praise for its bold, crude, original sculpture. The restless, excited Gothic of Amiens has been exchanged for monastic repose and a sense of eternal duration; yet the monasticism of Vézelay is felt to be enclosed, exclusive and outworn. Life has withdrawn from the monument, as it had from an old sanctuary occupied and then deserted by farm labourers; the essay ends with the words of a peasant explaining as much: 'Maintenant il n'y a personne là.'

No premonitions touched Pater. Far from withdrawing, he was almost feverishly engaged in tasks and willing to consider others. The first six months of 1894 were occupied by projects to write about Lovelace (considered and rejected), and to lecture on Rubens and on Pascal, apart from revising some earlier essays for re-publication and preparing further studies of French churches and Greek sculpture. Among the fragmentary work which was to be found among his papers after death was a study of Dr Johnson, and also essays begun on Hobbes, on Dante and on Newman's writings.

In early March he experienced the mild shock of William Rothenstein's drawing of him, a shock apparently fully shared by Hester and Clara. Pater had reached a rueful acceptance of his own appearance and to Mary Robinson's sister had even been able to make a joke of it. On learning that she was coming to see a performance of Aristophanes' *Frogs*, he said that she must come and see him: 'Look on me as one of the Frogs.' Nevertheless, Rothenstein's drawing, intended for publication, was disconcerting. To the artist he called it 'a clever likeness'. To Bussell he exploded, 'Do I look like a Barbary ape?' Hester and Clara were enlisted, no doubt willingly enough; and on Easter Sunday Pater warned John Lane that they would shortly be in London and would inspect the drawing. 'I will abide by their decision in the matter.' They vetoed publication, clearly to Pater's relief.

It was on Easter Monday, 26 March, that Pater had a visit from Moorhouse, become the vicar of a church at Bath and in 1894 invited to give the university sermon at Oxford. Moorhouse intermittently kept up the contact, and on this occasion, after some reminiscence, positively asked Pater if it was true – as he had heard – that he had changed his opinions about religion. The question was friendly, naïve and too direct. Pater, smiling, put it by, merely murmuring about what discussions he and Moorhouse had had in the old days. Perhaps Moorhouse felt a gleam of Christian hope when Pater went on to ask about his hymn-writing and said that good hymns were greatly needed. But the moment had passed. Marius-like, Pater had declined to commit himself. To both men there could be nothing special about this meeting. They looked forward to meeting again. Only in retrospect did it take on a certain significance; Pater remained, it seemed, in the mood he projected into Botticelli's Madonnas: neither for God nor for His enemies.

In talking to Moorhouse he may have mentioned that he was leaving Oxford two days later for a visit to the north of England and Scotland; and he may even have told him the reason. An honorary degree of LL.D. had been conferred on him by the University of Glasgow: the first and last such honour he received. Travelling slowly, staying in some of the 'Northern cathedral towns' on the route, Pater made his way to Glasgow, where the ceremony took place on 13 April.

One of the places he stopped at was York. From there he wrote again to Lane with the news of Hester and Clara's veto, and also to amend some lines he had contributed to go with the publication of Rothenstein's portrait of Bussell in the same series. The text had been brief, though enthusiastic ('His versatility is remarkable . . . He is capable of much.'). But now, for some reason, Pater proposed omission of the sentence, 'His friends love him; and he is popular with the Undergraduates he instructs.' In fact this omission was not made.

Before the end of April Pater was back in Oxford. He resumed his work, still obedient to Balzac's dictum about 'Le travail . . .', and probably feeling encouraged by the recognition implied by Glasgow. In June there appeared the article on Vézelay, the last to be published in his lifetime. And although he wrote of being 'very busy', he was not now to manage to finish any other article or lecture.

His gout was bad enough by mid-June to restrict him from walking about in Oxford. Already in May, it seems, he had begun to feel very unwell and was conscious of age coming on. Soon he was ill, seriously ill, with an attack of rheumatic fever. He remained in bed at 64, St Giles', looked after by Hester and Clara. Help in nursing him was given by John Addington Symonds's sister Charlotte, the widow of T. H. Green, who had taken up nursing after her husband's death and who had looked after Jowett during his final illness.

Although ill and weak (weaker than was quite realized), Pater began to recover. He had two engagements to lecture in Oxford at the end of July, to the University Extension Students, to whom his lecture on Raphael had been given in August two years previously. On Saturday 28 July, he was due to speak about Rubens – but that lecture was probably cancelled or postponed when he first became ill. On Monday 30 July it was intended that he would speak about Pascal, and preparing the text of this lecture became a task to which he attached himself obstinately.

The personality of Pascal – witty, sceptical, a stylist physically diseased and mentally doubtful until the end about the faith he wished to hold – was uncovered with a sympathy which was all empathy. The remarks about Pascal's maladies – with even a reference to 'the small compass of the sick chamber' – are at once understanding and yet partly irritable, as if Pater was irritated with his own body and impatiently determined to force himself back to his usual health. As he analyzes more closely Pascal becomes like Plato: someone in whom reason has been induced, as it were, to conceal the fundamental power of the imagination.

Pater appeared to have recovered sufficiently to come downstairs and take up work again on this manuscript. To Hester and Clara he seems to have shown himself cheerful and lively – and he probably felt instinctive relief at being once more active. As he lay ill in bed he may have remembered lying in bed as a child, experiencing with a sort of wonder the first sensations of bodily pain flowing and ebbing in 'that little white room' at Enfield, with its window across which the blossoms beat on gusty mornings. He had often enough put into his writing speculations about 'the last morning, the last recognition of some object of affection, hand or voice . . .', pondering fascinated on how death would come.

Sitting writing by an open window at 64, St Giles', Pater caught a chill which rapidly turned to pleurisy. The Pascal manuscript, not finished, was probably interrupted at this point. He had reached a sentence beginning, 'Now in him the imagination itself was like a physical malady, troubling, disturbing, or in active collusion with it – ' Or this sentence, the last one in the manuscript, may have been added by Pater as gradually he recovered from this attack too and became convalescent.

Yet it must have been clear that he was not going to be sufficiently well to lecture on Monday 30 July. That day was fixed, instead, for him and his sisters to travel down to Devon to stay in an old farmhouse which belonged to Bussell. Walks and drives in the countryside were planned: a relief for Hester and Clara, as well as himself, from the worrying weeks they had undergone. And there he would celebrate, on 4 August, his fifty-fifth birthday.

On the Sunday Pater was sufficiently recovered to leave his bedroom and spend the day downstairs. He had considered all the details of the following day's journey, when they would presumably have been met by Bussell, who was anyway going to be living nearby, and he had insisted on making a payment to Bussell's tenant in the farmhouse where they would stay. 'Not a tithe of the stimulus to one's imagination,' Pater had complained to Sharp after the one summer holiday spent in Cornwall, comparing it with visits to 'quite unrenowned places abroad'. Apart from the blueness of the sea in Devon, he perhaps hardly expected much stimulus – simply a quiet period in which to regain his strength before the autumn.

At ten o'clock on the Monday morning, he left his room and started down the stairs. Before he could go further, he had a sudden, violent heart-attack. Clara – possibly Hester as well – got to him as he was dying. He died on the staircase, Gosse recorded, 'in the arms of his sister'.

*   *   *

The funeral was held on 2 August in a mid-summer vacation Oxford doubtless largely deserted. Some university officials, however, were present, as well as Bussell and Shadwell, Mrs Green, Gosse and a few other friends, in addition to Hester and Clara.

It had all happened ironically and abruptly. Death had come to Pater quite unforeseen, and almost painlessly, after so many years of fearful anticipation. It was the most dramatic event in a quiet and unobtrusive life, leaving his reputation a little uncertain and his work unfinished. And yet, in a way, nothing – probably not even great age – would have fixed what was in its essence subjective, restlessly individual, an almost diseased sensibility (as he called it himself). He had done all he could. His life had broken off much as his essay on Pascal broke off: the imagination . . . He had suffered for it, proclaimed it, defended it and tried to build works of art out of it. Something had always eluded him. Perhaps he had failed, though at least he did not survive to experience the slow withering of what reputation he had, the suffocating of what for him had been an existence of agonizing intensity under dusty layers of neglect, indifference, misunderstanding and near-ridicule.

Not much could be done for Pater in death. What did it matter, he had asked about Emerald Uthwart's bitter experiences, reflecting on his own. Perhaps he would have savoured not only the expressed tribute of his family and friends but the sentence with which *The Times* seemed to hint at his ineradicable aestheticism, as it closed its brief notice of his funeral: 'The coffin was covered with beautiful wreaths.'

Notes on the text

INTRODUCTION

Pater's amusing qualities as a schoolboy, etc., are testified to by John Rainier McQueen in an important letter of 17 May 1906 to Thomas Wright, printed in his *Life of Walter Pater*, 1907, I, pp. xviii–xix. Benson does not record even the existence of McQueen.

Lionel Johnson's tribute ('Mr Pater's Humour') was printed in *The Academy* (51), 16 January 1897.

The acquaintance, later a close friend, was William Sharp, whose perceptive *Reminiscences of Pater* appeared in the *Atlantic Monthly*, December 1894, pp. 801–14.

Bywater's letter, to Dr Diels of Berlin, is printed in W. W. Jackson, *Ingram Bywater*, 1917, pp. 78ff.

The editorials of the *Daily Telegraph* and the *Evening News* after Wilde's conviction are quoted at length by H. Montgomery Hyde, *Trials of Oscar Wilde*, 1960 ed., pp. 11–12.

Pater's previously unpublished note to himself is quoted by Lawrence Evans, *Letters of Walter Pater*, 1970, p. xxix.

Bussell's sermon, with an additional note he made to it, is now conveniently printed in Samuel Wright, *A Bibliography of the writings of Walter H. Pater*, 1975, pp. 187ff.

Pater's childhood experiences referred to in the text come from *The Child in the House*, 1878.

CHAPTER ONE

No. 1, Honduras Terrace survives, though altered inside and with a later, stucco façade, as 368, Commercial Road and is occupied by the London Trustee Savings Bank. The fifth house of the terrace, formed between Johnson Street and Hardinge Street, has been demolished.

Queen Victoria's first letter of two written on 4 August 1839 to Lord Melbourne is printed in *The Letters of Queen Victoria*, ed. A. C. Benson and Viscount Esher, Vol. I, 1908, pp. 179–80.

On the history of Stepney, see for example N. Pevsner, *London* (Buildings of England series), 1952.

The memoirs of the Reverend William Quekett are '*My Sayings and Doings*', *with reminiscences of my life*, 1888.

Statistics for life expectancy in Stepney are quoted by Pevsner, *op. cit.*, p. 413, from Chadwick's *Report on the Sanitary Conditions of the Labouring Classes*, 1842.

John Thompson Pater, eldest son of Thompson Pater and Mary Church of Weston Underwood, Buckinghamshire, is recorded in *Holden's Triennial Directory* between 1805 and 1808 as 'surgeon and man midwife', living near the ponds, Highgate. That he moved to Commercial Road is proved by the tombstone at Enfield of his widow, transcribed by Wright: '. . . Relict of the late/MR THOMPSON PATER, Surgeon,/ of the Commercial Road, London.' A list of creditors published in *The Times* of 11 November 1808 includes 'T. Pater, Shadwell, Surgeon'.

The *Kent Poll Book* of 1802 records Richard Glode of Orpington; further information in *The Gentleman's Magazine*, 1804, Pt II, p. 984, mentioning his death in October of that year and giving the year of his knighthood as 1793.

The registers of St Swithin's, London Stone, record children of George and Elizabeth Grange born between 1759 and 1772. The relevant children are the girls Sophia (born 1 January 1761), Hester (1 March 1764) and Susanna (29 June 1769). Susanna did not marry. Elizabeth Grange died in the parish in 1793, aged 59. George Grange must then have gone to live with Sophia at Hadlow, where he died in 1809, aged 79, though buried with his wife in London.

The place of birth of Maria Pater, *née* Hill, is given by her in the 1851 census return. George Hill & Co. are recorded in *Kent's Directory for London* in 1801; by 1807 they are said to be warehousemen.

William and Matilda Pater had at least three children, though only one survived. From 6, Hardwick Place they moved to No. 1, Marine Place, Commercial Road; there on 10 November 1843 was born Josephina Clara (who is presumably the 'Myra' Pater known to Wright); on 22 September 1844 was born there Emily who died a few days later. Whether both Pater brothers gave the name Clara to one of their daughters for a specific reason is not known; it seems not to have been previously a family name.

The choice of Walter Horatio for Pater's names is discussed in Ch. 2.

The 'devoted nursing' of the cat was recorded, along with other detailed memories, by Mrs Humphry Ward, *A Writer's Recollections*, 1919 ed., p. 124.

William Pater died at Marine Place. His death was registered by Barbara Hill of 3, Strathmore Terrace, Shadwell, who had been present at it. Given that the surname is common, and that she is nowhere mentioned, it seems unlikely that Barbara Hill was related to Pater's mother.

The widowed Matilda Macdonald Pater married again on 3 February 1849, at the parish church of Hackney. Her second husband was a widower and a doctor of medicine living in Poplar, Dr Horatio Bloomfield, son of an army officer; she gave her father's profession as doctor of medicine.

The end of the sentence quoted from the 'Conclusion' to the first edition of *Studies in the History of the Renaissance* was modified in reprinting to the weaker and safer: '. . . and then our place knows us no more.'

Gosse's references to Pater's father are in his recollections of Pater, *The Contemporary Review*, July-Dec. 1894, p.796.

CHAPTER TWO

Benson, *op. cit.*, 1906, p. 2, refers to the house at Enfield as 'now demolished' and as being 'in the neighbourhood of Chase Side'. Gosse, *loc. cit.*, already speaks of it as gone. Lamb's reference to the stiles of Enfield comes in *Mrs Gilpin riding to Edmonton* (first published in *The Table Book*, 16 July 1827).

The associations Pater makes in discussing Rossetti's *The House of Life* sound as if Baudelaire was, consciously or not, inspiring him, cf. *Spleen* (LXXVIII) of *Les Fleurs du mal*:

> *Un gros meuble à tiroirs encombré de bilans,*
> *De vers, de billets doux, de procès, de romances,*
> *Avec de lourds cheveux roulés dans des quittances . . .*
> *Je suis un vieux boudoir plein de roses fanées*

The row of Lombardy poplars which 'formerly' stood in front of Enfield Court is mentioned in G. K. Hodson and E. Ford, *A History of Enfield*, 1873, p. 183.

References in the text to the various people named Pater living in the late 1830s and 1840s are drawn chiefly from certificates of birth, death and marriage. Lieutenant-General John Pater is referred to several times, along with places he gave his name to, in H. Davison Lowe, *Vestiges of Old Madras* (Indian Records Series), 1913, Vol. III.

The date of the marriage of Thompson Pater and Mary Church at Newport Pagnell is from the local parish register and has not previously been published. T. Wright, *op. cit.*, gives some entries for Roman Catholic baptism at Weston of their children and it was he who drew attention to Robert Pater of Thornton.

Some information about Walter Barton May (by a slip referred to as William) can be gleaned from the souvenir brochure *Hadlow – a thousand years of village life*, published there on the occasion of Hadlow's millennium in July 1975. A photograph of 'May's Folly' was reproduced in the London *Evening News*, 5 June 1976, on its purchase by a Danish student.

Maria Pater's will was signed on 7 January 1851.

Mary Susanna May's children who died young are buried in the elaborate May vault in Hadlow churchyard. Her grandson, Walter Reginald, is buried in the Porter-May vault (along with her own parents John and Sophia Porter); he died 16 April 1846 and his place of death is given simply as 'Hadlow', indicating almost certainly that he had not died at Fish Hall.

Susanna Grange died of bronchitis, 16 April 1855, at Fish Hall; she is buried in the Porter-May vault in Hadlow churchyard.

Mrs Humphry Ward's references to Hester and Clara are in *A Writer's Recollections*, 1919 ed., pp. 123–24; it is clear that she much preferred Clara, 'a personality never to be forgotten by those who loved her'.

Of Pater's appearance in his early Oxford days, a Brasenose undergraduate of the 1860s, S. Waddington, *Chapters of my Life*, 1909, p. 35, noted that it was 'by no means plain or ill-featured'.

Wright's story of the Pater brothers and the snake is in *The Life . . .*, Vol. I, p. 52, said to have occurred at Harbledown. The only other mention Wright makes of them together records William's scoffing attitude to Tennyson's *Morte d'Arthur* when Pater chose it to recite in 1858 at his last King's School speech day (p. 138) and see here Ch. 3.

William's clerkship in a merchant's office in 1851 is recorded in the March 1851 census. The *Army List* for August 1861 records him as an Assistant Surgeon in the East Kent Regiment (the 'Buffs'). Pater's reference to him in 1859 is to his having been at Portsmouth with his regiment, 'unless he has shifted his quarters recently' (*Letters . . .*, p. 1).

The manuscript of *Tibalt the Albigense* is now in the Houghton Library, Harvard

University, as is that of *Gaudioso the Second* referred to in the text below.

That Pater was called 'Parson Pater' when at Enfield Grammar School on account of his strange ways was recollected by a fellow-pupil G. J. Glass, speaking at an Old Boys' dinner in 1912; his unfortunately brief reference was reported in the *Enfield Observer* of 29 March 1912, and is also quoted in L. Birkett Marshall, *A Brief History of Enfield Grammar School*, 1958, p. 33.

The dissension in Enfield parish church between Daniel Harrison and David Waddington, M.P., took place in April 1854 and was the subject of an exchange of letters which Waddington had printed and circulated.

According to Wright, *The Life . . .*, Vol. I, p. 21, Pater himself was taught at Enfield to make flowers out of sealing-wax by a boy named first Howgrave, and afterwards Graham, the adopted nephew of the occupier of a nearby 'large and venerable mansion'. It may therefore be relevant to note that in 1855 a certain James George Graham lived at East Lodge, Enfield.

The headmaster of the Grammar School at Enfield from 1847 to 1874 was Charles Chambers, B.A. No connection seems established between him and the King's School at Canterbury, nor between that school and the May family.

Charles Sturges is recorded as a surgeon living at 1a, Sidney Square, Commercial Road.

CHAPTER THREE

It was Wright, *op. cit.*, who first linked the reference in *Marius* to the circumstances of Maria Pater's death. He specifically stated in a footnote (Vol. I, p. 74, note 1), 'I have proof that this is autobiographical'; but he did not provide it.

At Harbledown the Paters lived at No. 12, Harbledown Place (built in 1824, technically therefore a George IV period terrace). It has not proved possible to trace the ownership of this house which was probably rented by them.

Most of the detailed information in this chapter about Dombrain and McQueen – as well as Pater – comes from what McQueen told Wright, either in letters or verbally. Some of it was badly muddled by Wright as examination of the letters in the Lilly Library, Indiana University, establishes. The comparison of Haydock with a bull was actually (according to a letter of 10 Nov. 1903) McQueen's not Pater's, but it is clear they both admired Haydock.

The anti-Camden Society sermon of 1844 is referred to and quoted from by Kenneth Clark, *The Gothic Revival*, 1964 ed., pp. 150–51.

It was in 1859 that a group of parishioners at Enfield petitioned Parliament about the practices of the vicar, after the local bishop had expressly but vainly asked him to discontinue them.

McQueen's interesting reference to almost his first visit to Pater at Harbledown, and Pater's knowledge of architecture, is in a letter of 26 March 1904 to Wright, from which Wright failed to quote. Attention is drawn to the passage by Samuel Wright, *A Bibliography of the writings of Walter H. Pater*, 1975, p. 49.

McQueen's character is commented on frankly by Samuel Wright, *op. cit.*, p. 150, and he there tells the facts about McQueen ejecting his wife.

McQueen's will was made on 21 September 1908; Mrs Mary McQueen, his wife, received an annuity (dating from 21 June 1900) which was confirmed in the will. Magnus Rainier Robertson became a captain in the First World War and was killed in 1918; I owe to the Reverend Ivor Townley Clarkson (son of one of McQueen's executors) the information that Robertson had been educated at McQueen's expense.

Of Pater's very early verse all that has been printed in full is *The Chant of the Celestial Sailors* (by E. H. Blakeney at his private press, Winchester, 1928) and this is probably the least interesting piece he wrote.

That Pater did visit Pendergast is perhaps not strictly proven, but his letters from Oxford (Evans, Nos 3 & 4) speak of going to call when in London, as anyway their business will have required, and the style of address ('My dear Mr Pendergast') implies direct acquaintance.

For the King's School background during Pater's years there, apart from the information in Wright, there are factual details in D. L. Edwards, *A History of the King's School, Canterbury*, 1957, pp. 126ff.

CHAPTER FOUR

Oxford Life is printed in full by Samuel Wright, *A Bibliography . . .*, p. 154.

Jowett's prophecy about Pater (and Bywater) is variously recorded, sometimes said to have consisted in foreseeing 'firsts' for them both.

Bywater's comments about Pater, less favourable to the don than to the undergraduate, are to be found in W. W. Jackson, *Ingram Bywater*, 1917, 78ff.

McQueen's letter of 16 October 1858 to his grandmother is quoted by Thomas Wright, *The Life . . .*, Vol. I, p. 146.

Symonds's comment on Arnold's lecture was made in his diary in the winter term of 1860; it is printed by H. F. Brown, *John Addington Symonds, A Biography*, 1903, p. 84. Moorhouse (see under) is the source for Pater's enjoyment of Arnold's lectures.

Moorhouse's recollections were given by letter to Thomas Wright, who prints them *op. cit.*, Vol. I, *passim*.

Robert McQueen's letter of 12 November 1858 in quoted in Wright, *op. cit.*, Vol. I, p. 167.

Symonds' references to his ritualism at Harrow occur in his autobiography, printed by Brown, *op. cit.*, p. 54; the letter of 3 June 1860 to his sister, *ibid.*, p. 77.

I owe my awareness of Mackarness's strictures on *Studies in the History of the Renaissance* to the kindness of Dr Bernard Richards; they were made in *A Charge delivered to the Clergy of the Diocese of Oxford, At his Second Visitation in the Cathedral Church of Christ*, 20 April 1875.

Jowett's remark in his diary is given by Mrs Humphry Ward, *A Writer's Recollections*, 1919 ed., p. 131.

Wordsworth's sermon, and its effect on her, are referred to by Mrs Humphry Ward, *op. cit.*, pp. 167–68.

The 'enemy to all Gothic darkness' remark is recorded by Wright, *op. cit.*, Vol. I, p. 188 as Pater's 'very own words'.

Pater's unpublished, short letters in 1859 and 1860 to the King's School, Canterbury, about his exhibition remain in possession of the school.

Details of Symonds' income at Oxford, the pictures for his rooms and his breakfasts, are given in Phyllis Grosskurth, *John Addington Symonds, A biography*, 1964, pp. 44–46. According to Wright, *op. cit.*, Vol. 1, p. 194, Symonds did meet Pater briefly in these years, though he records that they never liked each other. Symonds asked McQueen what sort of person Pater was: 'Is he an able man?'

Ward's useful and detailed recollections were given to Benson, *op. cit.*, p. 18.

This comment by Capes, and that quoted later above about Pater's intellectual tendencies, occur in a letter of 1906 to Wright, *op. cit.*, Vol. I, pp. 160 and 165 respectively.

Wright seems to have been as solemn as Moorhouse and far more muddled about Pater's attitude to Browning (*op. cit.*, Vol. I, pp. 172–73). For Pater's real views it is sufficient to cite his letter to Arthur Symons in 1886, calling Browning 'one of my best-loved writers' (*Letters* . . ., p. 70), but he also thought that the admirable qualities of his finest verse were really those of imaginative prose (*Letters* . . ., p. 80). Quite possibly he was to say as much to Wilde, and hence Wilde's quip, 'Meredith is a prose Browning, and so is Browning.'

The incident of Pater reacting angrily to denigration of Flaubert was told by Douglas Ainslie, an undergraduate at Exeter College, who became friendly with Pater in the late 1880s, to Benson: *op. cit.*, p. 185.

Conceivably Pater entirely made up *Gertrude of Himmelstadt*, but the story in essence sounds traditional. No traceable castle or place called Himmelstadt seems to exist, though there is Seligenstadt and Himmelreich, and its 'heavenly' name may be part of some allegorical significance, as might also the choice of the name Gertrude (meaning literally 'spear-strength'). Perhaps Pater was aware, too, of

Bulwer-Lytton's *Pilgrims of the Rhine*, whose heroine is a Gertrude – and she dies at Heidelberg.

Moorhouse published his version of Pater's story as *The Rescue* (*Studies in Verse: By Land and Sea*, 1898 (see Samuel Wright, *A Bibliography* . . ., p. 140)). In one of McQueen's letters to Thomas Wright about Pater's version, he *does* refer to it as 'St Gertrude . . .', but this may be a slip of memory.

William Foster Pater (*c.* 1804–74) was the son of John Church Pater and thus a cousin of Pater's father. He is recorded at various addresses in Islington. He married Elizabeth Carter and they had at least five children: Sophia Elizabeth, Henry, Ann Matilda, Albert Foster and George Frederick. For the latter (who died the same year as his father) there is an East India connection; he is recorded as a merchant of Madras, 'but late of Rangoon', at the time letters of administration were granted. William Foster made his simple will in 1868, when living at 13, Richmond Villas, Seven Sisters Road, Islington; he later lived in St Peter's Square, Hammersmith. At the birth of Ann Matilda in 1837 the family was living at 6, Cloudesley Terrace, Islington. The effects after death of William Foster were sworn at under £400, afterwards re-sworn at under £800.

Pater's letter to Pendergast (*Letters* . . ., p. 2) is known only in this fragmentary form, with the addition to what is quoted above of a preceding sentence: '. . . I am going to take my B.A. on Thursday . . .'

Pater's cautious comments on the School of English Literature proposal were in a letter solicited and published by the *Pall Mall Gazette* in 1886 *Letters* . . ., pp. 68–69).

CHAPTER FIVE

McQueen's existing letters to Wright cover the period 1903–06 and are preserved in the Lilly Library, Indiana University. Copies of Pater's poems and letters which he sent Wright over the same period are not in the collection. The letter which enclosed his poem *John by the side of John* is dated 10 November 1903.

McQueen's diary references to Pater were printed by Wright, *The Life . . .*, Vol. 1, *passim*. His explanation of Pater's dualism (Wright, p. 201) was written as a note in F. Greenslet's *Walter Pater*, New York 1903, London 1904.

Moorhouse's recollections were given to Wright in letters which unfortunately appear not to have survived, but they are quoted extensively in *The Life . . .*, Vol. I.

Wright mentions Hoole very briefly and does not even give his full name.

McQueen told Wright (letter of 29 January 1904) that he knew none of Pater's friends at Queen's and that he and Moorhouse never met at Oxford: a fact Wright did not print.

Channing's recollection was given to Wright, *The Life . . .*, Vol. II, p. 141.

Rothenstein's reference to Pater assembling good-looking undergraduates for lunch parties occurs in his *Men and Memories*, Vol. I, 1931, p. 139.

There seems no basis for Wright's anecdote of Bessie Pater questioning Pater about his plans, 'after he had taken his degree' (*The Life . . .*, Vol. I, p. 209) and it barely makes sense. Wright had anyway, from some muddled source, got the year of her death wrong.

McQueen clearly stated (letter of 26

November 1903 to Wright) that the final estrangement took place before the Long Vacation of 1860, but Wright's circumstantial account of Dombrain's part in it and its happening in October must have some basis, possibly in what McQueen told him on a later visit and it is also borne out by W. K. W. Chafy.

The King's School boy was W. K. W. Chafy. Wright got into touch with him and there are letters from Chafy to him among the Lilly Library material; but none of these precedes publication of *The Life*.

Wright's account of the steps in McQueen's efforts to prevent Pater's ordination is on several points at variance with a long memorandum he received from McQueen; he even quotes from this inaccurately (*The Life . . .*, Vol. I, p. 207). What is narrated in the text above derives from McQueen's own written statements. Wright is also wrong in saying Liddon was 'at this time' Vice-Principal of St Edmund Hall (*The Life . . .*, Vol. I, p. 207, note 1), though McQueen told him he was. Liddon had given up the post, having been ill during the summer of 1862; in December 1862 he went into residence at Christ Church (see J. O. Johnston, *Life and Letters of Henry Parry Liddon*, 1904, p. 63).

Pater's comment on Liddon is recorded by Wright, *The Life . . .*, Vol. I, p. 194.

The correct date of Bessie Pater's death was first published by Evans, *Letters . . .*, p. 2, note 3. Her death was registered (among Overseas Records) by Henry Dale, British Chaplain at Dresden; her residence is given merely as 'Dresden'. Wright records that there was a stone to her memory at Dresden; there is no trace of her leaving a will proved in England after her death. McQueen probably never realized how closely her death and his last letter to Pater coincided.

CHAPTER SIX

Pater's letter of 8 April 1863 from Oxford to Pendergast in *Letters . . .*, p. 2; other letters to Pendergast, *passim.* By November his address at Oxford was 9, Grove Street (now Magpie Lane), see *Letters . . .*, p. 3, note 1, further.

Jowett's comments to Symonds about fellowships are recorded in the latter's diary, cf. H. F. Brown, *John Addington Symonds, a Biography*, 1903 ed., pp. 149-50.

For information about the dates of Pater and his sisters staying at Sidmouth, derived from Lethaby's *Sidmouth Journal*, I am indebted to Dr G. H. Gibbens, hon. curator of the museum there.

Wright, *op. cit.*, I, p. 211, prints the Brasenose entry on Pater's election as a fellow.

Ward's comments about Pater's early reputation and appearance in Benson, *op. cit.*, pp. 22 and 26.

The passage about being 'washed out beyond the bar . . .' was dropped by Pater when he utilized these paragraphs for the 'Conclusion' to *Studies in the History of the Renaissance*.

Hornby's tribute is printed by Wright, *op. cit.*, I, pp. 221–22.

Benson's comments on Pater's character, *op. cit.*, pp. 26, 181.

Manson's 'Recollections of Walter Pater' were printed in *The Oxford Magazine*, 7 November 1906, pp. 60–61; though brief, these recollections are vivid and clear.

Bywater's remarks were made in a letter to Dr Diels of Berlin; the letter is printed in W. W. Jackson, *Ingram Bywater*, 1917, pp. 78ff.

Colvin's attitude to Pater is referred to

by L. Evans in *Letters . . .*, pp. 5–6, note 5, with further reference.

The relevant passage from Pattison's M.S. diary is quoted by Evans, *op. cit.*, p. xxxiv.

For the history of the 'Old Mortality' society, see first the *Memoir of John Nichol*, ed. W. A. Knight, 1896. A complete list of the members is given in H. A. L. Fisher, *James Bryce*, 1927, Vol. I, p. 48; but J. W. Hook [sic] of Queen's must be a misreading for the name Hoole (there was no undergraduate there then called Hook).

For communicating S. G. Brooke's comments in his diary (at Corpus Christi College) I am indebted to Dr Bernard Richards of Brasenose.

Shadwell's life and career were the subject of a long obituary notice in *The Times* on the day after his death, 14 February 1919. For passages about him printed in *The Oriel Record* at the time of his retirement, and on his death, I am indebted to Dr William Parry, librarian of the College. Wright's comment is *op. cit.*, Vol. I, p. 218.

Benson's assertion ('it is not disputed . . .') that Shadwell's was the temperament delineated in *Diaphaneitè*, *op. cit.*, p. 10, note 1.

Pater's letter to Shadwell in *Letters . . .*, p. 4.

Suggestions that *The School of Giorgione* in a preliminary form was the essay prepared for *Studies in the History of the Renaissance* in 1872 and then cancelled are made by L. Evans in *Letters . . .*, p. 8, note 1.

The passage about Rossellino occurs in the essay on *The Poetry of Michelangelo*, first published in *The Fortnightly Review*, November 1871.

The male homosexual interests and literature of the period in England are dealt with in Brian Reade's anthology, *Sexual Heretics*, 1970. Some details about Solomon and extracts from his *Vision of Love Revealed in Sleep* are printed there.

Swinburne's letters to Solomon do not survive, apparently, but their tone may be gauged by Solomon's side of the correspondence and by Swinburne's letters to other friends of the period (e.g. D. G. Rossetti); see *The Swinburne Letters*, ed. Cecil Y. Lang, Vol. II, 1959 (covering the years 1869–75).

Pater gave the year Solomon exhibited his *Bacchus* at the R.A. as 1868, but it was in fact 1867. For the reference in Hopkins' diary for 1868 I am indebted to Miss Paddy Kitchen.

Swinburne's letter of 6 June 1873 to George Powell describes being at Oxford, speaking with Pater ('a great friend of poor Simeon's') and Pater's reactions: Lang, *op. cit.*, p. 253. Pater's letter of 9 August 1889 to Horne: *Letters . . .*, pp. 100–01.

It was in a letter (of 16 September 1871) to Powell that Swinburne made fun of Queen Victoria for putting up memorials to the Prince Consort; Lang, *op. cit.*, pp. 157–58.

The description of Swinburne as a talker is by Henry Adams; it is quoted by James Pope-Hennessy, *Monckton Milnes, The Flight of Youth*, 1951, p. 140; *op. cit.*, pp. 144–45 for Swinburne reading his poems in the presence of the Archbishop of York.

Pater's letter to Swinburne, of 9 December 1872, *Letters . . .*, pp. 11–12.

The relevant part of Swinburne's letter of 28 November 1869 to D. G. Rossetti, Lang, *op. cit.*, p. 58; in his letter

of 11 April 1873 to Morley, *op. cit.*, pp. 240–41. The 'mediaeval' carol was appended to a letter to Rossetti of 22 December 1869, *op. cit.*, p. 72.

CHAPTER SEVEN

Ward's comment on Pater's philosophy lectures occurs in his 'Reminiscences', *Brasenose Quatercentenary Monographs*, XIV, 2, (C) 1909, pp. 74–75.

The description of the Pater house in Bradmore Road is Mrs Humphry Ward's: *A Writer's Recollections*, 1919 ed., pp. 123–24.

Pattison's outburst about Pater in Benson, *op. cit.*, p. 192. Subsequent anecdotes come from Benson, *loc. cit.*, unless otherwise identified.

Leslie Stephen's comment about Tito in *Romola* is in his *George Eliot* (English Men of Letters series), 1902, p. 139.

Pater's admiration for Arnold's manner and his recollection of the remarks about Browning were recorded by W. Sharp in his reminiscences of Pater, in the *Atlantic Monthly*, Dec. 1894, p. 804.

His praise of the Eton schoolboy who was knowledgeable about Mérimée and Gautier is told in H. E. Wortham, *Oscar Browning*, 1927, p. 60 and quoted by Evans, *Letters . . .*, p. 16.

Pater's comparison of undergraduates to roses in a hedgerow, and of one to a sausage, are in Wright, *op. cit.*, II, p. 119. The first anecdote is, unacknowledged by Wright, taken from a letter of Creighton's to Gosse, *Life and Letters of Mandell Creighton*, 1904, Vol. II, p. 112.

The 'steam-engine' anecdote in A. Symons, *A Study of Walter Pater*, 1932, p. 93.

Benson, *op. cit.*, p. 194, tells the story of

Pater supposedly calling religion a 'loathsome' disease and connects it with the original written reference.

Wright, *op. cit.*, II, p. 131, for Pater's comment about marriage. He quotes Wilde's criticism of Pater's prose (*op. cit.*, II, p. 110) which was printed in the *Nineteenth Century*, July 1890, p. 131. Pater's review of *The Picture of Dorian Gray* appeared in *The Bookman*, November 1891; it is conveniently reprinted in *Oscar Wilde* (a collection of critical essays), ed. R. Ellmann, 1969, pp. 35–38.

The remark about 'nature running to excess' is recorded by Sharp, *loc. cit.*, p. 810; he also mentions that, having made it, Pater himself demurred at the sweepingness of his own remark.

Pater's letter to Moore: *Letters . . .*, p. 81. Moore's complaints about Pater are quoted (from the *Pall Mall Magazine*, Aug. 1904) by Wright, *op. cit.*, II, p. 96. Pater's review of *Modern Painting* – his last book review, as it happened – appeared in the *Daily Chronicle*, 10 June 1893.

The Bradmore Road dinner-party incident is related by Mrs Humphry Ward, *op. cit.*, p. 121. This is the clearest surviving record of Pater causing controversy in a social setting, but other, if less dramatic, scenes may have occurred.

CHAPTER EIGHT
Arsène Houssaye, editor of *La Presse* and *l'Artiste*, was the original dedicatee of Baudelaire's *Petits Poèmes en prose*.

Wilde's recollection of Pater's question about writing prose was the opening of his review of *Appreciations* in the *Speaker*, 22 March 1890 (reprinted in *A Critic in Pall Mall*, 1919, pp. 187–94).

Pater's letter of 5 June 1864 to

Pendergast, *Letters . . .*, p. 3. On 1 August of the same year he wrote to Pendergast from 414, rue St Honoré, Paris (*loc. cit.*, note 5).

The visit of Dickens and Forster to the Morgue in Paris in 1847 is recorded by J. Forster, *The Life of Charles Dickens*, 1873 ed., Vol. II, p. 303. Forster earlier records, *op. cit.*, p. 294, that Dickens had gone there rather frequently, 'until shocked by something so repulsive that he had not courage for a long time to go back.' In 1864 the new Morgue was opened, replacing the old one Dickens had known.

The impossibility of imagining the Paters in a crowded railway station, etc. was stated by Elizabeth Wordsworth (Principal of Lady Margaret Hall), *Glimpses of the Past*, 1912, p. 140.

The deaths of the two young Pater girls was published in *The Times* for 24 January 1866.

Mrs May made her will at Fish Hall on 8 May 1862. Her death certificate gives the details of her death at Sidmouth on 7 February 1872. For information about her visits there I am indebted to Dr G. H. Gibbens, hon. curator of the museum, Sidmouth.

CHAPTER NINE
A letter from Pater to Macmillan, dated 29 June [1872], refers to a meeting in London previously when the prospect of publishing a book had been discussed: *Letters . . .*, pp. 7–8. His letter of 14 September [1884] (quoted with a wrong date of 1876 by S. Wright, *A Bibliography*, p. 63) is in *Letters . . .*, pp. 55–56.

H. J. Nicholl was the journalist and miscellaneous author to whom Pater wrote, on 28 November 1881, about his publications, including the essay on

Botticelli: *Letters* . . ., p. 41, footnote 2, giving the facts as they concern Pater and Ruskin.

Pater's own casts or copies of della Robbia: the Madonna relief is referred to by Sharp in the *Atlantic Monthly*, Dec. 1894, p. 806 (and this is perhaps the 'Donatello' cast referred to in his room by the anonymous author of a memoir in the *Pall Mall Gazette*, 2 August 1894). S. Wright, *op. cit.*, p. 8, refers to two plaques in the Pater home.

Mrs Humphry Ward's comment about engravings at Bradmore Road in *A Writer's Recollections*, 1919 ed., p. 124. D. S. MacColl's recollections, with mention of a Botticelli, 'in crewel-work', were published in *The Week-end Review*, 12 November 1931, pp. 759–60.

Creighton's letter of 1 May 1871, *The Life and Letters of Mandell Creighton*, 1904, I, pp. 93–94. Mrs Humphry Ward, *op. cit.*, p. 141, refers to Creighton's 'beautiful Merton rooms . . . the Morris paper, and the blue willow-pattern plates upon it, that he was surely the first to collect in Oxford.' Mrs Creighton was one of the women involved with female education at Oxford.

Pater's comments before publication on *The Renaissance*, and his anxiety over its format, etc., in *Letters* . . ., pp. 8–12.

Mrs Pattison's review appeared, anonymously, in *The Westminster Review*, Jan.-April 1873, pp. 639–41. Symonds' review was in *The Academy*, 15 March 1873, pp. 103–05; his private comments on the book are quoted in P. Grosskurth, *John Addington Symonds*, 1964, p. 157. Morley in *The Fortnightly Review*, April 1873, pp. 469–77; for reactions to it and Pater's letter to Morley, *Letters* . . ., pp. 14–15.

Wordsworth's letter of 17 March 1873 to Pater is given in *Letters* . . ., pp. 12–14 (printed first in W. Watson, *Life of Bishop John Wordsworth*, 1915, pp. 89–91). I have followed Evans in omitting after 'momentary enjoyment' words Watson put in brackets thus: 'of course of a high and subtle kind'. Evans supposes them Watson's own gloss on the sentence, but I am much less sure, suspecting that Wordsworth was trying politely to be fair to Pater.

The sermon by W. W. Capes was reported at length in the *Oxford Undergraduate's Journal*, 27 November 1873: I owe my awareness of it and this reference to Dr Bernard Richards, who also kindly provided the source of the Bishop of Oxford's censure: *A Charge delivered to the Clergy of the Diocese of Oxford, At his Second Visitation* . . ., 20 April 1875; the sentence cited was that beginning, 'The theory, or idea, or system . . .', quoted fully at the end of Ch. 6 here.

The New Republic is often said, e.g. by T. Wright (*op. cit.*, II, p. 10) to have been published in 1877; it was then published in book form, having first appeared during June-December 1876 in the magazine *Belgravia*.

It is Gosse, *The Contemporary Review*, July-Dec. 1894, p. 799, who refers to the estrangement with Jowett; Sharp, *Atlantic Monthly*, Dec. 1894, p. 811, mentions the 'demoralizing moralizer' epigram, attributing it to Jowett. Both Benson and Wright record, at some length, Jowett's strong disapproval of Pater at this period.

Wilde's praise of *The Renaissance* came in his review of *Appreciations*, in *The Speaker*, 22 March 1890 (reprinted in *A Critic in Pall Mall*, 1919, pp. 187–94), His other reference, in *De Profundis*, conveniently in *The Letters of Oscar Wilde*, ed. R. Hart-Davis, 1962, p. 471.

Mrs Humphry Ward's recollection of the scandal caused by *The Renaissance* at Oxford in her *op. cit.*, p. 120; May Ottley's comment came in publishing *An English poet* in *The Fortnightly Review*, April 1931, p. 435.

CHAPTER TEN

Letters . . ., pp. 25–26, pp. 45–46, pp. 100–01, for the letters quoted to Gosse, Vernon Lee and Horne; the letter to Lane, *op. cit.*, p. 152.

Mrs Humphry Ward, *op. cit.*, pp. 123–24, on Bradmore Road, the source for further description by her cited in the text. The Bradmore Road house was not owned by Pater; from 3 December 1869 it was leased to a Mr Hall from whom Pater must have had a sub-lease (information from the Gloucester Land Registry).

Vernon Lee's Letters, ed. I. Cooper Willis, 1937, pp. 78–80, for her dinner with the Paters, the report on her Oxford landlady and her own first reaction to the Misses Pater; *op. cit.*, p. 224, having got to know better Clara, 'usually very reserved'. Her description in the text below of Hester and Clara's dresses, p. 152.

As Madame Duclaux Mary Robinson published 'Souvenirs sur Walter Pater' in the *Revue de Paris*, January 1925, pp. 339–58.

Pater's comment to Sharp on Cornwall: *Letters . . .*, p. 45.

D. S. MacColl's recollections referred to in the notes to Ch. 9 here.

Pater to Vernon Lee about his brother's illness: *Letters . . .*, p. 51

The story of Henry James's visit to Hester in *The Legend of the Master*, compiled by S. Nowell-Smith, 1947, p. 77.

For information about Clara, I am greatly indebted to the note prepared by Lady de Villers for her forthcoming history of Somerville College, which the author has kindly allowed me to use. From this are drawn facts about Clara's involvement with women's education at Oxford, her status at Somerville, the contemporary comparison of her and Hester to a sub-prior and prior, Wilde's fleeing of them at a dinner party and May Ottley's reminiscences.

Hester's letter of 24 February 1883 to Vernon Lee, *Letters . . .*, pp. 48–49. There is no record traced of Hester's birth, but she was baptized on 21 March (1837).

The information about the inscription on Pater's tombstone was given to Richard Jennings by Hester, and he recorded it in the *New Statesman*, 13 November 1948, p. 421.

Wilde's reference to 'Miss Pater . . .', *The Letters of Oscar Wilde*, ed. R. Hart-Davis, 1962, p. 195.

Pater's letter to Macmillan about translating Schnaase, *Letters . . .*, p. 22.

The MS presumed to be in Clara's hand is one of those in the Houghton Library at Harvard (see S. Wright, *A Bibliography . . .*, p. 106).

The references to Clara's tuition of Virginia Stephen are in Quentin Bell's *Virginia Woolf*, Vol. I, 1972, p. 68; they are quoted and discussed in Lady de Viller's study.

Benson, *op. cit.*, p. 21, for Pater as 'baffling . . .'; p. 209 for his 'dark moods of discouragement'. Hester's letter of 30 January (1903 ?) to Wright is at the Lilly Library, Indiana University.

Gosse's reminiscences cited in the notes to Ch. 9. He states that Pater thought

218

the portrait of himself as Mr Rose 'a little unscrupulous'. Pater's candidature for the Professorship of Poetry was omitted from all biographical accounts and seems first touched on in P. Grosskurth, *John Addington Symonds*, 1964, pp. 169, 172–73; it is mentioned by Evans in *Letters* . . ., p. xxi, with no reference to Grosskurth.

Pater's letter to Oscar Browning, *Letters* . . ., p. 16.

My attention kindly called to Pater's signature in a copy of Browne's *Pseudodoxia Epidemica*, 1658 (fourth edition), by Allan Braham; the copy was item 7 of a Supplementary List of books for sale (1977) by Paul Grinke of Devonshire Place, W.1.

Wright's *The Life* . . ., I, p. 139, records the speeches at the King's School Feast Day of 1858.

CHAPTER ELEVEN
Pater's letter of 17 April 1878: *Letters* . . ., p. 29.

The Bacchanals of Euripides was published in *Macmillan's Magazine* in October 1878.

The opening sentence of Flaubert's *La Légende de Saint Julien* is worth quoting: 'Le père et la mère de Julien habitaient un château, au milieu des bois, sur la pente d'une colline.' Pater's loan of *Trois Contes* to Wilde is documented by a letter of 15 November 1877, *Letters* . . ., p. 26; Evans, *loc. cit.*, note 2, records that this copy survives.

An English Poet was published by May Ottley in *The Fortnightly Review*, April, 1931, pp. 433ff.

Pater's letters to Macmillan in 1878 about the projected volume of essays: *Letters* . . ., pp. 32ff.

Mrs Ward in *A Writer's Recollections*, 1919 ed., pp. 121–22.

Vernon Lee's references to Pater in *Vernon Lee's Letters*, ed. I. Cooper Willis, 1937, pp. 78–80, 109.

Pater's letter of 4 November 1882 to Sharp: *Letters* . . ., pp. 43–45. Hester's letter to Vernon Lee, *op. cit.*, pp. 48–49. It was in the letter to Sharp that Pater referred to the very damp weather 'binding up one's arteries'.

Creighton's testimony about Pater's behaviour in hotels abroad: L. Creighton, *The Life and Letters of Mandell Creighton*, 1904, II, p. 111.

Sharp's reminiscences, cited in notes to Introduction.

William Pater's illness in 1883 is documented in two letters from Pater to Vernon Lee (*Letters* . . ., pp. 50–52); in the second he refers to 'what has been a depressing time to us'.

Mrs Ward's review of *Marius* was published under her initials in *Macmillan's Magazine* (LII), May-Oct. 1885, pp. 132–39.

CHAPTER TWELVE
Vernon Lee's Letters, p. 223.

Pater's letters to Ainslie in *Letters* . . ., *passim*, from 1887 onwards; Evans, *op. cit.*, p. 73, note i, says Wilde introduced him to Pater about that period. Pater's acquaintance with his uncle dated from about 1875 and is chiefly documented in Grant Duff's volumes *Notes from a Diary*, 1897–1905. The reference to Ainslie's *Escarlamonde* in *Letters* . . ., p. 121.

Bussell's reference to Pater's division of his day ('in the evening closing his books completely') was in his memorial sermon: conveniently in S. Wright, *A Bibliography* . . ., p. 188.

Letters . . ., p. 27, for Wilde's photograph(s) obtained by Pater; the other requests, etc., cited above are also in *Letters*.

For Walter Harte, Wright, *The Life . . .*, II, pp. 69ff.

Sharp, *loc. cit.* (in notes to Introduction, above), for his impression of Pater's appearance.

Vernon Lee's first impressions in her *Letters*, p. 78. 'Michael Field's' first meeting, from their unpublished Journal, quoted by Evans, *op. cit.*, p. 98, note 1. Benson, *op. cit.*, p. 178, for the 'military man' reference.

Holmes's recollections (he was an undergraduate at Brasenose in 1887–89) in C. J. Holmes, *Self & Partners (mostly Self)*, 1936, pp. 102–03. His drawings of Pater are reproduced facing p. 102.

Moore published his reminiscences in the *Pall Mall Magazine*, August 1904, p. 532. Lionel Johnson's remarks on visiting Pater in Kensington cited by Evans, *op. cit.*, p. xxiv.

Symons' reference to Pater and the Persian cat in *A Study . . .*, pp. 102–03; the 'almost bustling' reference given by Evans, *op. cit.*, p. xl.

Moore's paraphrase of Pater's letter about *A Mere Accident* reprinted in *Letters . . .*, p. 174.

Pater's letter to Harris, *Letters . . .*, p. 118. Harris on Pater in *Contemporary Portraits*, second series, New York 1919, pp. 203–26.

The Slade Professorship incident is referred to by Evans, *op. cit.*, p. xxi; it seems recorded only by Vernon Lee in her letters, *op. cit.*, pp. 178 and 192.

Pater's reference to being ill early in 1893: *Letters . . .*, p. 138.

Letters . . ., passim, for the various reactions to correspondents, gifts of books, etc.

Most of Wright's second volume of *The Life . . .* is obscured by the presence of Richard Jackson, whose pet animals – as well as houses, books, etc. – appear in the reproductions. There seems no record of any letter from Pater to Jackson, and many of the anecdotes reported by Wright have a dubious air.

The Harvard MSS include some notes headed 'Il Sartore'; Symons, *op. cit.*, p. 105, for a reference to this 'portrait' inspired by Moroni. 'S. Gaudioso the Second' (also a Harvard MS) was suggested by Romanino's portrayal of the saint in his National Gallery polyptych.

Jacques van Oost was in fact a seventeenth-century Bruges painter, but the National Gallery portrait (No. 1137) could easily pass as Dutch. The boy's fur-tipped hat and fur muff, combined with the picture's outstanding charm, might well be recollected by Pater, consciously or not.

Pater's letter to his cousin Frederic Loudon Pater about William's death (*Letters . . .*, p. 71) gives the details of his illness and resignation of his post; William's London address from his death certificate (where dropsy is recorded along with heart disease). Gosse, *loc. cit.* in Ch. 9, p. 796 for William's taste.

Wilde's review of *Appreciations* reprinted in *A Critic in Pall Mall*, 1919, pp. 187–94. Evans, *op. cit.*, p. 105, note 3, documents Watson's review in *The Academy*, 21 December 1889, pp. 399–400.

CHAPTER THIRTEEN

The relevant reviews of *Dorian Gray* are

quoted in R. Hart-Davis, *The Letters of Oscar Wilde*, 1962, pp. 263 and 265.

Details of the printings of *The Renaissance* in S. Wright, *A Bibliography . . .*, pp. 60–70. R. Le Gallienne's remark in *The Romantic '90s*, 1926, p. 74. For Beardsley's letter to Raffalovich, *The Letters of Aubrey Beardsley*, ed. H. Maas, J. L. Duncan and W. G. Good, 1971, pp. 192–93.

Symons, *A Study . . .*, p. 102, records Pater going into a church before lecturing. Pater's letter to the vicar of the Church of the Holy Redeemer, *Letters . . .*, pp. 141–42.

The text of Bussell's sermon, with some additional comment by him, conveniently in S. Wright, *op. cit.*, pp. 187ff.

The 'Michael Field' comment on Pater suppressing his essay on *Aesthetic Poetry* is quoted by Evans, *Letters . . .*, p. 113, note 3; Evans, *op. cit.*, p. xxiii, for Johnson's record of Pater's own comment.

MacColl's recollections, *loc. cit.*, in Ch. 9 here. 'An Undergraduate' published his sympathetic reminiscences of Pater in the *Pall Mall Gazette*, 2 August 1894.

Lionel Johnson's letter about Wilde's visit to him: Hart-Davis, *op. cit.*, p. 254, note 4.

Pater wrote to Symons declining to contribute to the first number of *The Yellow Book*: *Letters . . .*, pp. 147–48. His letter to Sharp dropping the 'Mr', *op. cit.*, pp. 43ff. Sharp records Pater's fondness for Balzac's saying 'Le travail . . .' The letter to Berenson, *Letters . . .*, p. 172. I owe to Mrs Luisa Vertova Nicolson the information that Berenson (who later met Pater and his sisters in Italy) felt he had been snubbed.

Impressions of Pater at his lecture in Oxford on Mérimée were given by Herbert Warren, President of Magdalen College, to Benson, *op. cit.*, p. 159.

Wilde's comment on *The Cornhill* parody of Pater: Hart-Davis, *op. cit.*, p. 276.

The unpublished passages of *Gaston* are discussed by G. d'Hangest, *Walter Pater. L'homme et l'œuvre*, 1961, II, pp. 94ff.

Pater wrote briefly about Bussell for the series *Oxford Characters* (1896), published by John Lane, illustrated by William Rothenstein; his letter to Rothenstein, *Letters . . .*, p. 150. Rothenstein's drawing of Pater was for the same series. The remark about Bussell being 'a little too reluctant' to publish, *op. cit.*, p. 144 (letter of 18 October 1893 to William Canton).

Pater's reference about 'exclusively personal . . .' literary work: *op. cit.*, p. 59 (letter of 1 March 1885 to Sharp). That *Marius* was the first of a trilogy, with *Gaston* the second part, etc., was stated by Pater in a letter of 28 January 1886 to Carl Wilhelm Ernst (*op. cit.*, p. 65) and repeated to at least one other correspondent.

May Ottley (when prefacing *An English Poet* in *The Fortnightly Review*, 1 April 1931, pp. 433–35) stated that Pater revisited the King's School in the summer of 1891 and that *Emerald Uthwart* was 'written soon after'.

T. Wright, *The Life . . .*, I, p. 16, deserves the credit of connecting 'Uthwart' with the Uthwatt family though he did not pursue the matter.

He is also the authority *op. cit.*, II, p. 165 for saying that Jowett congratulated Pater on *Plato and Platonism*. This is accepted by d'Hangest, *op. cit.*, II, p.

232, who speaks of the significance of their reconciliation.

The 'carp' anecdote is given in Mac-Coll's reconciliations (*loc. cit.*).

CHAPTER FOURTEEN

64, St Giles' was earlier lived in by Henry John Stephen Smith, Savile Professor of Geometry, and his sister Ellen; cf. B. Askwith, *Lady Dilke*, 1969, p. 68.

Reminiscences of Pater in later life quoted here, are by 'An Undergraduate' in the *Pall Mall Gazette* for 2 August 1894, by 'F' ('In Pater's Rooms'), *The Speaker*, 26 August 1899, p. 207, and E. B. Titchener in *Book Reviews* (New York), Oct. 1894, quoted by S. Wright, *op. cit.*, pp. 180–81.

Pater's ownership of Stenbock's poems, *The Shadow of Death*, is documented by an inscription of Lionel Johnson's in the actual copy (item 142 in the exhibition *Aubrey Beardsley*, Victoria and Albert Museum, 1966). Stenbock's friendship with Solomon is confirmed by a letter of Solomon's printed by B. Reade, *Sexual Heretics*, 1970, p. 37; *loc. cit.*, p. 307 for Stenbock's poem, 'Many are Dreams'.

The letter of 18 October 1893, on returning from France: *Letters . . .*, pp. 143–44. Letters of 17 December 1893 and 4 January 1894 record Pater's illness (*op. cit.*, pp. 146–47).

A letter of 11 March (*op. cit.*, pp. 149–50) speaks of attempting a 'little notice' of Lovelace and then deciding against it, given a shortage of time.

For the lost (?) essay on Johnson, see S. Wright, *op. cit.*, No. 111 (pp. 142–43). Other items mentioned exist among the Houghton Library MSS at

Harvard (*loc. cit.*, pp. 145–47). The Rubens lecture exists in no written form, but Evans, *Letters . . .*, p. 156, note 2, records that it was to be given.

The *Frogs* and frog story is told by M. Field, *Work and Days* (extracts from their journal), ed. T. and D. C. Sturge Moore, 1933, p. 202.

Letters . . ., pp. 147 and 150 for Pater's letters to Rothenstein; pp. 151 and 152 to Lane. W. Rothenstein, *Men and Memories*, Vol. I, 1931, p. 55, tells of Pater's remark to Bussell.

T. Wright, *The Life . . .*, II, pp. 212–15, records Moorhouse's last visit to Pater and gives the exact date (reliable doubtless as proved by Moorhouse himself).

T. Wright, *op. cit.*, II, p. 215, says Richard Jackson found Pater very unwell, 'apparently in the middle of May'. Wright, *loc. cit.*, confuses T. H. Green with the historian J. R. Green and marries Charlotte Symonds to the wrong man.

The details of Pater's final illnesses, etc., are given by Benson, *op. cit.*, pp. 175–76, and must derive from Hester and Clara.

Bussell told of the Devon holiday plans for 30 July (printed by S. Wright, *op. cit.*, p. 190).

Gosse (cited in Ch. 9, p. 805) for the exact circumstance of Pater's death. The death was registered on 1 August by Clara, who stated she had been present (she had also registered William's death but then was shown only as 'in attendance'). Pater left no will. Letters of Administration were granted to Clara in September 1894 and the estate valued at £2,599 4s. 3d. A report of the funeral appeared in *The Times* for 3 August.

A list of Pater's writings published in his lifetime

Coleridge's Writings: *Westminster Review*, January 1866
Winckelmann: *Westminster Review*, January 1867
Poems by William Morris: *Westminster Review*, October 1868
Notes on Leonardo da Vinci: *The Fortnightly Review*, November 1869
A Fragment on Sandro Botticelli: *The Fortnightly Review*, August 1870
Pico della Mirandula(sic): *The Fortnightly Review*, October 1871.
The Poetry of Michelangelo: *The Fortnightly Review*, November 1871
Children in Italian and English Design: *The Academy*, July 1872
STUDIES IN THE HISTORY OF THE RENAISSANCE, 1873 (reprinted as THE RENAISSANCE: STUDIES IN ART AND POETRY, 1877, 1888 and 1893)
On Wordsworth: *The Fortnightly Review*, April 1874
A Fragment on *Measure for Measure: The Fortnightly Review*, November 1874
Renaissance in Italy: The Age of Despots: *The Academy*, July 1875
The Myth of Demeter and Persephone: *The Fortnightly Review*, January and February 1876
Romanticism: *Macmillan's Magazine*, November 1876
A Study of Dionysus: *The Fortnightly Review*, December 1876
The School of Giorgione: *The Fortnightly Review*, October 1877
Imaginary Portraits: 1. The Child in the House: *Macmillan's Magazine*, August 1878
The Character of the Humourist:

Charles Lamb: *The Fortnightly Review*, October 1878
The Beginnings of Greek Sculpture
  I. The Heroic Age of Greek Art:
  II. The Age of Graven Images: *The Fortnightly Review*, February and March 1880
The Marbles of Aegina: *The Fortnightly Review*, April 1880
Samuel Taylor Coleridge: The English Poets: Selections, ed. T. H. Ward, 1880
Dante Gabriel Rossetti: The English Poets: Selections, ed. T. H. Ward, 1883 ed.
The English School of Painting: *The Oxford Magazine*, 25 February 1885
MARIUS THE EPICUREAN: HIS SENSATIONS AND IDEAS, 1885 (reprinted 1885 and 1892)
A Prince of Court Painters: *Macmillan's Magazine*, October 1885
On 'Love's Labour's Lost': *Macmillan's Magazine*, December 1885
Four Books for Students of English Literature: *The Guardian*, 17 February 1886
Amiel's Journal: The Journal Intime of Henri-Frédéric Amiel: *The Guardian*, 17 March 1886
Sebastian van Storck: *Macmillan's Magazine*, March 1886
Sir Thomas Browne: *Macmillan's Magazine*, May 1886
Denys l'Auxerrois: *Macmillan's Magazine*, October 1886
English at the Universities: *Pall Mall Gazette*, 27 November 1886
M. Feuillet's 'La Morte': *Macmillan's Magazine*, December 1886

Duke Carl of Rosenmold: *Macmillan's Magazine*, May 1887

IMAGINARY PORTRAITS, 1887 (reprinted 1890)

Vernon Lee's 'Juvenalia': *Pall Mall Gazette*, 5 August 1887

'An Introduction to the Study of Browning': *The Guardian*, 9 November 1887

M. Lemaitre's 'Serenus, and other Tales': *Macmillan's Magazine*, November 1887

'Robert Elsmere': *The Guardian*, 28 March 1888

Gaston de Latour: *Macmillan's Magazine*, June-October 1888

Their Majesties' Servants: *The Guardian*, 27 June 1888

The Life and Letters of Flaubert: *Pall Mall Gazette*, 25 August 1888

Style: *The Fortnightly Review*, December 1888

The Complete Poetical Works of Wordsworth . . .: *The Athenaeum*, 26 January 1889

The Complete Poetical Works of Wordsworth . . .: *The Guardian*, 27 February 1889

A Poet with something to say: *Pall Mall Gazette*, 23 March 1889

Shakespere's English Kings: *Scribner's Magazine*, 5 April 1889

'Toussaint Galabru': *The Nineteenth Century*, April 1889

The Bacchanals of Euripides: *Macmillan's Magazine*, May 1889

An Idyll of the Cevennes: *The Guardian*, 12 June 1889

Correspondance de Gustave Flaubert: *The Athenaeum*, 3 August 1889

Hippolytus Veiled: A Study from Euripides: *Macmillan's Magazine*, August 1889

Giordano Bruno. Paris 1568: *The Fortnightly Review*, August 1889

APPRECIATIONS: WITH AN ESSAY ON STYLE, 1889 (reprinted, 1890)

Noticeable Books: 3 – A Century of Revolution: *The Nineteenth Century*, December 1889

Tales of a Hundred Years Since: *The Guardian*, 16 July 1890

'On Viol and Flute': *The Guardian*, 29 October 1890

Art Notes in North Italy: *The New Review*, November 1890

Prosper Mérimée: *The Fortnightly Review*, December 1890

A Novel by Mr Oscar Wilde: *The Bookman*, November 1891

The Genius of Plato: *The Contemporary Review*, February 1892

A Chapter on Plato: *Macmillan's Magazine*, May 1892

Lacedaemon: *The Contemporary Review*, June 1892

Emerald Uthwart: *The New Review*, June and July 1892

Introduction to *The Purgatory of Dante Alighieri*, 1892

Raphael: *The Fortnightly Review*, October 1892

PLATO AND PLATONISM: A SERIES OF LECTURES, 1893

Mr George Moore as an Art Critic: *Daily Chronicle*, 10 June 1893

Apollo in Picardy: *Harper's New Monthly Magazine*, November 1893

The Age of Athletic Prizemen: *The Contemporary Review*, February 1894

Some Great Churches in France
1. Notre-Dame d'Amiens: *The Nineteenth Century*, March 1894
2. Vézelay: *The Nineteenth Century*, June 1894

Bibliography

THIS BIBLIOGRAPHY makes no attempt to be comprehensive. Many but not all of the books listed here are referred to in the notes. For convenience the list is divided into works on Pater and those which deal with him only in part. Both biographical and critical books are included. Place of publication is assumed to be London unless stated.

For a bibliography of Pater's own writings, see S. Wright, *A Bibliography of the writings of Walter H. Pater* (New York and London, 1975). His letters are edited by L. Evans, *Letters of Walter Pater* (Oxford, 1970).

1 Books on Pater:

A. C. BENSON, *Walter Pater* (1906)

E. CHANDLER, *Pater on style* (Copenhagen, 1958)

R. C. CHILD, *The Aesthetic of Walter Pater* (New York, 1940)

R. CRINKLEY, *Walter Pater: Humanist* (Lexington, 1970)

I. FLETCHER, *Walter Pater* (Harlow, 1971 ed.)

G. D'HANGEST, *Walter Pater. L'homme et l'œuvre* (Paris, 1961)

G. C. MONSMAN, *Pater's Portraits: Mythic Patterns in the Fiction of Walter Pater* (Baltimore, 1967)

A. SYMONS, *A Study of Walter Pater* (1932)

E. THOMAS, *Walter Pater. A Critical Study* (1913)

A. WARD, *Walter Pater: the Idea in Nature* (1965)

T. WRIGHT, *The Life of Walter Pater* (1907)

2 Some books referring to or partly dealing with Pater:

L. CREIGHTON, *Life and Letters of Mandell Creighton* (1904)

M. FIELD, *Works and Days* (1933)

E. GOSSE, *Critical Kit-Kats* (1896)

G. B. GRUNDY, *Fifty-five years at Oxford* (1945)

G. HOUGH, *The Last Romantics* (1949)

W. W. JACKSON, *Ingram Bywater* (1917)

F. KERMODE, *The Romantic Image* (1957)

J. D. DE LAURA, *Hebrew and Hellene in Victorian England: Newman, Arnold and Pater* (Austin, 1969)

VERNON LEE, *Vernon Lee's Letters*, ed. I. Cooper Willis (privately printed, 1937)

W. ROTHENSTEIN, *Men and Memories* (1934)

W. SHARP, *Papers Critical and Reminiscent* (1912)

G. TILLOTSON, *Criticism and the Nineteenth Century* (1951)

MRS HUMPHRY WARD, *A Writer's Recollections* (1918)

F. WEDMORE, *Memories* (1912)

Index

226

229